Scott Foresman

Practice Book

Editorial Offices: Glenview, Illinois • Parsippany, New Jersey • New York, New York
Sales Offices: Boston, Massachusetts • Duluth, Georgia • Glenview, Illinois
Coppell, Texas • Sacramento, California • Mesa, Arizona

ISBN: 0-328-14521-1

21 V0N4 13
CC:N3

Contents

Contents

Name

Family Times

Summary

Because of Winn-Dixie

Moving to a new town can be hard, and making new friends can be even harder. With the help of her dog, Winn-Dixie, Opal is able to get to know Miss Franny Block, the local librarian. Miss Block tells Opal an exciting tale about a bear that once wandered into the library.

Activity

Animal Stories With your family, share stories of personal experiences with animals. They can be stories about animals kept as pets, or animals seen in the zoo or in the wild.

Comprehension Skill

Sequence

Sequence is the order in which things happen in a story. When you read, think about what comes first, next, and last. Several events can occur at the same time. Words such as *meanwhile* and *during* give clues that two events are happening at the same time.

Activity

Foolish Fairy Tales Take turns telling fairy tales, like *Little Red Riding Hood* or *Cinderella,* with their events out of order. Talk about how these mix-ups changed the story. Did any of the stories sound better when the event order was changed?

Lesson Vocabulary

Words to Know

Knowing the meanings of these words is important to reading *Because of Winn-Dixie.* Practice using these words.

Vocabulary Words

grand excellent; wonderful

memorial helping people to remember a person, thing, or event

peculiar strange; unusual

positive without doubt; sure

prideful overly proud of oneself

recalls remembers

selecting picking out; choosing

Grammar

Declarative and Interrogative Sentences

Declarative sentences make statements. They end with periods. *For example: I like to go to the library.*

Interrogative sentences ask questions. They end with question marks. *For example: What time does the library open?*

Activity

Miscommunication Play a game in which two people have a conversation with each other. One player can only use declarative sentences and the other player can only use interrogative sentences. The conversation should be fast-paced: players are not allowed to stop and think before speaking.

Practice Tested Spelling Words

______	______	______	______
______	______	______	______
______	______	______	______
______	______	______	______
______	______	______	______

Name ______________________________

Sequence

- Events in a story occur in a certain order, or **sequence.** The sequences of events can be important to understanding a story.

Directions Read the following passage. Then complete the time line below by putting the events in the order in which they happen.

When Charlie came home from visiting his grandparents in Florida, he told his friend Bill all about his trip. He told him how fun it was to take his first airplane flight to Florida and to look down on the houses and cars from so far up.

His grandparents then took him to the beach to pick up sharks' teeth along the coast. Later in the week, he went to an amusement park to ride the roller coasters. Bill wished he could have gone to Florida too.

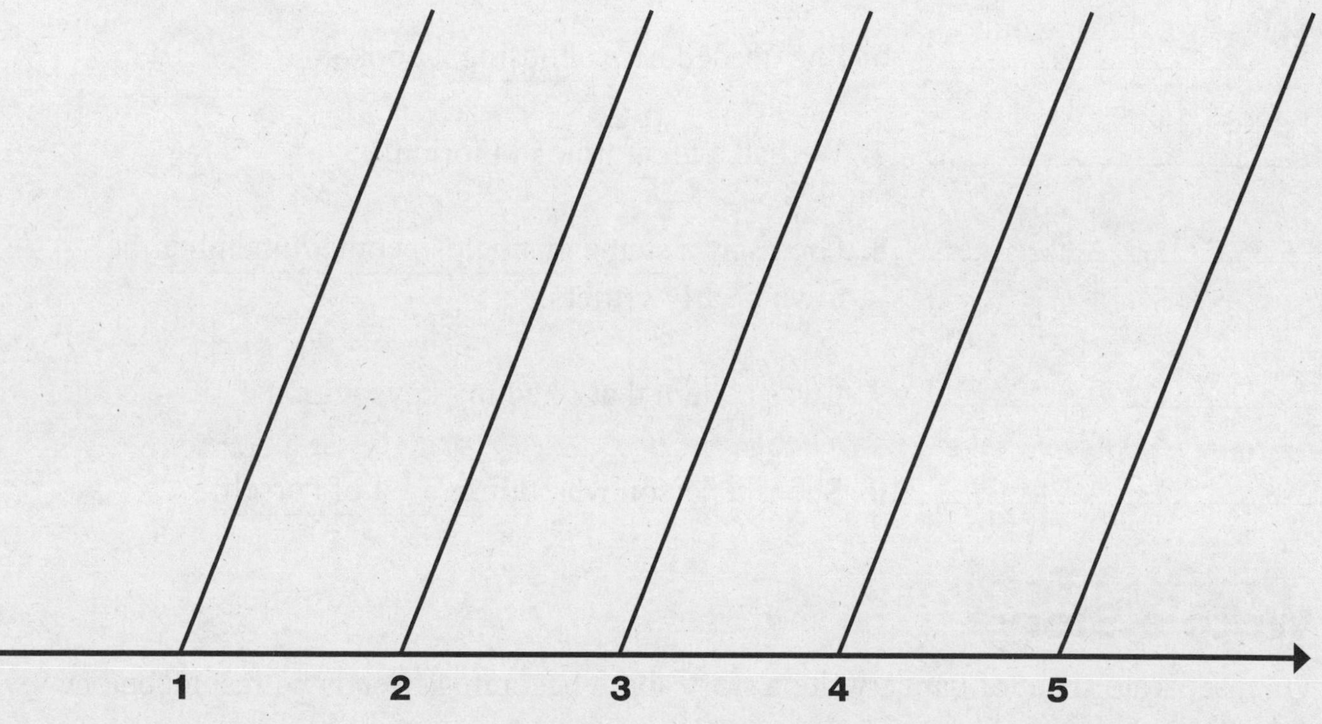

Home Activity Your child completed a time line with the order of events from a short passage. Talk together about the main events of a typical day. Ask your child to put those events in sequential order using a simple time line.

Name ______________________________

Vocabulary

Directions Choose the word from the box that best matches each definition. Write the word on the line shown to the left.

Check the Words You Know

- ___grand
- ___memorial
- ___peculiar
- ___positive
- ___prideful
- ___recalls
- ___selecting

______________ **1.** remembers

______________ **2.** without doubt

______________ **3.** excellent

______________ **4.** strange

______________ **5.** picking out

Directions Choose the word from the box that best matches the meaning of the underlined words. Write the word on the line shown to the left.

______________ **6.** She needed help choosing a book.

______________ **7.** We had a great time in Florida.

______________ **8.** Greg saw a statue that helps people remember the town's early settlers.

______________ **9.** I was certain that I had my keys with me.

______________ **10.** She is a person who thinks a lot of herself.

Write a Story

On a separate sheet of paper, write a story about becoming friends with someone new. Use as many vocabulary words as you can.

Home Activity Your child identified and used vocabulary words from *Because of Winn-Dixie.* With your child, create original sentences using the vocabulary words.

Name ______________________________

Vocabulary • Word Structure

- A **suffix** is a syllable added to the end of a base word to change its meaning or the way it is used in a sentence.
- The suffix *–ful* means "full of _____," as in *careful.* The suffix *–al* means "from, of, or like _____," as in *fictional.* You can use suffixes to help you figure out the meanings of words.

Directions Read the following story about a trip to the library. Then answer the questions below.

When I went to King Memorial School, there was a contest for telling a story about our town's original settlers. My friends and I formed a team and went to the local library. I was doubtful that our team would win until we talked to the town historian in the library. She told us the wonderful story of one brave pioneer family. To us, the story was a logical choice. I was really prideful when my team won the prize for telling our town's most colorful story.

1. What does the word *prideful* mean in the story?

____

2. What does the word *original* mean in the story?

____

3. What is the suffix in the word *wonderful*? What does *wonderful* mean?

____

4. What does the suffix mean in the word *logical*? What does *logical* mean?

____

5. Think of another word that ends with either *–ful* or *–al*. Tell the meaning of the word. Then use it in an original sentence.

____

____

Home Activity Your child identified suffixes in words to understand their meanings. With your child, read a short selection. Ask your child to point out words that use suffixes and what those words mean.

Name ______________________________

Author's Purpose

Directions Read the following story. Then answer the questions below.

The driver of the boat started to slow down as he entered the swamp. This made Minh a little nervous. He didn't know what kinds of creatures could be lurking around in the dark water. Minh thought the swamp looked very peculiar. The trees were unlike any he had ever seen. Some had moss hanging from their branches. It looked like spiderwebs in the light of the moon. All of a sudden, Minh heard a loud splash. He looked around, but saw nothing in the murky water. Then he heard another splash, much closer this time. He shined his flashlight out into the darkness just in time to see the tail of an alligator slip under the water.

1. What is most likely the author's purpose in writing the story?

____

____

2. Why do you think that is the purpose?

____

____

3. The author does not explain what made the splashing noise until the end of the story. Why do you think the author did this?

____

____

4. At what pace did you read the story? Why?

____

____

5. Do you think the author met his or her purpose? Why or why not?

____

____

Home Activity Your child analyzed the author's purpose in a short story. Read a short story, newspaper article, or advertisement with your child. Decide together what the author's purpose is in the selection.

Name ____________________________________

Sequence

- Events in a story occur in a certain order, or **sequence.** The sequences of events can be important to understanding a story.

Directions Read the following passage. Then answer the questions below.

After school, Kelly went over to Mrs. Jacobson's house to help her cook. Mrs. Jacobson was taking a pot of boiled potatoes off the stove when Kelly got there. "Ready to make potato salad surprise?" she asked.

First Mrs. Jacobson had Kelly peel the potatoes and put them in a large bowl. Then Mrs. Jacobson cut up celery, onions, and hard boiled eggs and mixed them with the potatoes.

Kelly added the mayonnaise and yellow mustard next. Now came time for the surprise. Mrs. Jacobson took a small bottle from the refrigerator. Kelly could not tell what it was. Mrs. Jacobson added a tiny bit of the secret ingredient to the mix. Kelly breathed in a tangy smell from the bowl. "What is the surprise?" she asked. Mrs. Jacobson said, "Horseradish. It gives it quite a kick!"

1. What is the first event in the passage? How do you know?

____

____

2. What is the last event in the passage?

____

3. What clue words help you know the order of the events?

____

4. What ingredients does Kelly add after Mrs. Jacobson puts the celery, onions, and hard boiled eggs into the potatoes?

____

5. Write a summary of the passage in one sentence.

____

Home Activity Your child identified the sequence of events in a short passage. Talk with your child about an activity, such as making a meal, in which the sequence of the steps is important to its success. Have your child write down the steps in the activity in the correct sequence.

Name ______________________________

Sequence

- Events in a story occur in a certain order, or **sequence.** The sequence of events can be important to understanding a story.

Directions Read the following passage. Then complete the diagram below.

Carlos started by building the base, or first level, of his sand castle. He made it about six inches thick. Then he dug a hole in front of the base. That way, when water rushed in, it would go through the hole. Carlos shaped the second level of the castle next. He made this level a little smaller than the base. For the last level of the castle, Carlos used very little sand. Finally, he added details to the castle using shells, stones, and feathers. Carlos even made a flag out of sticks and seaweed. He was very proud of his castle.

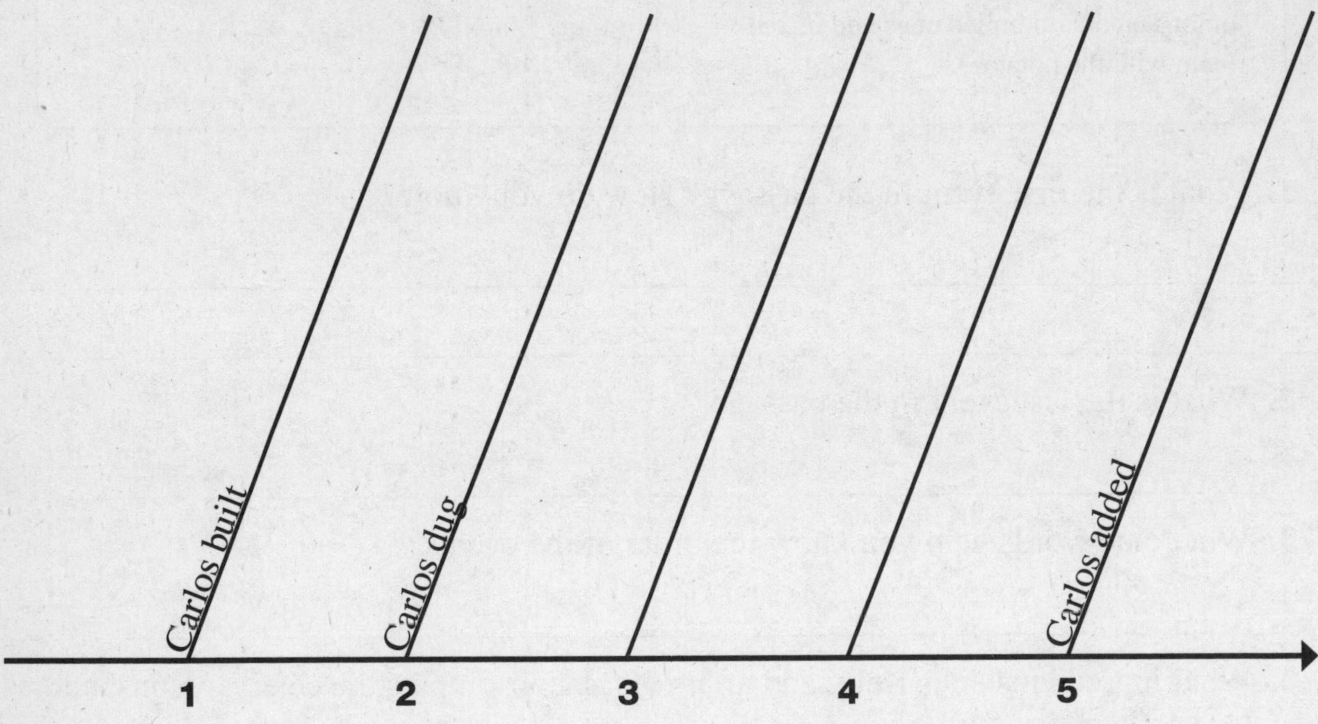

Home Activity Your child identified the sequence of events in a short passage. Have your child use a time line to write down five or six major events in his or her own life, starting with birth.

Name ______________________________

Map/Globe/Atlas

A **map** is a drawing of a place that shows where something is or where something happened. A map's **legend** has a **compass rose** to show direction, a **scale** to show distance, and a **key** to symbols. A **globe** is a sphere with a map of the world, and an **atlas** is a book of maps.

Directions Use this map of Florida to answer the questions below.

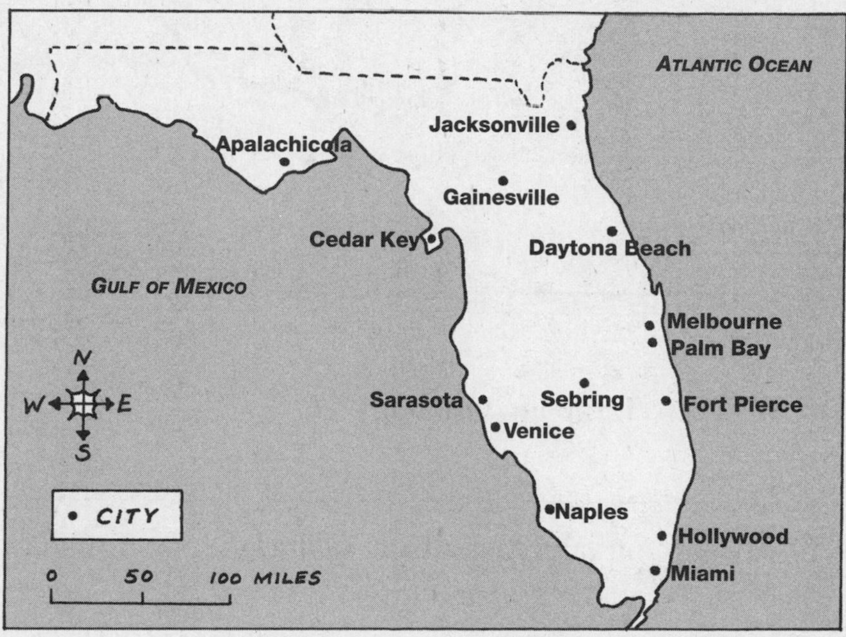

1. Which city is the farthest west?

____

2. Which city is on the Gulf of Mexico, Daytona Beach or Cedar Key?

____

3. Which city is north of Palm Bay, Melbourne or Fort Pierce?

____

4. Name the city that is closest to Hollywood.

____

5. Which city is approximately 75 miles east of Naples: Hollywood or Venice?

____

Name ______________________________

Directions Use this road map of Florida to answer the questions below.

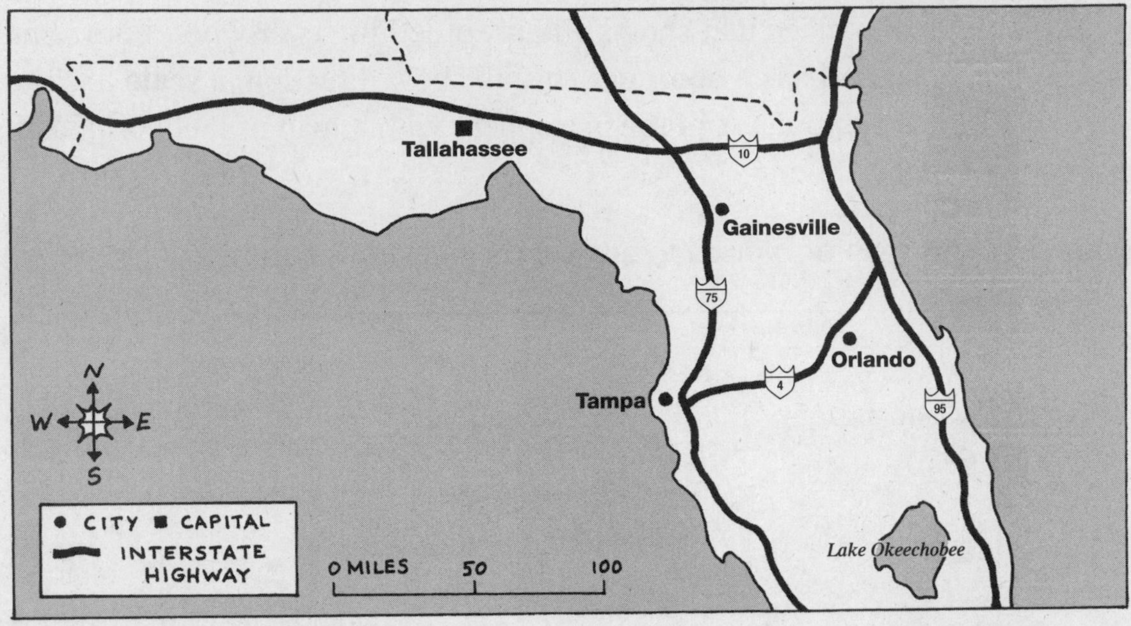

6. Which highway connects Tampa to Orlando?

____

7. Which highways would you take to get from Gainesville to Tallahassee?

____

8. Which highway runs north and south along the east coast of Florida?

____

9. What is the name of the lake shown on the map?

____

____

10. A road atlas of the United States provides road maps for all the states. When would you use a road atlas?

____

____

____

Home Activity Your child learned about using maps, atlases, and globes. Together, look at a map of your state. Examine the legend and locate significant cities or features with which your child is familiar.

Name

Family Times

Summary

Lewis and Clark and Me

You have probably never heard the story of Lewis and Clark's journey told from the point of view of a dog. But Seaman is no ordinary dog. He tells his version of Lewis and Clark's famous journey from his first meeting with the explorers to the moment when he was almost traded to the Native Americans.

Activity

Map It Out Pretend your family has just returned from an expedition to an unknown place. Draw a map showing the route your family took and the important places your family visited.

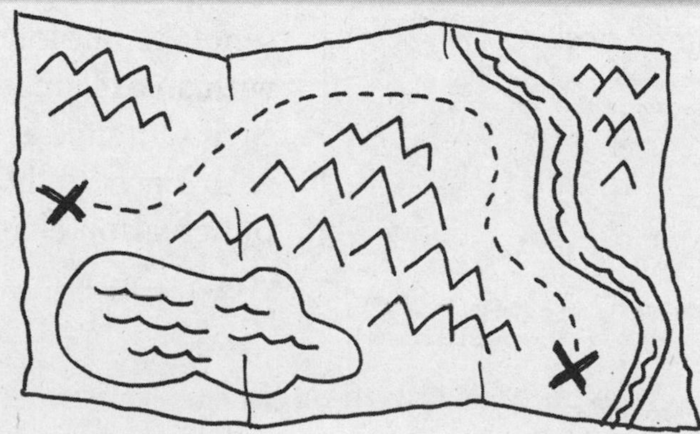

Comprehension Skill

Author's Purpose

The **author's purpose** is the reason or reasons the author has for writing. An author may write to persuade, to inform, to entertain, or to express ideas and feelings.

Activity

On Purpose Write the four different purposes for writing on four small pieces of paper. Fold them up and place them in a bowl. Choose a piece of paper and write a paragraph that meets the purpose written on the paper. Ask your friends or family to join you and pick a paper for themselves.

Lesson Vocabulary

Words to Know

Knowing the meanings of these words is important to reading *Lewis and Clark and Me*. Practice using these words.

Vocabulary Words

docks platforms built on the shore or out from the shore; wharfs

migrating moving from one place to settle in another

scan to glance at; look over hastily

scent a smell

wharf platform built on the shore or out from the shore beside which ships can load and unload; dock

yearned felt a longing or desire

Grammar

Imperative and Exclamatory Sentences

An **imperative sentence** gives a command or makes a request. The speaker of an imperative sentence wants the listener to do something. It ends with a period. *For example: Go play outside.* An **exclamatory sentence** shows strong feeling. It ends with an exclamation point. *For example: You really frightened me!*

Activity

Finishing Sentences Write two imperative sentences and two exclamatory sentences, but leave off the end punctuation. Take turns with a family member reading each sentence out loud as though it ended with an exclamation point. Then read each sentence as though it ended with a period. Discuss how the end punctuation changes each sentence.

Practice Tested Spelling Words

______	______	______	______
______	______	______	______
______	______	______	______
______	______	______	______
______	______	______	______

Name ______________________________

Author's Purpose

- The **author's purpose** is the reason or reasons the author has for writing.
- An author may write to persuade, to inform, to entertain, or to express ideas and feelings.

Directions Read the passage below. Use the graphic organizer to keep track of the author's purpose before and during reading, then answer the last question.

The Importance of Sacagawea

Even though it is hard to prove the facts about Sacagawea's life, many people believe that she was very helpful to Lewis and Clark on their expedition. Sacagawea was an Indian from the Shoshone tribe. She guided the explorers during their journey. She taught them about the wild plants and found them food in the wild. She even helped smooth the meetings between Lewis and Clark and the tribal leaders they met. Without Sacagawea's help, Lewis and Clark's journey would have been more difficult and dangerous.

	Author's Purpose	**Why do you think so?**
Before you read: What do you think it will be?	**1.**	**2.**
As you read: What do you think it is?	**3.**	**4.**

5. Do you think the author met his or her purpose? Why or why not?

____

____

____

Home Activity Your child identified the author's purpose in a passage. Work with your child to identify the author's purpose in an editorial in the newspaper.

Name ________________________________

Vocabulary

Directions Choose the word from the box that best matches each definition. Write the word on the line.

Check the Words You Know

- ___docks
- ___migrating
- ___scan
- ___scent
- ___wharf
- ___yearned

________________ **1.** platforms built on the shore or out from it; piers

________________ **2.** to look over hastily

________________ **3.** a smell

________________ **4.** moving from one place to settle in another

________________ **5.** another word for dock

Directions Choose the word from the box that best completes each statement. Write the word on the line shown to the left.

________________ **6.** Josh ______ for home while he was on a long journey.

________________ **7.** Tanya could smell the ______ of the ocean in the air.

________________ **8.** Like the wharf in our hometown, these ______ are filled with sailors.

________________ **9.** The people ______ to the West had to bring enough supplies to last the whole trip.

________________ **10.** I had to ______ the pages of the manual to find the diagram.

Write a Journal Entry

On a separate sheet of paper write a journal entry you might make after discovering a new part of the world. Use as many vocabulary words as you can.

Home Activity Your child identified and used vocabulary words from *Lewis and Clark and Me.* With your child, imagine you are walking along a busy waterfront. Write a short story together about your imaginary walk. Use as many vocabulary words as you can.

Name ______________________________

Vocabulary • Word Structure

- An **ending** is a letter or letters added to the end of a base word. Recognizing an ending will help you figure out the word's meaning.
- The ending *-ed* is added to a verb to make it past tense. The ending *-ing* is added to a verb to make it tell about present or ongoing actions.

Directions Read the following passage about a journey. Look for words ending in *-ed* and *-ing*. Then answer the questions below.

Enrique yearned for the unsettled land of the West. He was tired of living in such a busy town. So one day he packed up his things and headed for the docks. He started his journey migrating by boat. He planned to meet his uncle downriver. His uncle was also moving west and had offered him a ride on his wagon. When he arrived at the wharf, Enrique hopped off the boat and headed into town. The scent of freshly baked bread was in the air, which made him hungry. Enrique stopped to scan the row of shops for the bakery. Just then, Enrique heard his name being called from across the street. It was his uncle. "Are you ready for the journey of a lifetime?" asked his uncle. Enrique shouted, "More than you know!"

1. What does *yearned* mean? How does the ending change the base word?

____

2. What does *migrating* mean? What is the base word?

____

3. Rewrite the ninth sentence in the passage so that it uses the word *scanning.*

____

4. If you added *-ed* to the noun *scent,* what kind of word does *scent* become?

____

5. Write a sentence using an *-ed* and an *-ing* word.

____

____

Home Activity Your child identified and used word endings to understand words in a passage. Have your child make a list of common verbs. Ask your child to change the meaning of the word by adding *-ed* and *-ing* to each word.

Name ____________________

Cause and Effect

Directions Read the article. Then answer the questions below.

As more and more people wanted to move West, the ways they traveled changed to meet their needs. Many early settlers moved across the country by wagon. Wagons carried much more than saddlebags could carry on a horse. Wagons were also covered, which protected travelers from bad weather. Some people joined wagon trains. A wagon train was a group of wagons that traveled together. Traveling together in a wagon train kept people safer. Wagon trains were carefully planned out before they left for their journeys. People agreed to follow certain rules and elected officers to keep order along the way. Soon technology changed again, however, and people said good-bye to wagons and hello to railroads.

1. Why did people start using wagons instead of horses?

____

____

2. What was an effect of having a cover on a wagon?

____

____

3. Why did people join wagon trains?

____

____

4. What was an effect of new technology?

____

____

5. On a separate sheet of paper, explain why you think people stopped using wagons and started traveling on trains.

Home Activity Your child read an article and answered questions about cause and effect. Read a short story with your child. Ask your child to identify causes and effects in the story.

Author's Purpose

- The **author's purpose** is the reason or reasons the author has for writing.
- An author may write to persuade, to inform, to entertain, or to express ideas and feelings.

Directions Read the following passage. Then answer the questions below.

Crossing the river was dangerous for the backpackers. If they lost their balance, the river's current could take them far downriver. But it was nearing sunset, and it would take too long for them to get back to the camp if they took another route. Elizabeth went first. She was a good swimmer and was not afraid of water. She made it safely to the other side. John followed her. The rushing water made him very nervous. He took one shaky step after another. All of a sudden, John was knocked off his feet. He was being carried downstream in the current. Elizabeth dove in after him, and luckily was able to tow John to shore.

1. What is most likely the author's purpose of the passage?

____

2. Why do you think that is the purpose?

____

____

3. Where in the passage did the author write the most exciting detail? How do you know?

____

4. At what pace did you read this passage—fast, medium, or slow? Did you need to change your normal reading pace to understand it? Why or why not?

____

____

5. Do you think the author met his or her purpose? Why or why not?

____

____

Home Activity Your child identified the author's purpose in a passage. Have your child write a short story with a clear purpose in mind. See if you can determine your child's purpose after reading the story.

Name ______________________________

Author's Purpose

- The **author's purpose** is the reason or reasons the author has for writing.
- An author may write to persuade, to inform, to entertain, or to express ideas and feelings.

Directions Read the passage below. Use the graphic organizer to keep track of the author's purpose before and during reading, then answer the last question.

Don't Forget York

One special member of Lewis and Clark's expedition who was not in history books until recently was York. York was an African American slave of Clark's. In Clark's journals, it says that York hunted and found food for Clark and his men. It also says that York tried to make sure that Clark was safe during the trip. York was an important part of the expedition and will no longer be forgotten.

	Author's Purpose	Why Do You Think So?
Before you read: What do you think it will be?	**1.** ______________	**2.** I looked at the ______ It helps ______________
As you read: What do you think it is?	**3.** to inform us ______	**4.** ______________

5. Do you think the author met his or her purpose? Why or why not?

____

____

____

Home Activity Your child identified the author's purpose in a passage. Read an article or short story with your child. Ask your child the author's purpose before, during, and after reading.

Skim and Scan

To **scan** is to move one's eyes quickly down the page, seeking specific words and phrases. Scanning is used to find out if a resource will answer a reader's questions. Once a reader has scanned a document, he or she might go back and skim it.

To **skim** a document is to read the first and last paragraphs as well as using headings and other organizers as you move down the page. Skimming is used to quickly identify the main idea. You might also read the first sentence of each paragraph.

Directions Scan the passage to answer the questions below.

School's largest yard sale. Northside School will hold its largest yard sale ever on Saturday, March 16. It will be located on the soccer field from 9 a.m. until 4 p.m.

Raising money for a class field trip. The school is holding the sale to collect money for a class field trip to study the route taken by Lewis and Clarke. This is a cross-country trip, and the students need money for transportation, food, and lodging.

Toys, clothing, and furniture for sale. Students' families will set up booths on the field. We've heard reports that many of the items for sale will be toys, games, clothes, furniture, and antiques.

Come early for the best selection. It is best to arrive at the sale early to have the best pick of items. But, if you are not an early bird, you might find some half-price bargains at the end of the day.

1. When you scan this passage, what helps you find specific information?

____

2. In which paragraph would you find out if antiques will be for sale?

____

3. In which paragraph would you find out why the yard sale is being held?

____

4. In which paragraph would you find out the best time to go to the sale?

____

5. Can you find out about the prices of items by scanning this passage?

____

Name ______________________________

Directions Skim this letter to answer the questions below.

Dear Mr. Lewis and Mr. Clark,

I am a student at Gardner School in Portland, Oregon. My class is getting ready for a field trip that will cover part of the route you took to the Pacific Ocean.

I can hardly imagine a two-year journey across half of the country without a car, train, or airplane. I think I would have gotten tired and lonely. I would have missed my home and family.

But it must have been an amazing trip. Were you excited to see new landscapes? Were the people who you met along the way different from what you expected? Did you learn a lot from them? I think I would have liked traveling on horseback and in canoes.

I wonder, were you ever scared? Did you worry about getting lost or getting sick? Were the wild animals frightening? You didn't have a map, although you had about 40 people traveling with you.

I can't wait to see the route you took with my own eyes!

Sincerely,
Justin

6. What is a good way to skim this letter?

____

7. What is the topic of this letter?

____

8. Is the letter about the modern-day city of Portland? How can you tell?

____

____

9. Does the letter indicate if Justin is impressed by Lewis and Clark's journey? How can you tell?

____

____

10. Is Justin excited about the trip? What in the letter gave you that impression?

____

Home Activity Your child learned about scanning and skimming to help find a main idea or information. Look at a newspaper or magazine with your child and have him or her skim it to find the main idea. Then ask your child to scan it for a particular piece of information.

Name

Family Times

Summary

Grandfather's Journey

A grandfather's experiences, his journey to America, and his life in Japan all inspire the narrator to find parts of Japan and America that he loves and cannot do without.

Activity

Dynamic Dialogue Together, reread *Grandfather's Journey*. Notice that there is no dialogue. Choose one of the events in the story, and rewrite it using lively and active dialogue.

Comprehension Skill

Sequence

Sequence means the order in which things happen. Dates, times, and clue words such as *first*, *then*, *next*, and *last* can help you understand the order of events.

Activity

Good Directions Teach your family to perform a dance move, special handshake, or anything that they may not know how to do, without demonstrating it for them. You must use specific language and clue words only. See if they complete the trick or task correctly.

Lesson Vocabulary

Words to Know

Knowing the meanings of these words is important to reading *Grandfather's Journey.* Practice using these words.

Vocabulary words

amazed surprised greatly; struck with sudden wonder; astounded

bewildered completely confused; puzzled

homeland country that is your home; your native land

longed wished very much; desired greatly

sculptures works of art made by carving, modeling, casting, etc.

still to make or become calm or quiet

towering very high

Grammar

Subjects and Predicates

No sentence is complete without both a subject and a predicate. The **subject** is the word or group of words about which something is said in the sentence. The **predicate** of a sentence is the word or group of words that tell something about the subject. All the words in the subject are called the **complete subject.** The subject's central noun or pronoun is called the **simple subject.** All the words in the predicate are called the **complete predicate.** The predicate's verb is called the **simple predicate.** *For example: My friend Paul likes Mexican food.* In the example, "My friend Paul" is the *complete subject,* and "Paul" is the *simple subject.* "Likes Mexican food" is the *complete predicate,* and "likes" is the *simple predicate.*

Activity

Collaborative Tale Write a short story together. Have one person write the subject of every sentence and the other person write the predicate. Switch roles halfway through the story.

Practice Tested Spelling Words

______	______	______	______
______	______	______	______
______	______	______	______
______	______	______	______
______	______	______	______

Name ______________________

Sequence

- **Sequence** is the order in which things happen.
- Dates, times, and clue words such as *first, then, next,* and *last* can help you understand the order of events.

Directions Read the following passage. Then complete the diagram.

One rainy afternoon, Grandmother told me about the many places she had lived in her lifetime. The first place she lived was Austria, where she was born in 1920. But by 1925, her family had moved to Paris, France, and then later to a small village in Belgium. After her eighteenth birthday, Grandmother came to New York City by herself. She hated the cold winters and knew the big city was not for her. Finally, Grandmother packed her bags and moved for the last time to a farm in North Carolina, where she has lived ever since.

First Event

1.

Second Event

2.

Third Event

3.

Fourth Event

4.

5. What clue words in the passage helped you to figure out the sequence of events?

____

Home Activity Your child used a graphic organizer to identify the sequence of events in a passage. With your child, draw a picture or write a summary of each of the main scenes in a favorite story on note cards. Arrange the note cards in the order in which the events occurred in the story.

Name ______________________________

Vocabulary

Directions Choose the word from the box that best completes each sentence. Write the word on the line shown to the left.

Check the Words You Know

- ___amazed
- ___bewildered
- ___homeland
- ___longed
- ___sculptures
- ___still
- ___towering

_______________ **1.** The strange language of the country completely ____ her.

_______________ **2.** She felt scared when she saw the ___ mountains.

_______________ **3.** The trip took her many miles from her ___.

_______________ **4.** She was ____ by the size of the city.

_______________ **5.** The ____ at the museum were made out of marble.

_______________ **6.** She ____ to see a familiar face.

Directions Circle the word that has the same or nearly the same meaning as the first word in each group.

7. longed	called	yearned	stretched
8. bewildered	confused	happy	angry
9. still	stir	calm	annoy
10. amazed	depressed	sleepy	surprised

Write an E-mail Message

Pretend you have just moved to a new country. On a separate sheet of paper write an email message to a friend back home explaining how you have adapted to life in this new place. Use as many vocabulary words as you can.

Home Activity Your child identified and used vocabulary words from *Grandfather's Journey.* With your child, go on an imaginary trip halfway around the world. Use the vocabulary words to describe how you are feeling on the trip.

Name ____________________

Vocabulary • Dictionary/Glossary

- **Dictionaries** and **glossaries** provide alphabetical lists of words and their meanings.
- Sometimes looking at the words around an unfamiliar word can't help you figure out the word's meaning. If this happens, use a dictionary or glossary to find the meaning.

Directions Read the following story about traveling in the United States. Then answer the questions below. Use your glossary or a dictionary for help.

One year for summer vacation, my family took a long road trip around the United States. We visited national parks, where we drove along roads that went through towering mountains. I had to still my nerves just to look over the bluff.

We went to art museums and studied sculptures carved ages ago. I was amazed to learn that people had created art before they could even read or write.

At the end of the trip, I longed for my home and my friends. But I will never forget the wonders I saw.

1. What is the meaning of the word *towering* as it is used in the story?

____

2. What is the other meaning of *bluff* not used in the story? What part of speech is it?

____

3. What is the meaning of *still* in the story?

____

4. Write an original sentence using the other meaning of *still* not used in the story.

____

____

5. To find the meaning of *longed,* you need to look at the entry for *long.* Which definition is used in story?

____

____

Home Activity Your child used a glossary to identify the intended definitions of multiple meaning words. Create and draw a comic together in which the confusion over the different meanings of a word has caused a funny outcome.

Name ______________________________

Main Idea and Details

Directions Read the article. Then answer the questions below.

Japanese immigrants did not find an easy life when they came to America. When they arrived, they had to take any jobs they could. The plantations in Hawaii had plenty of work but did not allow the Japanese people very much freedom.

The Japanese settlers in California found other problems. Harmful rumors were spread about them, and soon the U.S government passed laws that would not allow as many Japanese immigrants into the country. Then when the nation of Japan became an enemy in World War II, the U.S. imprisoned many innocent Japanese immigrants in internment camps. It took the Japanese immigrants a long time to live the life they had dreamed of living.

1. What is the topic of this article?

____

2. What is the main idea of the passage?

____

____

3. What is one detail that supports this main idea?

____

____

4. If the main idea of another article was that the Japanese were treated unfairly during World War II, what detail could you use from this passage to support it?

____

____

5. On a separate sheet of paper, draw a graphic organizer to show the relationship between the main idea and the supporting details in this passage.

Home Activity Your child identified the main idea and details in an article. Pretend that you were asked to write an article about your family for the local newspaper. Discuss what the main idea of the article would be and how it could be supported with details.

Sequence

- **Sequence** is the order in which things happen.
- Dates, times, and clue words such as *first, then, next,* and *last* can help you understand the order of events.

Directions Read the passage. Then answer the questions below.

The 442nd Regimental Combat Team, a brave team of Japanese American soldiers during World War II, had an interesting history. The team was made up of Japanese Americans from Hawaii and from the continental United States. These two groups grew up very differently. When they met for the first time in April of 1943 for training, they did not get along very well. They fought with each other constantly. But after they took a trip to an internment camp and saw how Japanese Americans were treated, they learned to respect each other. They trained hard from May until February of 1944.

In the spring, they left for combat in Europe. There they were joined by other battalions, including the 100th Infantry Battalion. The 442nd Regimental Combat Team served their country well and were honored with more than 9,000 Purple Hearts.

1. What major event is described first?

____

2. When did the team learn to appreciate each other?

____

3. What words tell you when the team left for combat in Europe?

____

4. Did the 100th Infantry Battalion join the 442nd Regimental Combat Team before or after they arrived in Europe? How do you know?

____

____

5. On a separate piece of paper, write the information from the passage in order using a graphic organizer.

Home Activity Your child has identified the order of events in a nonfiction article. Discuss the activities your child has to do in the upcoming week. Help your child put these activities in sequential order.

Name ______________________________

Sequence

- **Sequence** is the order in which things happen.
- Dates, times, and clue words such as *first, then, next,* and *last* can help you understand the order of events.

Directions Read the passage. Then complete the diagram below.

Before the first settlers came to build our town, it looked very different from the busy place it is today. Wild horses roamed the land. Then immigrants came from Western Europe, including Ireland and the Netherlands. They plowed the fields and built schools and churches.

Years later, people from Asian countries, like China and Japan, came to the area to help construct railroads. Instead of moving on after the work was done, they stayed in the town to raise their families.

First Event

1. Wild ______________________________

Second Event

2. Immigrants ______________________________

Third Event

3. They plowed ______________________________

Fourth Event

4. Years later ______________________________

5. What do you think happened to the town after the fourth event in the passage?

____

Home Activity Your child identified the order of events in a passage. Discuss the order of events that led your family to live in the community that you do.

Name ______________________

Electronic Media

- There are two types of **electronic media**—computer and non-computer. Computer sources include computer software, CD-ROMs, and the Internet. Non-computer sources include audiotapes, videotapes, films, film strips, television, and radio.
- To find information on the Internet, use a search engine and type in your keywords. Be specific. It's a good idea to use two or more keywords.

Directions Use the list of electronic media below to answer the questions.

Electronic Media Source List

- "Interviews with Japanese Travelers" (Public Radio taped interview program)
- *Traveling in Japan* (CD-ROM with printable navigation maps)
- *The Japanese History Site* (Internet site that describes Japan's history)
- *Food in Japan* (DVD of Japan's most exotic foods)
- *The Japanese in America During World War II* (Filmstrip that shows life in the Japanese internment camps)

1. Which source would be helpful in writing a report on Japan for school?

____

2. Why would *Traveling in Japan* be a helpful source if you were planning a road trip around Japan?

____

3. Which source do you think was produced more recently: *Food in Japan* or *The Japanese in America During World War II*? Why?

____

4. What keywords might you type into a search engine to get the Web site *The Japanese History Site*?

____

5. If you needed to use a quote in your report about what travelers think about the United States, what source would you use?

____

Name ______________________________

Directions Use the Internet search results found on a search engine to answer the questions below.

WEB SEARCH

Results 1-3 of about 25,000

Search Results

History of **Immigration**

Use the tool bar below to search through 1,000 primary source documents. First, type in the year of **immigration** and then the country from which the immigrants came.

My Story

Hi! Welcome to my home page. My name is Ken, and I moved to this country 25 years ago with my wife and family. Learn about my story and my family by clicking on the icons to the right.

Japanese in the United States

The *Japanese Immigrant Society,* together with the *Foundation to Support Diversity,* has supported the research found on this site. All information is for educational use only.

6. If you click on the underlined link entitled History of Immigration, what kind of site will you be taken to?

____

7. What does the information after each link tell you?

____

8. What keyword was typed in to receive these search results?

____

9. Why might Ken's Web site not be useful for a school report?

____

10. Why might you be able to trust the information on the third link?

____

____

Home Activity Your child learned about electronic media. With your child, review the rules of safe Internet searching and how to find helpful research articles on the Internet.

Name

Family Times

Summary

The Horned Toad Prince

On the windy prairies of the Southwest, Reba Jo meets a horned toad who makes a deal with her. When Reba Jo doesn't hold up her end of the bargain, the horned toad is offended and asks for a simple kiss to end the deal. That little kiss unlocks a magical spell, and the once-ugly toad becomes a prince!

Activity

Inside a Fairy Tale Rewrite your favorite fairy tale with your family members as characters and your community as the setting. Write the story in common, everyday language.

Little Red Baseball Cap, on her way to Grandma's apartment

Comprehension Skill

Author's Purpose

The **author's purpose** is the reason or reasons the author has for writing. An author may write to persuade, to inform, to entertain, or to express ideas and feelings.

Activity

News Clues Find an article in the newspaper with pictures. Read only the headline and look only at the pictures. Then work with a family member to try to guess the author's purpose. Finally, read the article to see if your guess was correct.

Lesson Vocabulary

Words to Know

Knowing the meanings of these words is important to reading *The Horned Toad Prince*. Practice using these words.

Vocabulary Words

bargain an agreement to trade; deal

favor act of kindness

lassoed roped; caught with a lasso

offended hurt the feelings of someone; made angry

prairie a large area of level or rolling land with grass but few or no trees

riverbed a channel in which a river flows or used to flow

shrieked made a loud, sharp, shrill sound

Grammar

Compound Sentences

A **compound sentence** contains two simple sentences joined by a comma and a joining word. Joining words are *and*, *but*, and *or*. *For example: She wanted to play outside, but it was raining.* Be careful not to confuse compound sentences with sentences that have compound predicates. A compound predicate associates two or more verb phrases with a simple subject. *For instance: Paul brushed his teeth and went to bed.*

Activity

Keep It Simple On two note cards write *Keep It Simple* and *Make It Compound.* Place these cards face down. When the players are ready, turn over one of the cards. If the card says *Keep It Simple*, each player should write down two simple sentences. If the card says *Make It Compound*, each player should write down a compound sentence. The first player to write a correct sentence or sentences wins.

Practice Tested Spelling Words

______	______	______	______
______	______	______	______
______	______	______	______
______	______	______	______
______	______	______	______

Name ______________________________

Author's Purpose

- The **author's purpose** is the reason or reasons for writing. An author may write to persuade, to inform, to entertain, or to express ideas and feelings.
- The kinds of ideas in the text, and the way the author organizes and states these ideas, can help you determine the purpose.

Directions Read the following passage. Then complete the diagram below.

When I smelled chili cooking in the kitchen, I knew I was in trouble. This wasn't just ordinary chili. This was "fibber's chili," which was invented by my great-aunt. She fed this chili to anyone she thought had told a fib or a lie. "One bite," she used to say, "and they can't help but tell you the whole truth."

I knew my mom was making it for me now. Why? Yesterday I kicked a soccer ball into a window, and it broke. Of course, then I told my mother that the window smashed when a bird flew into it. I suppose now I could tell her that I'm too sick to eat. But then she'd serve me fibber's chili a second time! I've got to get up my courage and tell the truth.

Examples of Ideas

1. A special chili

2. The narrator has not told the truth about

Author's Purpose

5.

Content of Text

3.

4.

Home Activity Your child identified the author's purpose in a text. Have your child choose something to write in a letter to a friend or relative. What would your child's purpose be, given the subject matter, and how could information be presented to serve that purpose? Then have your child write the letter.

Name ______________________________

Vocabulary

Directions Draw a line to connect each word on the left with its definition on the right.

1. riverbed	a large area of level or rolling land with grass but few or no trees
2. favor	a channel in which a river flows or used to flow
3. prairie	an agreement to trade; deal
4. lassoed	act of kindness
5. bargain	roped; caught with a lasso

Directions In each statement below, the first pair of words has a certain relationship (such as the same meaning). To complete the statement, add a word that gives the second pair of words the same relationship as the first pair. For example, *neat* is to *messy* (opposite meanings) as *happy* is to *sad* (opposite meanings). Choose the word from the box and write it on the line shown to the left.

____________________ **6.** *Laughed* is to *cried* as *whispered* is to _____.

____________________ **7.** *Remembered* is to *recalled* as *angered* is to _____.

____________________ **8.** *Tree* is to *forest* as *grass* is to _____.

____________________ **9.** *Train* is to *track* as *river* is to _____.

____________________ **10.** *Disagreement* is to *fight* as *deal* is to ____.

Check the Words You Know

___bargain
___favor
___lassoed
___offended
___prairie
___riverbed
___shrieked

Write a Fairy Tale

On a separate sheet of paper, write your own fairy tale about making a bargain. Use as many vocabulary words as you can.

Home Activity Your child identified and used vocabulary words from *The Horned Toad Prince*. Together, create additional analogies, as shown in the second activity, to use with the vocabulary words.

Name ______________________________

Vocabulary • Context Clues

- Sometimes when you are reading, you see a word you don't know. The author may give you a **synonym** for the word. Synonyms are words with the same or similar meanings.
- Often you can recognize a synonym by noting a word set off by commas and preceded by the word *or* and *like.*

Directions Read the following passage. Then answer the questions below.

Once upon a time, there lived an old man. He lived on a prairie, or the plains, that seemed to stretch forever. One day, the old man took a walk and came upon two little boys fighting. One of the boys shrieked, or screeched, that the other boy had not carried out his half of a bargain.

"The deal," he screamed, "was that we would both dig for the treasure—not just me!" The little boy was obviously offended, or insulted, to be doing all the work. "I'm not asking for favors. I just want you to do your share of digging," he said.

The boys stopped fighting when they saw the old man standing before them. The old man reached in his pocket and took out the largest ruby the boys had ever seen.

"If you agree never to fight again," said the man, "I will show you a treasure that is a million times greater than the one you are digging for."

1. What is the synonym for *prairie* used in the passage?

____

2. What synonym for *shrieked* does the author use? How do you know?

____

3. Where in the passage is the synonym for *bargain*?

____

4. In the passage, the synonym for *offended* is *insulted.* What is another synonym?

____

5. After reading the passage, you might describe the old man as mysterious. What is a synonym for *mysterious?*

____

Home Activity Your child identified synonyms that appeared as context clues in a passage. Play a naming game with your child by taking turns saying words that describe a feeling—such as *happy*, *sad*, or *angry*—and having the other person provide one or more synonyms.

Name ____________________________

Sequence

Directions Read the following passage. Then answer the questions below.

Today I learned how to make green chili pie. First you must gather the ingredients—6 or 7 green chilies, 1 cup of grated Fontina cheese, 4 eggs, 2 cups light cream, salt, and pepper. Then preheat the oven to 425°. Butter the bottom of a pie pan and line it with chilies. Sprinkle the cheese over them. Mix the eggs, cream, salt, and pepper together in a bowl. Pour this mixture over the cheese. Bake the pie for 15 minutes. Then lower the heat to 325° and bake for 20–30 minutes longer. Test the pie for doneness by removing it from the oven and inserting a knife into the center. If the knife comes out clean, the pie is done. You may serve the pie hot or cold.

1. What is the first step in making green chili pie?

____

____

2. What is the last step in making the pie?

____

____

3. What step follows baking the pie for fifteen minutes? How do you know this is the next step?

____

____

4. If these steps were written in a different order, would it matter? Why or why not?

____

____

5. On a separate sheet of paper, explain the steps of a process you know well.

Home Activity Your child identified the steps in a process. Perform a household chore with your child, like making a bed, and have your child name the steps that make up the process.

Name ______________________________

Author's Purpose

- The **author's purpose** is the reason or reasons for writing. An author may write to persuade, to inform, to entertain, or to express ideas and feelings. The kinds of ideas in the text, and the way the author organizes and states these ideas, can help you determine the purpose.

Directions Read the following passage. Then answer the questions below.

Riding in a hot-air balloon during the Albuquerque International Balloon Fiesta is inspiring. It is the chance of a lifetime. You would not believe the number of balloons that soar through the air at the same time. Each one's vibrant, colored patterns are unique. Peering over the edge of the balloon's basket, you can see tiny cars and buildings below. Even the mountains in the distance look small from this height. A rush of excitement fills your heart as the balloon soars higher into the clear, blue sky. All your worries and troubles are miles away.

1. Give an example of an idea expressed in this passage.

____

2. How does the author organize ideas in the passage?

____

____

3. What do you think is the author's purpose?

____

4. Do you think the author succeeds in meeting this purpose? Why or why not?

____

____

5. Change the structure of this passage by creating a problem, rising action, a climax, and an outcome. What would be different about the passage with these additions?

____

____

Home Activity Your child answered questions to identify the author's purpose in a passage, and he or she created elements of a story structure. Read a favorite short story together. As you discuss the story, identify the problem, rising action, climax, and outcome.

Name ______________________________

Author's Purpose

- The **author's purpose** is the reason or reasons for writing. An author may write to persuade, to inform, to entertain, or to express ideas and feelings.
- The kinds of ideas in the text, and the way the author organizes and states these ideas, can help you determine the purpose.

Directions Read the following passage. Then complete the diagram below by telling the ideas of the text, how they are organized, and the author's purpose.

Once upon a time, in a small, southwestern town, lived a wise jackrabbit. The jackrabbit gave advice to the people of the town. He told them where to dig for water and how to plant their crops.

One day, a boy named Jorge asked the jackrabbit what he should get his sister for her birthday. The jackrabbit said, "Some long-stemmed grass from the fields far, far away."

Jorge collected the grass and gave it to his sister. She thought it was the worst gift she had ever received.

The next day, Jorge yelled at the jackrabbit for giving bad advice. The jackrabbit replied, "I said I give advice. I never said it was *good* advice."

Examples of Ideas

1. A jackrabbit ______________________________

2. Jorge accepts ______________________________

Content of Text

3. The sister's response is ______________________________

4. The jackrabbit's response is ______________________________

Author's Purpose

5. ______________________________

Home Activity Your child answered questions to identify the author's purpose. Read an article or short story with your child. Ask him or her to guess the author's purpose before reading, based on any titles or headings. During and after reading, have your child determine the author's purpose based on the ideas and organization of the text.

Name ___________________________

Illustration/Caption/Label

- **Illustrations** and pictures can help readers understand information about characters and events in a story or a subject in a nonfiction article.
- A **caption** is the text that explains or gives more information about an illustration or picture. Captions usually appear below or to the side of the image.
- **Labels** also use text to provide information about illustrations and pictures. They can appear inside the image or above or below it.

Directions Study the illustrations and captions below.

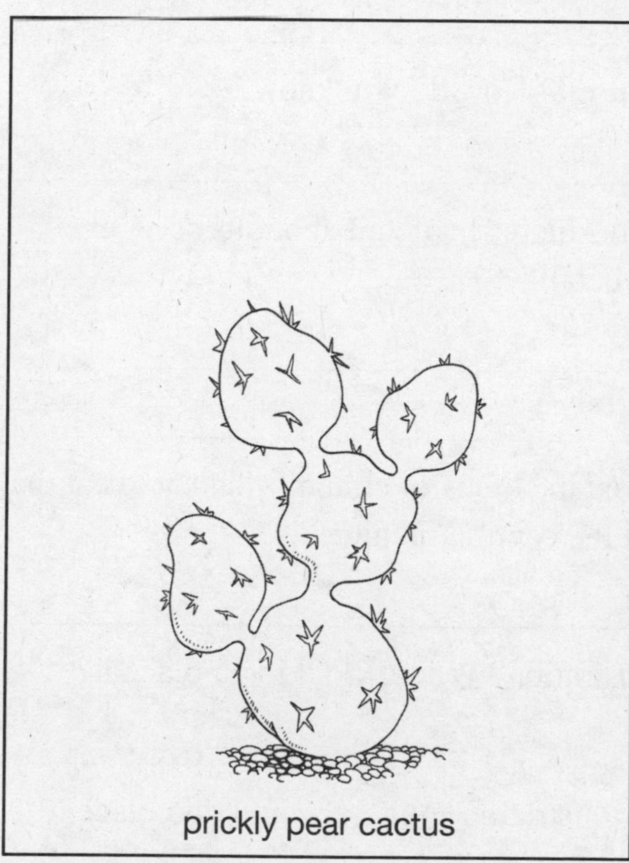

prickly pear cactus

The prickly pear cactus, which grows in the American Southwest, has flat stems called pads. These stems are good at holding in water. For this reason, desert animals try to eat them. However, the prickly pear cactus protects itself with sharp, pointy spines that keep animals away.

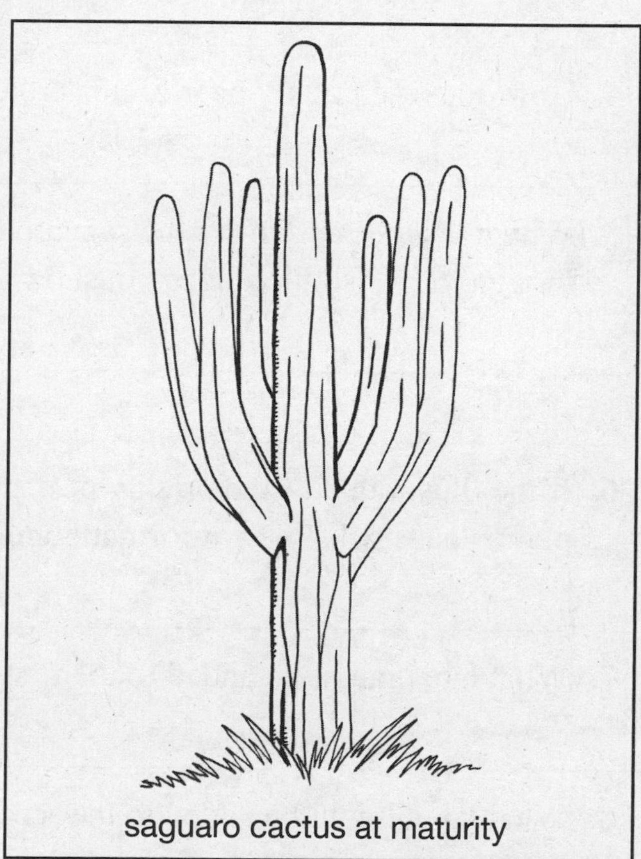

saguaro cactus at maturity

The very large saguaro cactus grows from a very small seed. It takes many years for the saguaro to grow to its full size. These plants sometimes live 150 years. At that age, a saguaro may measure up to fifty feet high.

Name ________________________________

Directions Use the illustrations and captions to answer the questions.

1. What is shown in these illustrations?

____

2. What do the illustrations themselves show about the differences between the prickly pear cactus and the saguaro cactus?

____

3. How large can a saguaro cactus grow?

____

4. How does the prickly pear cactus protect itself? How do you know?

____

5. Why does the caption for the saguaro cactus include a detail about its seed, even though the illustration does not show this detail?

____

____

6. If the illustration of the prickly pear showed the kinds of animals that try to eat the plant's pads, what new information might the caption include?

____

7. What label might be added to the first illustration? Where would you place it?

____

8. What label might be added to the second illustration? Where would you place it?

____

9. What kind of article might include these illustrations?

____

10. Write a new caption that could be used for both images at once.

____

Home Activity Your child learned how to analyze illustrations and captions. Read a nonfiction article that contains no illustrations. Together, discuss what illustration you could add to help the reader understand the information in the article.

Name

Family Times

Summary

Letters Home from Yosemite

Yosemite National Park is an amazing place. In one visit, you can see giant trees, towering mountains, and interesting wildlife.

Activity

Picture Postcards Pretend your family is on a camping trip at a local park. Cut a piece of paper to be about the size of a postcard. Draw pictures of your campsite on one side. Write a message about your trip on the other side.

Comprehension Skill

Main Idea and Details

A passage's **main idea** makes a point about the passage's topic and has at least one supporting detail. **Details** are smaller pieces of information that tell more about the main idea.

Activity

What's the Big Idea? Take turns with one or more family members delivering short speeches about any topic that you wish. At the end of your speech, ask your audience, "What's the big idea?" Have them identify your main point and supporting details.

Lesson Vocabulary

Words to Know

Knowing the meanings of these words is important to reading *Letters Home from Yosemite*. Practice using these words.

Vocabulary Words

glacier a great mass of ice moving very slowly down a mountain or along a valley

impressive able to have a strong effect on the mind or feelings

naturalist a person who studies living things

preserve to keep from harm or change; protect

slopes land that goes up and down at an angle

species a set of related living things that share certain characteristics and that can interbreed

wilderness a wild region with few or no people living in it

Grammar

Clauses and Complex Sentences

A **clause** is a group of related words that has a subject and a predicate. A **dependent clause** has a subject and a verb, but cannot stand alone. *For example: Whenever she goes to the forest.* An **independent clause** can stand alone. *For example: Avery brings her camera.* A **complex sentence** is made up of two clauses, one dependent clause and one independent clause. *For example: When it is hot outside, I like to go swimming.*

Activity

Geometric Sentences Read an article in a magazine or newspaper with a family member. Underline three complex sentences. Then circle the dependent clauses and put a rectangle around the independent clauses.

Practice Tested Spelling Words

______	______	______	______
______	______	______	______
______	______	______	______
______	______	______	______
______	______	______	______

Name ______________________________

Main Idea and Details

- The **main idea** is the most important idea from a paragraph, passage, or article.
- **Details** are small pieces of information that tell more about the main idea.

Directions Read the following passage. Then complete the diagram below.

Several people helped make Yellowstone National Park a protected place. In the 1600s and 1700s, fur trappers came through the area. They noticed its amazing features, such as geysers that shoot hot water high into the air. When they returned to towns and camps, they told stories about what they had seen.

Soon expeditions were organized to explore Yellowstone. The expedition led by Ferdinand Hayden in 1871 included a photographer and an artist who captured the beauty of Yellowstone in their pictures. They showed their pictures to Congress. In 1872, President Grant signed a law that made sure Yellowstone would be protected forever by making it the first national park.

Main Idea
1.

Supporting Details
2.
3.
4.
5.

Home Activity Your child read a short passage and identified the main idea and supporting details. Work with your child to create a graphic organizer that identifies the main idea and supporting details of an article about a natural area.

Name ____________________________________

Vocabulary

Directions Choose the word from the box that best matches each definition. Write the word on the line.

Check the Words You Know

- ___glacier
- ___impressive
- ___naturalist
- ___preserve
- ___slopes
- ___species
- ___wilderness

____________________ **1.** a mass of ice moving very slowly down a mountain or along a valley

____________________ **2.** a wild place with few or no people living in it

____________________ **3.** to keep from harm or change

____________________ **4.** a person who studies living things

____________________ **5.** a set of related living things with similar characteristics

Directions Choose the word from the box that best matches the meaning of each underlined word. Write the word on the line.

____________________ **6.** We went skiing down the snow-covered mountains.

____________________ **7.** The scenery in the national park was magnificent.

____________________ **8.** The park rangers want to keep changes from happening in the park.

____________________ **9.** Long ago a large sheet of ice covered this whole area.

____________________ **10.** We camped out in a wild, isolated area.

Write a Poem

On a separate sheet of paper, write a poem about your favorite natural place. Use as many vocabulary words as you can.

Home Activity Your child identified and used vocabulary words from *Letters Home from Yosemite.* Read a nonfiction article about a natural place with your child. Have your child create sentences in response to the article using the vocabulary words.

Name ______________________

Vocabulary • Word Structure

- A **suffix** is a syllable added to the end of a **base word** to change its meaning. You can use a suffix to figure out the meaning of an unfamiliar word.
- The suffix *-ist* can make a word mean "one who is an expert in." The suffix *-ive* means "tending or inclined to ____."

Directions Read the following passage. Then answer the questions below.

On our sunrise hike through the extensive wilderness, the naturalist told us that the park was filled with many species of animals. It was impressive to think that so many different animals could live in the same place. She also told us that to preserve the park, we needed to leave it like we had never been there. We couldn't take any flowers or plants with us, and we shouldn't leave our garbage there either. Unfortunately, visitors in the past had not been so careful. Restoring the park to its natural state is a massive job.

1. What is the suffix in the word *extensive*? What does it tell you about the meaning of the word?

____

2. What does *naturalist* mean? How do you know?

____

____

3. What does *impressive* mean? How do you know?

____

4. What does the word *massive* mean?

____

5. Write two other words that end in either *-ist* or *-ive.*

____

Home Activity Your child read a short passage and identified suffixes to understand words in a passage. Read an article with your child. Help your child to identify and circle the suffixes added to words in the article.

Name ______________________________

Fact and Opinion

Directions Read the article. Then answer the questions below.

Redwood National Park is a great place to visit where you can see some very tall trees. Some of the trees stand hundreds of feet tall. Besides being tall, the trees can also be very old. In fact, redwood trees can live for 2,000 years. I think it is very impressive that these old, great trees grow from tiny seeds.

The park's location near the Pacific Ocean helps the trees stay healthy. The trees soak in the water that is in the air, which keeps them alive in case of drought.

Other kinds of plants grow in the park as well. Douglas fir, western hemlock, ferns, and mosses all grow in the same soil as the massive redwood trees. This means that the soil is rich in nutrients from the different kinds of plants growing there. If you love trees, you will love Redwood National Park.

1. How do you know the last sentence is a statement of opinion?

____

2. Write an example of another statement of opinion in the passage.

____

____

3. Write an example of a statement of fact in the passage.

____

____

4. Which part of the first sentence is a statement of fact and which part is opinion?

____

____

5. On a separate sheet of paper, write one statement of fact and one statement of opinion about a natural place you have visited.

Home Activity Your child read a short passage and identified statements of fact and opinion. Talk to your child about the events of your day. Use statements of fact and opinion. Have your child identify which statements were facts and which were opinions.

Name ____________________

Main Idea and Details

- The **main idea** is the most important idea from a paragraph, passage, or article.
- **Details** are small pieces of information that tell more about the main idea.

Directions Read the following passage. Then answer the questions below.

I can't believe our summer camping trip is over. We did so many fun things in so little time. First we found a perfect camping spot on the edge of a grassy meadow. The ground was nice and soft there—perfect for sleeping on. Then we headed to the river, where we went rafting. The ride was bumpy and fast. When we finished rafting, we took a long hike back up the river. Along the hike we stopped to pick wild berries. They were sweet. Finally we got back to our camp and built a fire. We sang songs around the fire until it was time for bed.

1. In one or two words, what is this passage about?

____

2. What is the main idea of the passage?

____

____

3. What is one important detail that tells more about the main idea?

____

____

4. What is another detail that tells more about the main idea?

____

____

5. On a separate piece of paper, make a graphic organizer that shows the main idea and the details that support the main idea.

Home Activity Your child identified the main idea and supporting details of a nonfiction passage. Read a magazine article about a different wild animal with your child. Work together to identify the main idea and supporting details of the article. Then write a short summary.

Name ______________________________

Main Idea and Details

- The **main idea** is the most important idea from a paragraph, passage, or article.
- **Details** are small pieces of information that tell more about the main idea.

Directions Read the passage. Then complete the diagram below.

Yosemite National Park has many rules for people to follow in order to preserve the park. One rule is that hunting of any animals is not allowed. Hunting would change the food supply for animals in the park. Hunting in a busy park could also be dangerous to humans. Riding a bike off an official trail is against the rules too. This could ruin the plant life growing in natural areas. Another rule prohibits people from feeding animals. It is not safe for the animals or the visitors. Wild animals might get used to being fed and be unable to feed themselves in the wild. Finally, people cannot remove plants or rocks as souvenirs. If visitors follow these and other rules of the park, Yosemite will continue to be a beautiful, natural place to visit.

Main Idea
1. Yosemite has

Supporting Ideas
2. Hunting
3.
4. Feeding animals
5.

Home Activity Your child read a short passage and identified its main idea and supporting details. Have your child write a paragraph about his or her favorite place. Then help your child create a graphic organizer that identifies the main idea and supporting details of the paragraph.

Name ___________________________

Print Sources

- Libraries contain many sources of information for students to use. You can use a library database or a card catalog to identify and locate these materials. In both cases, you can search for materials by author, title, or subject.
- **Print sources** include encyclopedias, newspapers, magazines, dictionaries, and other reference books.

Directions Study this school's list of available print resources.

Newspapers

Hillside School News (school newspaper)

Hillside Streets (community paper)

Daily Globe (metropolitan city paper)

Magazines

History for Young People

Mathematics Today

The Natural World

Go Go Go Travel Monthly

Sports U.S.A.

Encyclopedias

Encyclopedia of History Makers, vol. I

Encyclopedia of the Nation, vol. I–X

Encyclopedia of Nature, vol. I–II

Encyclopedia of Science, vol. I–IV

Encyclopedia of Women, vol. I–II

Dictionaries

Kenner's Dictionary of Common Words and Phrases

The Student's Dictionary

Theisen's Dictionary of Medicine

Name ________________________________

Directions Imagine that you are writing a report on Yosemite National Park. Use the list of print sources to answer the questions below.

1. What print source would you use first for your report on Yosemite? Explain.

2. Why might a newspaper not be the first place you looked for information?

3. What magazine(s) might have information you could use for your report?

4. Which source(s) might have interesting photographs for your report?

5. How might you use a dictionary while writing your report?

6. Suggest a topic you might check in a library's card catalog for information.

7. Name three listed sources unlikely to have much information on Yosemite.

8. Which encyclopedia might help you find information on animals in Yosemite?

9. How might you use an author's name to find information for this report?

10. What print sources would have up-to-date information on a fire at Yosemite?

Home Activity Your child learned about print sources. Take a trip together to your local library. Find and browse through the sections of print sources.

Name

Family Times

Summary

What Jo Did

Imagine that you could jump as high as a basketball rim. That's exactly what Joanna Marie, or Jo, could do. Jo makes new friends when she shows off her talent during a basketball game in which she is the only girl.

Activity

Not-So-Hidden Talents With your family, discuss the special talents each of you has. What can you do that is unlike what everyone else can do? If you could have a superhuman talent, what would it be?

Comprehension Skill

Cause and Effect

A **cause** is why something happens. An **effect** is what happens. Sometimes a cause may lead to more than one effect. Some effects may have more than one cause.

Activity

A Cause-and-Effect Game Play this game with one or more family members. Each person in the group takes a turn and announces an event that is the cause of other events. Everyone else then takes one minute to think of an effect. The person who thinks of the best effect wins.

Lesson Vocabulary

Words to Know

Knowing the meanings of these words is important to reading *What Jo Did.* Practice using these words.

Vocabulary Words

fouled in sports, made an unfair play

hoop a ring or round band

jersey a shirt that is pulled on over the head

marveled was filled with wonder; was astonished

rim an edge, border, or margin on or around anything

speechless not able to speak

swatted hit sharply or violently away

unbelievable incredible

Grammar

Common and Proper Nouns

Common nouns name any persons, places, or things. Common nouns begin with lower case letters unless they are at the beginnings of sentences. *For example: goldfish, eggplant, shoelace, boy.* **Proper nouns** name particular persons, places, or things. They begin with capital letters. Some have more than one word. *For example: Kelly, Martin, Mrs. Yee, Alaska.*

Activity

Commonly Known As Divide a sheet of paper into two columns. Label the left column *Proper Noun* and list the names of five important or famous people. Label the right column *Commonly Known As.* Work with a family member to write the common noun or nouns associated with each person. For instance, if you had *Ben Franklin* in your left column, you might put *inventor, politician,* or *writer* in the right column.

Practice Tested Spelling Words

____	____	____	____
____	____	____	____
____	____	____	____
____	____	____	____
____	____	____	____

Name ______________________________

Cause and Effect

- A **cause** is why something happens. An **effect** is what happens.

Directions Read the following passage. Then complete the diagram.

Today's soccer game was full of action! Tina kicked the ball to Michael, but she kicked it too hard. Michael's kick made the ball go out of bounds. Jackie, on the other team, had the chance to throw it in. She threw the ball so hard, it almost went into Tina and Michael's goal. Andre, the goalie, jumped to the side and blocked it. He kicked it back into the field. Michael tripped while running and couldn't get to the ball. This left the ball right in front of Jackie. Jackie gave it one swift kick, sending the ball soaring past Andre and into the goal.

Cause		Effect
1.	→	Michael kicked the ball out of bounds.
The ball went out of bounds.	→	2.
Jackie threw the ball.	→	3.
4.	→	He couldn't get to the ball.
Jackie gave it one swift kick.	→	5.

Home Activity Your child identified causes and effects in a short passage. Read an article about a sporting event with your child. Ask your child to identify causes and effects in the article you read.

Name ______________________________

Vocabulary

Directions Choose the word from the box that best matches each definition. Write the word on the line shown to the left.

Check the Words You Know
___fouled
___hoop
___jersey
___marveled
___rim
___speechless
___swatted
___unbelievable

______________ **1.** not able to speak

______________ **2.** hit sharply away

______________ **3.** was filled with wonder

______________ **4.** a ring or round band

______________ **5.** incredible

Directions Choose the word from the box that best matches each clue. Write the word on the line.

______________ **6.** You might wear this while playing a sport.

______________ **7.** This is part of a basketball hoop.

______________ **8.** This is when someone made an unfair play in a sport.

______________ **9.** This is what you are when you don't have anything to say.

______________ **10.** This is something you thought was not possible.

Write a News Report

On a separate sheet of paper, write a news report about a sporting event. Use as many vocabulary words as you can.

School + Home **Home Activity** Your child identified and used vocabulary words from *What Jo Did*. Work with your child to make a crossword puzzle with the words and to write original clues for it.

Name ____________________

Vocabulary • Word Structure

- **Prefixes** and **suffixes** have their own meanings and are added to base words. They change the meanings of base words.
- The prefix *un-* means "the opposite of ____" or "not ____." The suffix *-able* means "able to be ____ed." The suffix *-less* means "without ____."

Directions Read the following passage about a basketball game. Look for the prefix *un-* and the suffixes *-able* and *-less* as you read. Then answer the questions below.

It was the most unforgettable basketball game I ever saw. When the referee said a foul had been made against our star player, I was speechless. The fans for our team were unable to stop yelling. It was useless to try to quiet them. They couldn't believe we were so lucky. We had played an unbelievable game and we were tied with a few seconds to go. It was up to our guard at the free-throw line. As I uncovered my eyes, I saw the effortless shot soar through the hoop like a bird. We won!

1. What does *unbelievable* mean? What are its prefix and suffix?

____

2. What does *useless* mean? Does it have a prefix or suffix?

____

3. How are *speechless* and *effortless* alike? What does each word mean?

____

____

4. What does *unforgettable* mean? What are its prefix and suffix?

____

5. Write a sentence using two words that have a prefix or a suffix. Tell the meaning of those words.

____

____

Home Activity Your child identified and used prefixes and suffixes to understand words in a passage. With your child, make a list of words associated with a favorite sport or activity. Ask your child how the meanings change when you add a prefix, a suffix, or both.

Name ______________________________

Draw Conclusions

Directions Read the article. Then answer the questions below.

You didn't have to see the last race to know how the track meet had gone. All you had to see were the faces of the Cardinals' runners. No one was smiling. Tracy, who usually couldn't stop laughing about something, was completely silent. The team dragged their bags onto the bus.

At the next track meet, the girls' spirits were high. They were singing their school's fight song as they entered the other team's stadium. Tracy was her usual self, giggling like crazy.

The meet started off well. The Cardinals won the 800-meter relay by more than two seconds. But then the Cardinals started to lose race after race.

This time things were different, however. The girls weren't sad or angry. Instead they kept on cheering as loudly as they could. One of the fans asked Tracy how she could be so cheerful when her team was losing. She answered, "Doing our best and having fun is more important than winning or losing."

1. What conclusion can you draw about how the first meet went?

____

2. What details in the passage support this conclusion?

____

____

3. What conclusion can you draw about what happened between the track meets?

____

____

4. What details in the passage support this conclusion?

____

____

5. On a separate sheet of paper, draw a graphic organizer that shows one conclusion you drew from the passage and the details that supported that conclusion.

Home Activity Your child has drawn conclusions using details in a short passage. Watch a sporting event in your local area or on television. Ask your child to draw conclusions about why the event turned out the way that it did.

Name ______________________________

Cause and Effect

- A **cause** is why something happens. An **effect** is what happens.
- Clue words such as *because, so,* and *since* sometimes signal a cause-effect relationship. Sometimes you must figure out for yourself that one thing causes another.

Directions Read the following passage. Then answer the questions below.

Ana's brothers said she couldn't play baseball with them because she was younger than they were. This made Ana angry. She knew she was good at throwing, and she also had a strong swing. "They're just worried about what their friends will say," thought Ana. She took a seat behind the dugout to watch the game. During the first inning, Ana's brother Jose jammed his finger while trying to catch a fast grounder. He had to leave the game to get some ice. This was Ana's chance. She volunteered to take his place. Everado, her other brother, stared her down with an irritated look. "Of course you can play," said one of the other players. "Do you have your mitt?" asked another. Ana did, and she ran onto the field with a smile on her face.

1. At the beginning of the passage, what was the cause of Ana not being able to play?

____

____

2. What was the effect of this event?

____

3. What was the cause of Jose's jammed finger?

____

4. What was the effect of this event?

____

5. Have you ever been told you could not do something you knew you were able to do? How did it make you feel? Compare your situation with Ana's.

____

____

Home Activity Your child identified causes and effects in a short passage. Have your child write a short story about a sporting event or other event. Ask your child to underline the causes and effects of the events in the story.

Name ______________________________

Cause and Effect

- A **cause** is why something happens. An **effect** is what happens.
- Clue words such as *because, so,* and *since* sometimes signal a cause-effect relationship. Sometimes you must figure out for yourself that one thing causes another.

Directions Read the following passage. Then complete the diagram.

The blue team's score was zero because no one could get the ball past Ricky. The blue team's coach told them to take shots before Ricky had a chance to block them. Linda quickly took a shot. She was too far away from the hoop, so the ball bounced off the rim. Half the blue team surrounded Ricky. This left the ball open for Linda to get it again. She shot the ball. She was much closer to the basket this time, so the ball made it in. The blue team cheered because they had finally scored a point!

Cause		Effect
No one could get the ball past Ricky.	→	**1.** ______________________
2. Linda was ______________________	→	The ball bounced off the rim.
Half the blue team surrounded Ricky.	→	**3.** ______________________
Linda shot the ball. She was much closer to the basket this time.	→	**4.** The ball ______________________
They finally scored a point.	→	**5.** ______________________

Home Activity Your child identified causes and effects in a short passage. Talk with him or her about an event that happened during the day. Ask your child what the causes and effects of that event were.

Name ______________________________

Chart/Table

- **Charts** show data or information visually. Most charts have titles and use a combination of words and numbers. A chart often takes the form of a list, diagram, or table.
- A **table** is a special kind of chart that shows information in rows and columns. A single box in a table is often called a **cell**.
- Charts and tables can be created easily using word-processor software.

Directions Examine the images below from the ZipWriter word processor program. Then answer the questions.

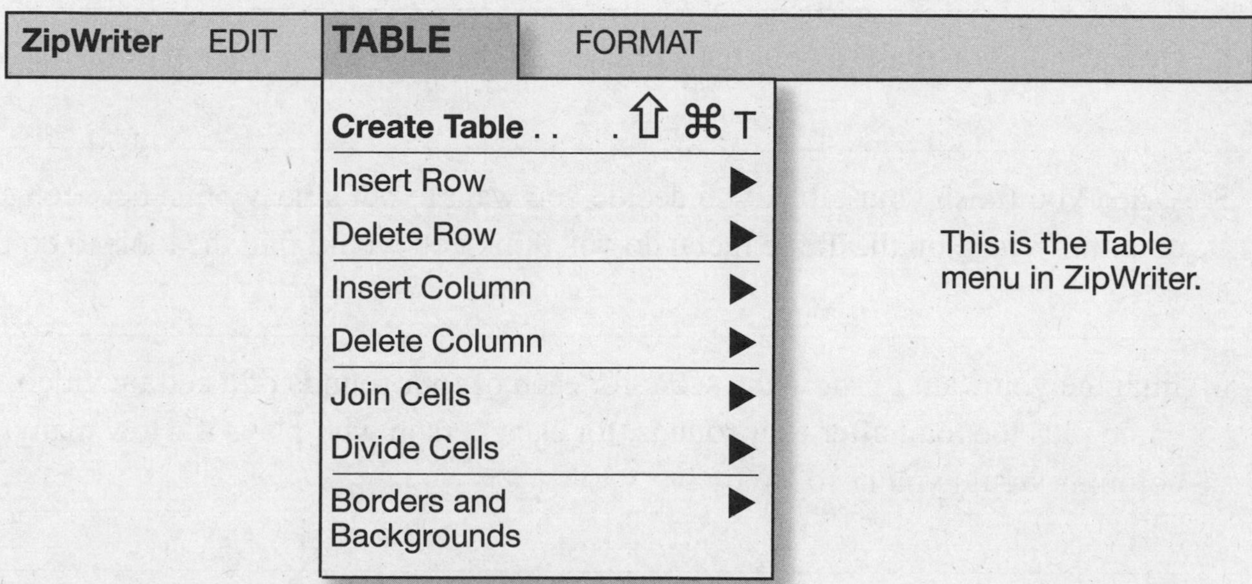

This is the Table menu in ZipWriter.

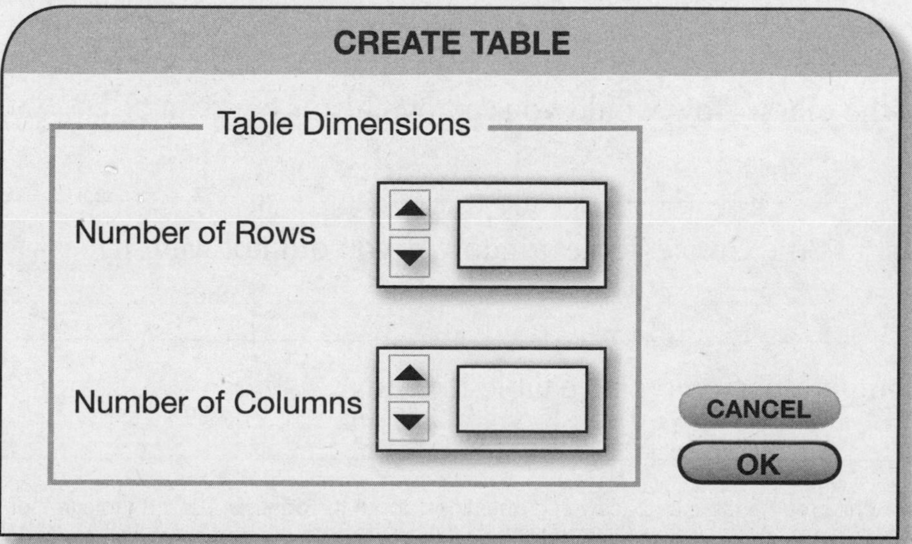

This is the Create Table window. It appears when you select the Create Table command from the Table menu.

Name ________________________________

1. You want to create a table showing 31 students' high scores at a certain video game. How many columns would you ask for in the Create Table window?

2. What command in the Table menu would you use to erase an extra row?

3. Now you want to add another column to the table, to show each student's high score at a different game. What command from the Table menu would you use?

4. How would you make a cell that stretched all the way across the top of the table?

5. When you finish your table, you decide you want to put a heavy line between each column. Where on the Table menu do you think you would find the tools to do this?

6. Imagine you want to show the score for each of four rounds of a certain video game plus the total after four rounds, for each person who plays it. How many columns would you need? Why?

7. Two new students join the class. What should you do to update your table?

8. One student leaves the class. How would you remove his or her data?

9. How would you dismiss the Create Table window if you did not want it?

10. For what purpose might a person create a table like this?

Home Activity Your child read a table and answered questions about it. Together, draw a table (either by hand or using a computer) to show your family's activities each day during the course of a week. Before drawing the table, have your child decide how many columns and rows you will need.

Name

Family Times

Summary

Coyote School News

Ramón Ernesto Ramírez, known as Monchi, lives on a ranch in the southwestern United States. Life, like the bumpy road to school, isn't perfect. Still, he enjoys writing for the school newspaper, celebrating Nochebuena, and helping with the roundup. Monchi is asked to help brand the cattle, so he has to decide whether to win the Perfect Attendance Award or to follow in the tradition of the vaqueros.

Activity

Roundup! With your family, imagine you are joining some cowboys to drive cattle to market. Write a story together about your roundup adventure.

Comprehension Skill

Draw Conclusions

Drawing a conclusion is forming an opinion based on what you already know or on the facts and details in a text. Check an author's conclusions or your own conclusions by asking: Is this the only logical choice? Are the facts accurate?

Activity

What's the Conclusion? Describe a person, place, or thing. Have a family member draw a conclusion about what you have described. Ask for facts and details that support the conclusion. Then switch roles and draw a conclusion about something your partner describes.

Lesson Vocabulary

Words to Know

Knowing the meanings of these words is important to reading *Coyote School News.* Practice using these words.

Vocabulary Words

bawling crying out in a noisy way

coyote a small, wolflike mammal living in many parts of North America

dudes people raised in the city, especially Easterners who vacation on a ranch

roundup the act of driving or bringing cattle together from long distances

spurs metal points worn on a rider's boot heels for urging a horse onwards

Grammar

Regular Plural Nouns

Nouns that name more than one person, place, or thing are **plural nouns.** Nouns that name only one person, place, or thing are called **singular nouns.** To make most nouns plural, add *–s* or *–es* to the singular noun: *pet* becomes *pets*, *fox* becomes *foxes*, *monkey* becomes *monkeys*, and *horse* becomes *horses.* Plural nouns that are created this way are called **regular plural nouns.**

Activity

Plural Poems Together, write a poem using as many regular plural nouns as you can. The poems do not have to rhyme.

Practice Tested Spelling Words

Name ______________________________

Draw Conclusions

- **Drawing a conclusion** is forming an opinion based on what you already know or on the facts and details in a text.
- Check an author's conclusions or your own conclusions by asking: Is this the only logical choice? Are the facts accurate?

Directions Read the following passage. Then complete the diagram below by finding facts and details to support a conclusion.

A cowboy's job changed with the seasons. In the fall, the cowboys brought cattle roaming on the open land to the ranch. They branded the cattle, so they could keep track of them. Then during the winter months, the cowboys fed the cattle and raised them.

When spring arrived, the ranchers chose the cattle they wished to sell. Next, the cowboys would take the cattle on a long journey to a busy town so that others could buy the cattle. After the cowboys sold the cattle, they rested a little while before they started the process all over again.

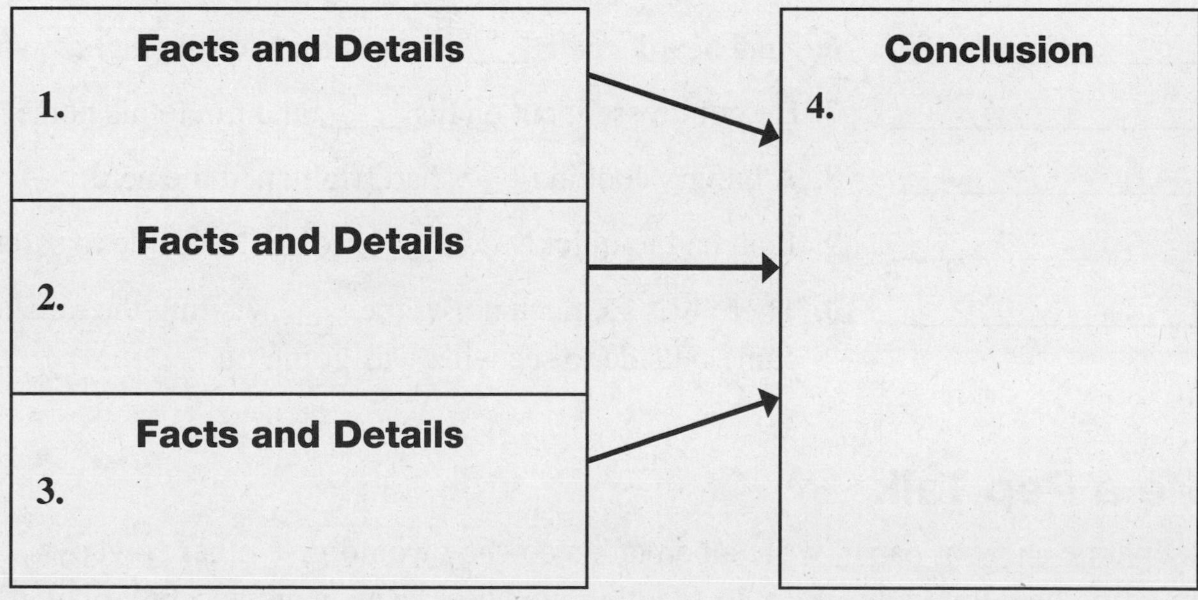

5. How would you decide if the facts and details are accurate?

____

____

Home Activity Your child read a short passage and drew a conclusion using facts or details. Tell your child about a job you once had. Have your child draw a conclusion about this job based on the facts and details you provide.

Name ________________________________

Vocabulary

Directions Choose the word from the box that best matches each definition. Write the word on the line.

Check the Words You Know
___bawling
___coyote
___dudes
___roundup
___spurs

________________ **1.** people who were raised in the city but vacation on a ranch

________________ **2.** metal points worn on a horse rider's boot heel

________________ **3.** small, wolf-like animal

________________ **4.** the act of driving or bringing cattle together from long distances

________________ **5.** shouting or crying out in a noisy way

Directions Choose the word from the box that best completes each sentence. Write the word on the line shown to the left.

________________ **6.** Juan heard a calf ____ in the middle of the night.

________________ **7.** He got dressed, put on his ____, and ran to his horse.

________________ **8.** A hungry-looking ____ had frightened the herd.

________________ **9.** Juan had to quickly do a ____ to get the cattle to safety.

________________ **10.** There was so much noise, the ____ visiting the ranch came outside to see what was going on.

Write a Pep Talk

On a separate sheet of paper, write a pep talk a cowboy would give other cowboys before going on a long journey to do a cattle roundup. Use as many vocabulary words as you can.

Home Activity Your child identified and used vocabulary words from *Coyote School News.* With your child, create a word search using the words from this selection.

Name ______________________

Vocabulary • Dictionary/Glossary

- **Dictionaries** and **glossaries** provide alphabetical lists of words and their meanings.
- Sometimes looking at the words around an unfamiliar word can't help you figure out the word's meaning. If this happens, use a dictionary or glossary to find the meaning.

Directions Read the following passage. Then answer the questions below.

At the crack of dawn, my uncle went around to the tents to wake up the dudes at the ranch. Today they were going on a roundup and needed to get everything ready before they left. The dudes sat down for breakfast and then got dressed for the trip. Some of them had never ridden a horse before, so putting on their chaps and spurs took a lot of time. They heard some cattle bawling far in the distance. Before long, the group headed out into the open plains.

1. How would you define *dudes* by looking at the words that are near it?

____

2. Look up *dudes* in a glossary or dictionary. How is the meaning that you looked up different from the meaning you thought it had by looking at the words near it?

____

____

3. How would you define *bawling* by looking at the words that are near it?

____

4. Look up *bawling* in a glossary or dictionary. How is the meaning that you looked up different from the meaning you thought it had by looking at the words near it?

____

____

5. Look up *roundup* in a glossary or dictionary. What part of speech is it?

____

Home Activity Your child read a short passage and used a dictionary or glossary to understand unfamiliar words. Have a conversation about your day with your child. When your child hears an unfamiliar word, help your child to find the word's meaning in a dictionary.

Literary Elements • Setting

Directions Read the passage. Then answer the questions below.

The sleepy little town was barely recognizable that night. It was alive with excitement about the upcoming fiesta. The streets were covered with decorations. Red, green, and white streamers were wrapped around the light posts. Mexican flags were hung outside of building windows. The sounds of a Mariachi band tuning up were heard in the town's central square—first, a sweet scale on the trumpet, then the soft plucking from a guitar and a violin. People were walking toward the central square carrying all kinds of foods, from spicy beans, tortillas, and meats, to sweet desserts freshly made that day. Some of the women were dressed in long, flowing white skirts and shirts with ruffles. Their hair was pulled back with beautiful ribbons and colorful flowers. These were the dancers who would soon perform for the crowds. It surely was going to be a fiesta to remember.

1. In a few words, tell what is going on in the passage.

____

2. Where and when does this passage take place?

____

____

3. How do you know that the town is different from what it is usually like?

____

____

4. How does the author use senses to describe this setting?

____

____

5. On a separate sheet of paper, draw a picture of the setting described in the passage.

Home Activity Your child read a short passage and answered questions about its setting. Read a short story to your child. Have your child explain how the story would be different if the setting were to be changed.

Name ______________________________

Draw Conclusions

- **Drawing a conclusion** is forming an opinion based on what you already know or on the facts and details in a text.
- Check an author's conclusions or your own conclusions by asking: Is this the only logical choice? Are the facts accurate?

Directions Read the following passage. Then answer the questions below.

It took quite a bit of teamwork for the first issue of the Wide Valley School Newspaper to come out successfully. The editor, Sally Jo, did a good job of making sure everything ran smoothly. Candice read through the reporters' articles to correct any errors. Brian then took Candice's edited articles and entered them into the classroom computer. Then Taylor arranged the articles and added graphics. Finally, Ms. Jackson had the newspaper printed.

1. Draw a conclusion about how much time it took to put together the paper's first issue.

____

2. What details support this conclusion?

____

____

3. What do you think was Sally Jo's main duty as editor?

____

4. Draw a conclusion about the teamwork it takes to put together a newspaper.

____

____

5. Describe any prior knowledge that helped you draw these conclusions.

____

____

Home Activity Your child read a short passage and drew conclusions using facts and details. Read an article with your child. Have your child draw a conclusion from the article and explain to you how prior knowledge helped him or her to do so.

Name ____________________

Draw Conclusions

- **Drawing a conclusion** is forming an opinion based on what you already know or on the facts and details in a text.
- Check an author's conclusions or your own conclusions by asking: Is this the only logical choice? Are the facts accurate?

Directions Read the following passage. Then complete the diagram below by finding facts and details to support a conclusion.

One thing that cowboys had to be careful of while driving cattle was a stampede. A stampede is what happens when the cattle get scared by an unexpected noise and start to run very fast and wildly. Even breaking a twig could scare cattle into a stampede. Stampedes could cause harm to the camp, the cowboys, the horses, and the cattle themselves. It was hard to control the stampedes. Sometimes cowboys would try to direct the stampede to run in a circle. Other times, they let the cattle get tired from running and stop on their own.

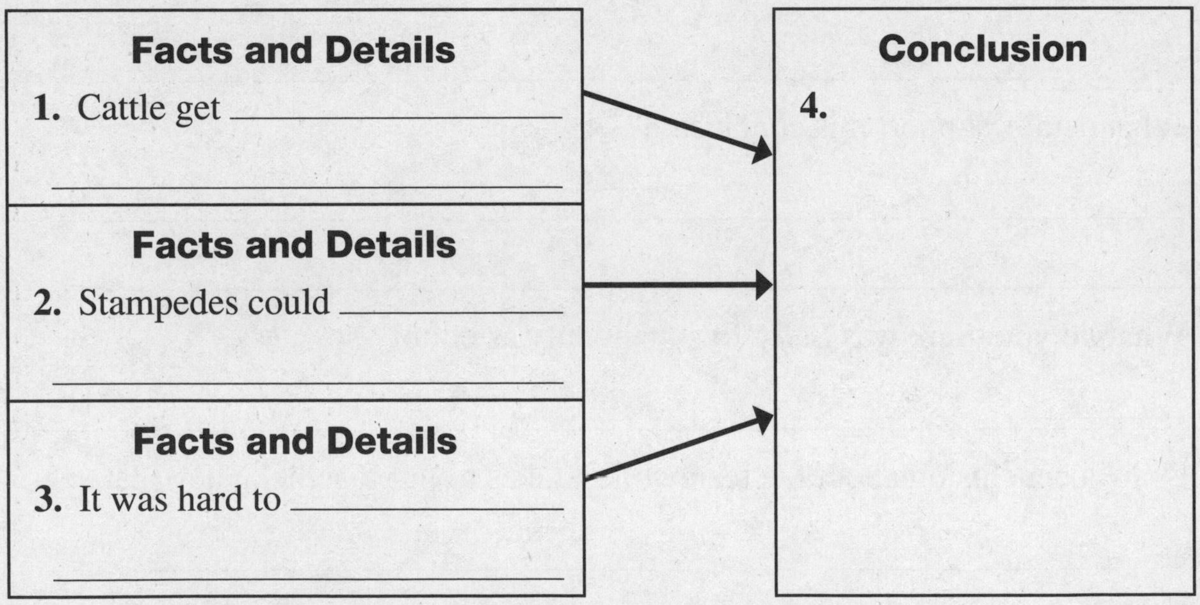

5. How would you decide if the facts and details are accurate?

____

____

Home Activity Your child read a short passage and drew a conclusion using facts and details. Describe a person, place, or thing. Ask your child to draw a conclusion about what you described based on facts and details in your description.

Name ______________________________

Newspaper/Newsletter

Newspapers are daily or weekly publications printed on large sheets of paper folded together. They include such sections as current news, advertisements, feature stories, and editorials. **Newsletters** are short publications for groups and include news that interests the groups' members.

Directions Use this index from a school newspaper to answer the questions below.

1. In what section would you find information about the mayor's upcoming visit to the school?

____

____

2. On what page would you find the score of the last basketball game?

____

3. On what page would you find comments from students about last week's newspaper?

____

4. In what section would you find comics or cartoons?

____

5. Would the school newspaper be a good place to find out information about world events? Why or why not?

____

____

Name ______________________________

Directions Use the school newspaper article to answer the questions below.

Gallup Ranch School to Have New Bus

Most of the students who attend Gallup Ranch School have to take the bus in the morning. The surrounding ranches are too far away for students to be able to walk or ride a bicycle to school. Since the bus has to start out early to make all of its stops, many students have to wake up very early in the morning to catch the bus. Teachers are aware of the problem, and that is why they have asked for funding from the county government. Just yesterday, the principal of the school announced that the county will buy us a second bus. Now there will be two bus routes instead of one, and students won't have to be on the bus so long.

6. What does the headline of this article tell you about the article?

____

____

7. Why do you think a school newspaper would include an article like this?

____

____

8. Where would you expect to find an article like this in the school newspaper?

____

____

9. Name the *who, what,* and *when* in this article.

____

____

____

10. What kind of group might include this story in their newsletter? Explain.

____

____

Home Activity Your child learned about using newspapers/newsletters as resources. Work with your child to create a family newspaper. Challenge your child to think of the sections to include in the newspaper and the topics to write about in the articles.

Name

Family Times

Summary

Grace and the Time Machine

Grace and her friends build a time machine powered by imagination. Using the memories of Grace's grandmother and Mrs. Myerson, a neighbor, everyone has fun experiencing far-off places such as The Gambia, Trinidad, and Heidelberg.

Activity

Traveling Through Time Ask your family members the following question: If you could visit a different year, in the past or the future, what year would it be? Why? Have a conversation about your time-travel destinations.

Comprehension Skill

Draw Conclusions

Drawing a conclusion is forming an opinion based on what you already know or on the facts and details in a text. Check an author's conclusions or your own conclusions by asking: Is this the only logical choice? Are the facts accurate?

Activity

Working Backwards State a conclusion or opinion about a period of history. Ask a family member to name some facts and details that could support the conclusion. Then switch roles and try to support an opinion suggested by your partner.

Lesson Vocabulary

Words to Know

Knowing the meanings of these words is important to reading *Grace and the Time Machine*. Practice using these words.

Vocabulary Words

aboard on board; in or on a ship, train, bus, airplane, etc.

atlas book of maps

awkward not graceful or skillful in movement or shape

capable having fitness, power, or ability

chant to call over and over again

mechanical like a machine

miracle a wonderful happening that is contrary to the known laws of nature

reseats sits again

vehicle device for carrying people or things, such as a car, bus, airplane etc.

Grammar

Irregular Plural Nouns

Most nouns are changed from their singular forms to their plural forms by adding an *–s* or an *–es*. *For example: bird/birds, beach/beaches.* Some nouns, however, are made plural in other ways, such as by changing their spelling. *For example: tooth/teeth.* Some nouns have the same singular and plural forms. *For example: sheep/sheep, fish/fish.* Plural nouns that are made by one of these other methods are called **irregular plural nouns.**

Activity

Animal Memory On separate note cards, write the names of the following animals and draw a picture of each of them: fish, deer, goose, ox, mouse, and moose. On separate note cards, write the plural form of each name and draw a picture to go with it. Mix the cards up and turn them facing down. Try to match the singular nouns to their irregular plural forms by playing a game of memory with a family member.

Practice Tested Spelling Words

______	______	______	______
______	______	______	______
______	______	______	______
______	______	______	______
______	______	______	______

Name ______________________________ Grace

Draw Conclusions

- **Drawing a conclusion** is forming an opinion based on what you already know or on the facts and details in a text. Facts and details are the small pieces of information in an article or story.
- Facts and details "add up" to a conclusion. Conclusions formed by the author or the reader must make sense.

Directions Read the following passage. Then complete the diagram and answer the question.

Traveling can teach you many things. It can teach you about land features, such as deserts, mountains, and mesas, and the differences between them. Traveling can teach you about a new climate, whether it's hot and humid or cold and windy, and how the people deal with the climate from day to day.

Visiting a new city or country also can tell you much about the people who live there. You can hear the language they speak, eat the foods they eat, dress in the clothes they dress in, and appreciate the art they make.

Fact or Detail 1.	+	Fact or Detail 2.	+	Fact or Detail 3.	=	Conclusion 4.

5. What do you think would happen if people did not travel?

____

____

Home Activity Your child drew a conclusion using facts or details in a passage. Talk to your child about any traveling you have done in your life, such as visiting another city, state, or country. Ask your child to draw a conclusion about your travel experiences.

Name ______________________________

Vocabulary

Directions Choose the word from the box that best completes each sentence. Write the word on the line.

Check the Words You Know
___aboard
___atlas
___awkward
___capable
___chant
___mechanical
___miracle
___reseats
___vehicle

__________________ **1.** At first, it felt ____ to be in a new country.

__________________ **2.** We rode in a special ____ to tour the city and its rivers.

__________________ **3.** My sister is ____ of getting around by herself.

__________________ **4.** Sharon opened the ____ to see where we were.

__________________ **5.** We listened to the tribe ____ as they danced.

Directions Choose the word from the box that best matches each clue. Write the word in the puzzle.

Across

6. like a machine

9. on or in a car or train

10. book of maps

Down

7. seats again

8. a wonder

Write an E-mail Message

On a separate sheet of paper write an e-mail message to a friend about an imaginary trip you took to another country. Use as many vocabulary words as you can.

Home Activity Your child identified and used vocabulary words from *Grace and the Time Machine.* With your child, make up a story about living in another part of the world. Use as many of the vocabulary words as you can.

Name ____________________

Vocabulary • Word Structure

- A **prefix** is a syllable added at the beginning of a base word to change its meaning.
- The prefix *re-* means *to do over* or *again.*

Directions Read the following passage. Then answer the questions below.

I love to retell how much fun it was to ride the train while traveling abroad with my family. We carried an atlas to keep track of how many miles we'd crossed. It was amazing how quickly we moved from city to city! There were no mechanical problems with the train, so nothing slowed down our trip.

The best thing about the train trip my family took was the lunch breaks. At these times, everyone got off the train to have a picnic in a beautiful meadow or to walk around a tiny village. Then the conductor reseated us, and when everything was reorganized, ZOOM! We were off to explore more of the country.

1. What is the prefix in the word *retell*? What does the word mean?

____

2. What does the word *reseated* mean?

____

3. Why did the conductor need to *reseat* the passengers?

____

____

4. If you *reorganized* your bedroom, what did you do?

____

5. Write a sentence using a word with the prefix *re-*.

____

____

Home Activity Your child identified the prefix *re-* to understand the meanings of new words. Have a conversation with your child and try to use as many words that begin with *re-* as you can. Count how many you can use in one sentence.

Name ______________________

Grace

Compare and Contrast

Directions Read the passage. Then answer the questions below.

The countries of Brazil and Bolivia both are located in South America. The two countries are right next to each other, but Brazil is many times larger than Bolivia.

The northern part of Brazil has a tropical climate. You will find the rain forests of the Amazon River there. But in the southern part of Brazil, it is cooler and better for farming. Bolivia also has tropical rain forests. The rain forests cover the land in the eastern part of the country. Yet, in the western part, there are high, cold mountains and plateaus.

People in Brazil mostly speak Portuguese, while people in Bolivia speak Spanish and native languages. Yet many people in both countries, no matter the language, are Roman Catholics.

1. How are the sizes of Brazil and Bolivia different?

____

2. What land feature do Brazil and Bolivia share?

____

3. What land features does Bolivia have that Brazil does not?

____

____

4. What is similar about the people in these two countries? What is different?

____

____

____

5. On a separate sheet of paper, put the information above into a Venn diagram.

Home Activity Your child has compared and contrasted two countries. Read an encyclopedia article about another country. With your child, compare and contrast the country's land and people with that of the United States.

Name ______________________________

Draw Conclusions

- **Drawing a conclusion** is forming an opinion based on what you already know or on the facts and details in a text. Facts and details are the small pieces of information in an article or story.
- Facts and details "add up" to a conclusion. Conclusions formed by the author or the reader must make sense.

Directions Read the following passage. Then answer the questions below.

If you ever travel to Trinidad, you might hear a calypso song. This special kind of song is an important part of the culture of Trinidad. Calypso songs make fun of an event in society or in politics that everyone in the area knows about. The song might be sung with Spanish, African, and Creole words. The calypso singer can sing the words to a popular melody or a made-up one. The musical instruments that back up the singer play an offbeat rhythm. These instruments might include a guitar, a shak-shak, which is like a maraca, a stringed instrument called a cuatro, a bamboo instrument called a tamboo-bamboo, and steel drums.

1. Draw a conclusion about the purpose of the calypso song.

____

2. What detail(s) supports this conclusion?

____

____

3. In a few of your own words, describe calypso music.

____

4. What detail(s) supports this description?

____

____

5. Describe an event where you might hear calypso music.

____

Home Activity Your child drew conclusions using facts or details in a passage. While reading an article or short story with your child, stop periodically and ask him/her to draw conclusions about the paragraphs you have just finished.

Name ______________________________ Grace

Draw Conclusions

- **Drawing a conclusion** is forming an opinion based on what you already know or on the facts and details in a text. Facts and details are the small pieces of information in an article or story.
- Facts and details "add up" to a conclusion. Conclusions formed by the author or the reader must make sense.

Directions Read the following passage. Then complete the diagram and answer the question.

When I got off the boat and stepped onto the island, I was amazed by what I saw. The sand was white and soft, almost like powder. It felt so soothing on my tired feet. There were palm trees that stretched up into the sky. Large flowers of every color surrounded the bases of the trees. Butterflies with spots and stripes fluttered in the light of the summer sun. A small path led through the trees to an open-air market, where travelers were greeted by friendly faces, delicious-smelling foods, and sweet island music.

Fact or Detail		Fact or Detail		Fact or Detail		Conclusion
1. The sand was	+	**2.** There were palm	+	**3.** Butterflies	=	**4.** The island was a ________ place.

5. What conclusion could you draw about the people of this island?

____

____

School + Home **Home Activity** Your child drew a conclusion using facts or details in a passage. Describe to your child your idea of a perfect island. Have your child draw conclusions from your description.

Name ______________________ Grace

Advertisement

- All **advertisements** sell a product or service. Advertisers want their product or service to appear at its best or most appealing.
- There are four parts to an advertisement: a photo or other picture of what is being sold, a headline in large type that "yells" about the product, information about the product, and who makes the product or service.

Directions Use this advertisement to answer the questions below.

The Sunny Fun Cruise will give your family the trip of a lifetime! The Sunny Fun Cruise ship sails to such locations as Jamaica, the Bahamas, and the Florida Keys. Your family will love the ride aboard this beautiful ship that has five refreshing swimming pools, three fine-dining restaurants, and two state-of-the-art game rooms. At any of the ship's ports you can enjoy water activities like snorkeling, shopping, and touring the local town. Contact the Sunny Fun Travel Company today to book a family vacation everyone will love!

1. What is this advertisement trying to sell?

____

2. What is the headline in this advertisement?

____

3. Who wants you to book this cruise?

____

4. How does the ad appeal to families?

____

____

5. In what kind of magazine would you see an ad like this?

____

Name ________________________________ Grace

Directions Use the advertisement below to answer the questions.

Ever wanted to go back in time? Now you can!

With the Time Machine 3000 you can be swept away to the past or the future! Using the Time Machine 3000 is as easy as setting your watch. Simply set the day, date, and year you wish to travel to, hit the "Go" button, and you're off to a place you've been before or one you've never seen! The Time Machine 3000 is a product of the famous Gail Scientific Research Group—the same company that brought you the Teleporter 2000. Imagine the places you could go and the things you could do with the Time Machine 3000! Buy it today!

6. How does the headline grab your attention?

____

____

7. Why does the ad include a picture of the Time Machine 3000?

____

8. Why does the ad tell you that using the machine *is as easy as setting your watch?*

____

____

9. Why do you think the ad told you that the Gail Scientific Research Group was the same company that brought you the Teleporter 2000?

____

____

10. Based on this ad, would you buy the Time Machine 3000? Why or why not?

____

____

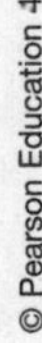

Home Activity Your child learned to identify the parts of an advertisement. Look through a newspaper or magazine with your child. Ask your child to indicate the different parts of the advertisements that appear in the periodical.

Name

Family Times

Summary

Marven of the Great North Woods

When Marven Lasky is a little boy, he leaves his family to become a bookkeeper at a lumber camp. At first, it is difficult for Marven because the lumberjacks speak French and do not follow his Jewish traditions. But after Marven befriends Jean Louis, a lumberjack who Marven mistakes for a bear in the woods, he learns to accept his new home.

Activity

A Job Well Done Ask your family members to tell you why they think it is important to do a job well. Record their thoughts on a piece of paper. Then, together, summarize their ideas into a neat and well-organized paragraph that can be displayed in a room of your home.

Comprehension Skill

Fact and Opinion

A **statement of fact** can be proved true or false. A **statement of opinion** cannot be proved true or false, because it expresses a belief or a judgment.

Activity

That's Your Opinion Read a short article aloud together. After every statement, stop to discuss whether it is a statement of fact or opinion. If it is a statement of fact, discuss what sources you could use to prove the statement true or false.

Lesson Vocabulary

Words to Know

Knowing the meanings of these words is important to reading *Marven of the Great North Woods.* Practice using these words.

Vocabulary Words

cord measure of quantity for cut wood, equal to 128 cubic feet. A pile of wood 4 feet wide, 4 feet high, and 8 feet long is a cord.

dismay sudden, helpless fear of what is about to happen or what has happened

grizzly a large, gray or brownish bear

immense very large; huge; vast

payroll list of persons to be paid and the amount that each one is to receive

Grammar

Singular Possessive Nouns

A **singular possessive noun** is a singular noun that shows ownership. *For example: Lisa's shoes are green. The dog's ears are floppy.* "Lisa's" and "dog's" are *singular possessive nouns.* Singular possessive nouns are formed by adding *–'s* to the end of the noun. It does not matter whether or not the noun already ends in *s. For example: the table's legs, Tess's toy.*

Activity

Whose Is This? Together, take a walk around your house. Point to items that belong to a certain member of the family. In a notebook, fill in the following sentence for each item you see: The ____ is _____. *For example: The book is Kari's.*

Practice Tested Spelling Words

____	____	____	____
____	____	____	____
____	____	____	____
____	____	____	____
____	____	____	____

Fact and Opinion

- A **statement of fact** can be proved true or false. You can look in a reference book, ask an expert, or use your own knowledge and experience.
- A **statement of opinion** cannot be proved true or false. It is a belief or a judgment. It often contains a word of judgment, such as *best, should,* or *beautiful.* It may begin with the words *in my opinion* or *I believe.*

Directions Read the following passage. Then complete the table. Read each statement and answer the questions at the top of each column.

I am a forester. My job is to take care of forests. Sometimes I recommend cutting trees to keep the forest healthy. If this happens, the loggers' work must follow laws that protect the environment, so the loggers should know these laws. There are other times when I suggest not cutting down trees. I disagree with people who think we should never cut down any trees. I believe we should preserve forests for the future as we use forest resources today.

Statement	Does it state a fact or an opinion?	If an opinion, what are the clue words? If a fact, how could you prove it?
I am a forester.	Fact	Check the person's job.
My job is to take care of forests.	**1.**	**2.**
I disagree with people who think we should never cut down any trees.	**3.**	**4.**

5. Find one sentence that contains both a statement of fact and a statement of opinion.

____

____

Home Activity Your child identified statements of fact and statements of opinion in a short paragraph. Listen to or watch a news program with your child. Ask your child to tell you when he or she hears the news announcer expressing an opinion. Ask your child to explain why it is an opinion rather than a fact.

Name ______________________________

Vocabulary

Directions Choose the word from the box that best matches each definition. Write the word on the line.

Check the Words You Know
___cord
___dismay
___grizzly
___immense
___payroll

______________ **1.** very big; huge; vast

______________ **2.** a pile of cut wood measuring 128 cubic feet

______________ **3.** a sudden, helpless fear about what is about to happen

______________ **4.** large, fierce North American bear

______________ **5.** a list of people to be paid and the amount each one is to receive

Directions Choose the word from the box that best completes each sentence. Write the word on the line shown to the left.

______________ **6.** Anil named his dog "Bear" because it reminded him of the _____ bear he'd seen in a picture.

______________ **7.** Charlotte looked with _____ at the flat tire on her bicycle.

______________ **8.** Mr. Ramos told me that I need to be on the _____ in order to be paid.

______________ **9.** We will need at least a _____ of firewood to keep warm this winter.

______________ **10.** Marta could not move the _____ rock from the trail.

Write a Journal Entry

On a separate piece of paper write a journal entry about a day you spent in a forest chopping firewood. Use as many vocabulary words as you can.

Home Activity Your child identified and used vocabulary words from *Marven of the Great North Woods*. Read a selection with your child. List any unfamiliar words and try to figure out the meaning of each word by using other words that appear near it. Use a dictionary when necessary.

Name ______________________________

Vocabulary • Dictionary/Glossary

- **Dictionaries** and **glossaries** provide alphabetical lists of words and their meanings.
- Sometimes looking at the words around an unfamiliar word can't help you figure out the word's meaning. If this happens, use a dictionary or glossary to find the meaning.

Directions Read the following story. Then answer the questions below.

When Stella heard the low, growling sound, she hid quietly behind the cord of cut wood. She remembered the story about the grizzly bear who roamed the nearby woods. The bear was immense. A moment later, her Uncle Seth called out, "Stella, why are you hiding behind that pile of wood?" Stella could not hide the dismay in her voice. "I heard the bear growling," Stella answered in a fearful whisper. Stella's uncle laughed. "Didn't you know we have a new dog on the payroll?" he said. "His bark sounds more like a growl than a regular bark!"

1. Which words around the word *cord* can help you figure out its meaning?

____

2. What is the meaning of *immense?* How did you determine its meaning?

____

3. What words around the word *dismay* help you figure out its meaning?

____

4. What is the meaning of the word *grizzly?* How did you determine its meaning?

____

5. Use a dictionary or glossary to find the definition for one of the words you couldn't use nearby words to understand. Write down the definition.

____

____

____

Home Activity Your child identified unfamiliar words that could be defined using a dictionary or glossary. Work with your child to identify unfamiliar words in a newspaper or magazine article. Ask your child if he or she needs to use a dictionary to find the meaning of the words. If so, ask your child to look up at least one definition in a dictionary or glossary.

Name ______________________________

Main Idea and Details

Directions Read the article. Then answer the questions below.

A hundred years ago, lumberjacks worked in forests all over North America. They were known for their hard work, their strength, and the immense amount of food they ate. Today, lumberjacks are mostly just a memory. You can learn about lumberjacks by reading books, visiting museums, or attending lumberjack competitions. History comes alive at a lumberjack competition. In these competitions, modern-day lumberjacks compete in events like logrolling and wood chopping. Lumberjack music, food, and costumes are also part of these events.

1. In one or two words, what are all of the sentences about?

____

2. What is the main idea of the passage?

____

____

3. What is one supporting detail that tells more about the main idea?

____

____

4. What is another supporting detail for the main idea?

____

____

5. On a separate sheet of paper, write a summary of the passage in one or two sentences.

Home Activity Your child identified the main idea and supporting details of a nonfiction passage and wrote a summary of it. Read a short magazine or newspaper article with your child. Work together to identify the main idea and supporting details of the article. Then use this information to write a short summary.

Fact and Opinion

- A **statement of fact** can be proved true or false. You can look in a reference book, ask an expert, or use your own knowledge and experience.
- A **statement of opinion** cannot be proved true or false. It is a belief or a judgment. It often contains a word of judgment, such as *best, should,* or *beautiful.* It may begin with the words *in my opinion* or *I believe.*

Directions Read the following passage. Then answer the questions below.

Logging is the most dangerous occupation in the United States. Logging is a job that combines dangerous tools with a dangerous environment. Chainsaws are very frightening to use. Everyone should agree about how dangerous it is to be around a sliding and rolling log weighing more than a ton.

Every year, loggers are injured by the equipment they use and by the trees they cut down. Loggers are injured almost twice as often as workers in other industries. To protect loggers, the United States has created many logging-safety laws.

1. Is the third sentence a fact or an opinion? How can you tell?

____

2. Is the fourth sentence a fact or an opinion? How can you tell?

____

3. Is the sixth sentence a fact or an opinion? How can you tell?

____

4. Is the seventh sentence a fact or an opinion? How can you tell?

____

5. Why do you think someone would want to have the dangerous job of being a logger? Use at least one fact and one opinion to support your answer.

____

____

Home Activity Your child identified statements of fact and opinion in a short paragraph. Read a letter to the editor from the newspaper with your child. Ask your child to tell you when he or she reads an opinion. Ask your child to explain why it is an opinion rather than a fact.

Name ______________________________

Fact and Opinion

- A **statement of fact** can be proved true or false. You can look in a reference book, ask an expert, or use your own knowledge and experience.
- A **statement of opinion** cannot be proved true or false. It is a belief or a judgment. It often contains a word of judgment, such as *best, should,* or *beautiful.* It may begin with the words *in my opinion* or *I believe.*

Directions Read the following passage. Read each numbered statement in the boxes. Draw a line from each box to the oval titled "fact" or "opinion."

The first lumberjack I ever met was named William. He was shopping for a new pair of boots. I pointed to a pair of brown boots in the window. "I don't like wearing brown boots," said William. He bought a pair of black boots instead. William smiled when he put them on. "These are the most beautiful boots in the world," he said.

FACT

1. The first lumberjack I ever met was named William.	**2.** He was shopping for a new pair of boots.	**3.** I don't like wearing brown boots.	**4.** He bought a pair of black boots instead.	**5.** These are the most beautiful boots in the world.

OPINION

Home Activity Your child identified statements of fact and statements of opinion in a short paragraph. Read information on a cereal box with your child. Ask your child to tell you which information is fact and which is opinion and why.

Graph

- **Graphs** show data in visual form. Graphs can quickly show how one piece of information compares to other pieces of information. There are several types of graphs.
- A **bar graph** uses vertical or horizontal bars to show different amounts of something.
- A **circle graph** has a pie shape. It shows how something can be divided into parts.
- A **line graph** contains lines that connect a series of points on a graph. Line graphs are good for showing changes that happen over time.
- A **picture graph** uses pictures to show amounts or numbers of things.

Directions The North Woods Logging Company wants to see how much wood their lumberjacks are chopping. Remember, wood is measured in cords. Study the bar graph and the circle graph below. Then answer the questions on the next page.

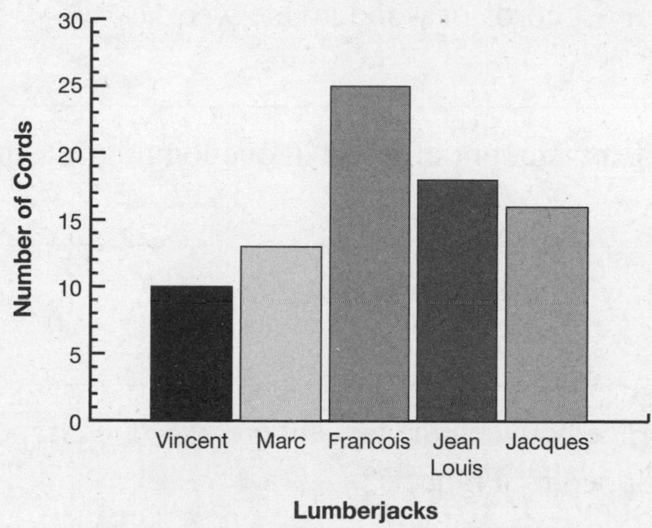

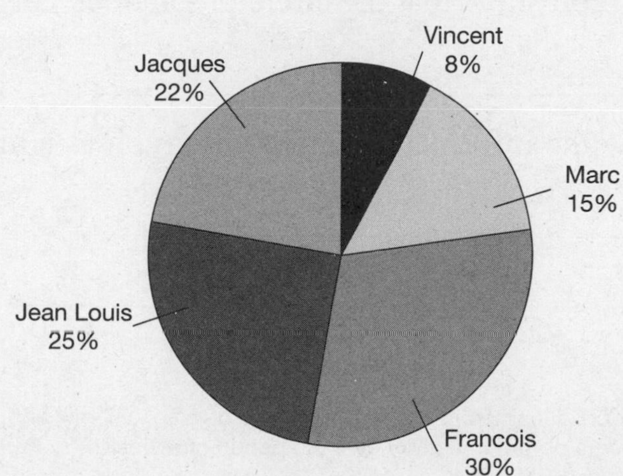

Directions Use the graphs to answer the following questions.

1. How do you know what each graph shows?

2. What unit is used in the bar graph to measure the amount of wood chopped?

3. Whose names appear along the bottom of the bar graph?

4. How is the information in each graph similar? How is it different?

5. Who chopped the most cords of wood in one week?

6. Who chopped the least amount of wood in one logging season?

7. In the circle graph, what is being divided into parts?

8. What is the difference between the percentage of wood chopped by Jean Louis and the percentage chopped by Francois?

9. What does the bar graph show that the circle graph does not?

10. How could you show the information in the bar graph as a picture graph?

Home Activity Your child learned about different kinds of graphs. Draw and label a line graph to show the hours you spent doing a common activity over the period of a week.

Name

Family Times

Summary

So You Want to Be President?

President of the United States is a tough job that many people strive to get. This book tells you what it takes to be president, but also how our past presidents stayed true to themselves and their unique personalities while in office.

Activity

Presidential Decisions With your family, talk about the types of changes and decisions you would make if you were president of the United States. Explain why these changes are important to you and the country.

Comprehension Skill

Main Idea and Details

The **main idea** of a passage makes a point about the passage's topic and has at least one supporting detail. **Details** are smaller pieces of information that tell more about the main idea.

Activity

Radio News Together with a family member, listen to a news report on the radio. Pay close attention to what is being discussed. On a piece of paper, write down what you think is the main idea of the report and two supporting details. Compare your notes. Did you agree?

Lesson Vocabulary

Words to Know

Knowing the meanings of these words is important to reading *So You Want to Be President?* Practice using these words.

Vocabulary Words

Constitution the written set of fundamental principles by which the United States is governed

howling very great

humble not proud; modest

politics the work of government; management of public business

responsibility the act or fact of taking care of someone or something; obligation

solemnly seriously; earnestly; with dignity

vain having too much pride in your looks, ability, etc.

Grammar

Plural Possessive Nouns

Plural possessive nouns show that something is owned by more than one person, place, or thing. Like singular possessive nouns, plural possessive nouns are created by adding an *–'s* to the noun. However, if the noun already ends in *s*, add only an apostrophe to the end of the word. *For example: men's shoes, geese's feathers, books' covers, buildings' windows.*

Activity

Animal Parts Describe a recognizable feature of a certain type of animal. *For example: These are long, spotted, and stretch into the trees.* Have a family member respond with the plural possessive name of the animal and the feature. *For example: giraffes' necks.*

Practice Tested Spelling Words

____	____	____	____
____	____	____	____
____	____	____	____
____	____	____	____
____	____	____	____

Name ______________________________

Main Idea and Details

- The **main idea** is the most important idea from a paragraph, passage, or article.
- **Details** are small pieces of information that tell more about the main idea.

Directions Read the following passage. Complete the diagram by stating the main idea and three supporting details. Then answer the question below the diagram.

The President has a difficult job, but at least there are people to help the President along the way. These special people are called the Cabinet. The President gets to choose the members of the Cabinet, but the members of the United States Senate must approve them.

Each member of the Cabinet represents a department of the government. Some examples of these departments arc Education, Homeland Security, and Transportation. The Cabinet meets with the President to talk about issues that affect their departments. In these meetings, the President gets good advice on what decisions to make.

Main Idea

1.

Supporting Details

2.

3.

4.

5. What is a one-sentence summary of this passage?

____

____

Home Activity Your child used a graphic organizer to identify the main idea and supporting details of a passage. Work with your child to identify the main idea and supporting details for individual paragraphs in a magazine or newspaper article about government. Challenge him or her to summarize the entire article.

Name ________________________________

Vocabulary

Directions Choose a word from the box that best completes each sentence. Write the word on the line shown to the left.

Check the Words You Know
___Constitution
___howling
___humble
___politics
___responsibility
___solemnly
___vain

__________________ **1.** A ____ person might look in a mirror all the time.

__________________ **2.** The President has much ____.

__________________ **3.** He behaved ____ as he took the oath.

__________________ **4.** The ____ is an important document.

__________________ **5.** Many people voted, so the election was a ____ success.

Directions Choose the word from the box that best matches each numbered clue below. Write the letters of the word on the blanks. After you are finished, the boxed letters will spell a secret word.

6. seriously

7. government work

8. the act of taking care of someone

9. having too much pride

10. not proud

6. ___ ___ ___ [ ] ___ ___ ___ ___

[x]

[e]

7. ___ ___ ___ ___ ___ ___ ___ [ ] ___

[u]

[t]

8. ___ ___ ___ ___ ___ ___ ___ ___ [ ] ___ ___ ___ ___ ___

9. [ ] ___ ___ ___

10. ___ ___ ___ ___ ___ [ ]

Write a Speech

Pretend you have just been elected President of the United States. On a separate sheet of paper, write a short speech you would give to the public. In the course of explaining how you will approach your new job, use as many vocabulary words as you can.

Home Activity Your child identified and used vocabulary words from *So You Want to Be President?* Together, read an article about politics or government. Discuss the article, using as many vocabulary words from the selection as you can.

Name ______________________

Vocabulary • Dictionary/Glossary

- **Dictionaries** and **glossaries** provide alphabetical lists of words and their meanings.
- Sometimes looking at the words around an unfamiliar word can't help you figure out the word's meaning. If this happens, use a dictionary or glossary to find the meaning.

Directions Read the following letter. Then answer the questions below. Use your glossary or a dictionary to help you with unfamiliar words.

Dear Mr. President,

I became interested in politics after studying the Constitution in school. I hope this doesn't sound vain, but I think I'm a pretty smart student, and I believe that my ideas are worth hearing. I think that the government should take on the responsibility of making sure that every person in the country knows how to read and write. Then everyone would be able to communicate better and solve problems easier. I solemnly believe this. Please look at the plan I've written on the following pages.

Sincerely,
Benita

1. Look up the word *Constitution* in your glossary. What part of speech is it?

____

2. What is the meaning of the word *communicate*?

____

3. Why does Benita want to avoid sounding *vain*?

____

____

4. Write a *responsibility* that you have in your life.

____

5. Write an example for the glossary entry for the word *solemnly*.

____

____

Home Activity Your child used a glossary to identify the definitions of unfamiliar words. Read a short story together. Create a glossary for the story by writing down all the unfamiliar words and using the definitions from a dictionary.

Name ______________________________

Generalize

Directions Read the following passage. Then answer the questions below.

There have been forty-two Presidents of the United States. Eight of these men were born in Virginia. Seven were born in Ohio. The states of Massachusetts and New York each can claim four presidents as native sons. Two presidents were born in North Carolina, Vermont, and Texas. Thirteen other states have each produced one President.

Eighteen Presidents have been members of the Republican party. Fourteen others have been Democrats. Presidents have been members of four other parties, all of which have now disappeared. The Whig party and the Democratic-Republican party each claimed four Presidents. Two presidents (in fact, the first two) were Federalists.

1. Write a valid generalization based on the information in the first paragraph.

____

____

2. Write a valid generalization based on information in the second paragraph.

____

____

3. What examples support your second generalization?

____

____

4. Here is a generalization based on this passage: Northern states have produced few Presidents. Why is this generalization faulty?

____

____

5. On a separate sheet of paper, write a paragraph about why some states might have produced more Presidents than other states. Use at least one generalization.

Home Activity Your child made generalizations based on information in an article. Together, write a list of generalizations you could use to describe your family.

Name ______________________________

Main Idea and Details

- The **main idea** is the most important idea from a paragraph, passage, or article.
- **Details** are small pieces of information that tell more about the main idea.

Directions Read the passage. Then answer the questions below.

The government of the United States has its share of responsibilities, but so do you. In order for the nation to do well, citizens have to do their part.

One responsibility of citizens is taking part in elections. Once you turn eighteen years old, you are given the right—and the responsibility—to vote. Citizens vote for officials to be their representatives. In this way, each citizen has a say in governing the country.

Another responsibility of all citizens, no matter what age, is to obey laws. The nation's laws are written to keep citizens safe and protected.

1. In three or four words, tell what the passage is about.

____

2. What is the main idea of the passage?

____

3. What is one important detail that tells more about the main idea?

____

____

4. What is another detail that supports the main idea?

____

____

5. In one sentence, write a summary of this passage.

____

____

Home Activity Your child identified the main idea and supporting details in a short nonfiction article and wrote a summary of it. Read a magazine or newspaper article about citizens' involvement in government. Work together to write a short summary of the article.

Name ________________________________

Main Idea and Details

- The **main idea** is the most important idea from a paragraph, passage, or article.
- **Details** are small pieces of information that tell more about the main idea.

Directions Read the passage and complete the diagram. State the main idea and three supporting details. Then answer the question below the diagram.

Rosalynn Carter, the wife of President Jimmy Carter, took her role as First Lady seriously. She did not let her time in the White House pass her by. Mrs. Carter attended official meetings and represented the United States on business trips. Mrs. Carter also supported programs to help needy citizens. For example, she worked to improve the lives of elderly people and citizens with mental health problems. Another accomplishment of Mrs. Carter was pointing out the importance of the performing arts to our society.

Main Idea

1. Rosalynn Carter took

Supporting Details

2. She attended

3. She represented

4.

5. What is a one-sentence summary of this passage?

____

____

Home Activity Your child identified the main idea and supporting details in a nonfiction passage. Together, read an article about a famous person. Work with your child to identify the main idea and supporting details of the article. Then ask your child to summarize the article.

Name ______________________________

Time Line

A **time line** is a chart that shows a sequence of events. A time line uses a bar divided into periods of time to show the order of events.

Directions Study the time line below. Then answer the questions that follow.

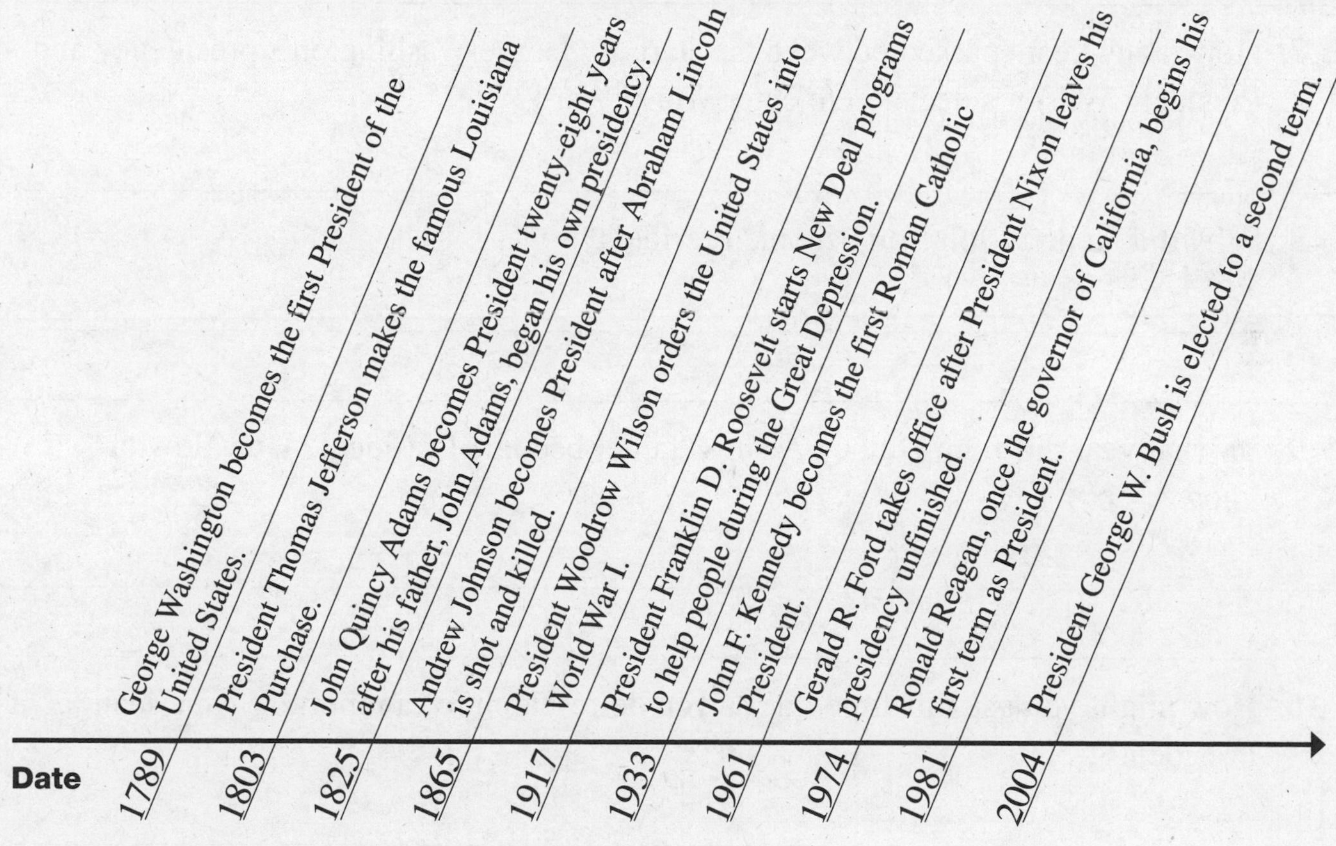

1. What information does this time line provide?

____

____

2. How are the dates organized on this time line?

____

____

3. According to the time line, what event happened most recently?

____

4. When did President Jefferson make the Louisiana Purchase?

____

5. What happened in 1974 before Gerald R. Ford became President?

____

6. What happened for the first time in 1961?

____

7. How many years passed between the start of George Washington's presidency and President Wilson's decision to enter World War I?

____

8. Why did Andrew Johnson become President?

____

____

9. In what year did John Quincy Adams' father become President? How do you know?

____

____

10. How might you use this time line as you do research for a report on American Presidents?

____

____

____

Home Activity Your child learned about time lines and used a time line to answer questions. Together, read an encyclopedia entry about an American President. Write key facts about the President's life and career in a time line. Encourage your child to illustrate the time line with pictures, where appropriate.

Name ______________________

Family Times

Summary

The Stranger

In late summer, a farmer hits a man in the road with his truck. The speechless stranger then spends several weeks on the farm. The weather stays warm into autumn, and the leaves around the farm remain green. The stranger realizes something is wrong. He leaves the farm, and the weather returns to normal.

Activity

Seasonal Characters Imagine what the different seasons might be like if they were people. What would summer look and sound like? What kind of clothes would winter wear? Draw or describe a season as a person. See if a family member can guess which season it is.

Comprehension Skill

Cause and Effect

A **cause** is why something happens. An **effect** is what happens. Sometimes a cause has more than one effect. To find an effect, ask yourself, "What happened?" To find a cause, ask yourself, "Why did it happen?"

Activity

If and Because Make up an "if" sentence that contains a cause and an effect. *For example: If I stumbled with a full glass of milk, the milk would spill on the floor.* Have a family member add to the story with a "because" sentence that uses the effect from your sentence. *For example: Because the milk spilled on the floor, Mark got out the mop.* Keep adding to the story, switching between "if" and "because" sentences.

Lesson Vocabulary

Words to Know

Knowing the meanings of these words is important to reading *The Stranger*. Practice using these words.

Vocabulary Words

draft current of air

etched engraved: placed a design on a metal plate or glass surface using acid, which eats away the lines

fascinated interested greatly; attracted very strongly; charmed

frost moisture frozen on or in a surface; feathery crystals of ice formed when water vapor in the air condenses at a temperature below freezing

parlor formerly, a room for receiving or entertaining guests; sitting room

terror great fear

timid easily frightened; shy

Grammar

Action and Linking Verbs

Verbs are words that tell what the subject of a sentence does or what the subject is like. Verbs that show action are called **action verbs.** *For example: flew, thinking, climb.* Yet not all verbs show action. **Linking verbs** tell what the subject is or what the subject is like without showing action. *For example: am, was, seemed, feel.*

Activity

Verb Charades On strips of paper, write twelve simple sentences, six containing action verbs and six containing linking verbs. Underline the verb in each sentence. Then put the strips into a pile. Take turns with family members picking a sentence from the pile and acting it out silently for the rest of the group. The person who guesses the verb should tell if it is an action verb or a linking verb.

Practice Tested Spelling Words

______	______	______	______
______	______	______	______
______	______	______	______
______	______	______	______
______	______	______	______

Name ______________________

Cause and Effect

- A **cause** is why something happens. An **effect** is what happens.
- Sometimes clue words such as *because, so,* and *since* signal causes and effects. Other times you must figure out the causes and effects for yourself.

Directions Read the following passage. Complete the diagram to show causes and effects. Then answer the question below the diagram.

As Casey walked home from the store, the air felt crisp and dry. Casey could see small white clouds made by her breath. Since the wind blew sharply, the leaves on the elm tree rustled. She tightened her coat around her.

As she hurried down the street, the sky grew darker. Casey had a feeling something was about to happen. Just as she reached her house, a big fluffy, white snowflake fell onto her coat. She looked up and smiled. The first snowfall of the season, she thought. How exciting!

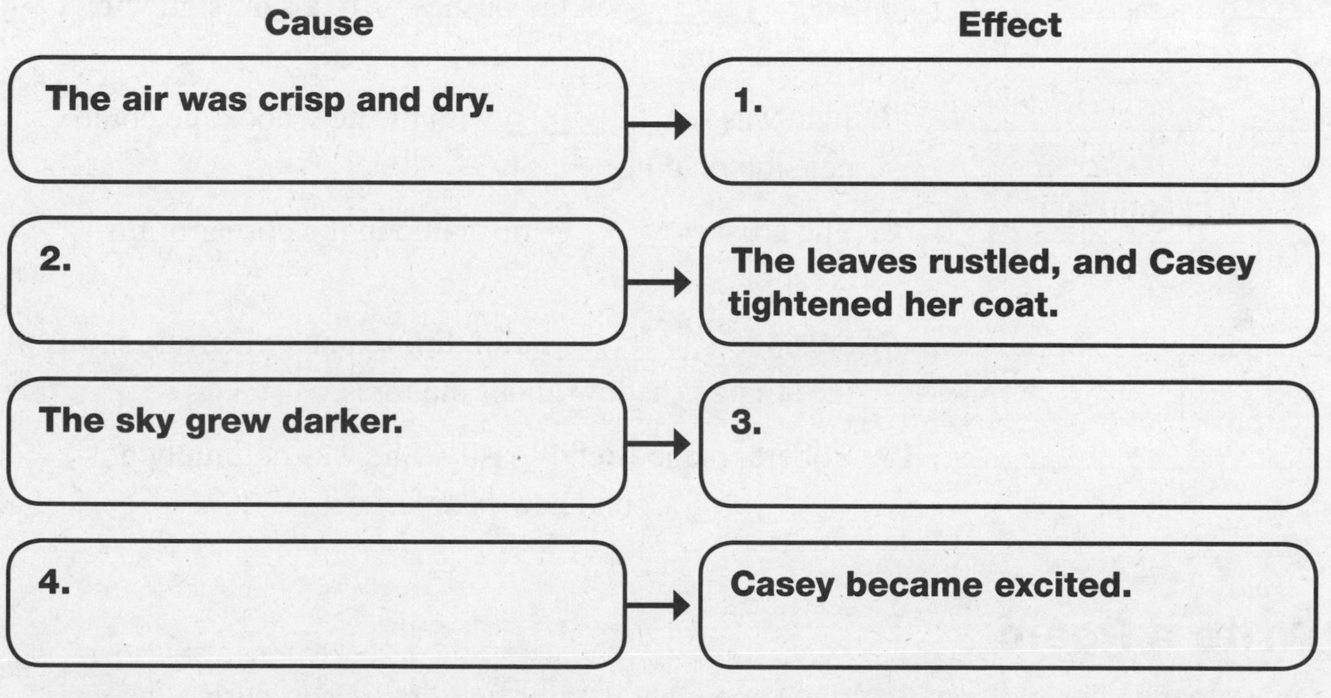

Cause	Effect
The air was crisp and dry.	**1.**
2.	**The leaves rustled, and Casey tightened her coat.**
The sky grew darker.	**3.**
4.	**Casey became excited.**

5. What are two effects of snowfall?

____

Home Activity Your child identified causes and effects in a brief passage. Work with your child to identify the causes and effects of three important events in his or her own life.

Name ______________________________________

Vocabulary

Directions Choose the word from the box that best matches each clue. Write the word on the line.

Check the Words You Know
___draft
___etched
___fascinated
___frost
___parlor
___terror
___timid

____________________ **1.** a room for receiving guests

____________________ **2.** engraved

____________________ **3.** crystals of frozen water on a cold surface

____________________ **4.** a current of air

____________________ **5.** easily frightened; shy

Directions Choose the word from the box that best completes each sentence below. Write the word on the line shown to the left.

____________________ **6.** The _________ on the bushes were a sure sign winter was coming.

____________________ **7.** Juan was so _________ with his new book, he could not stop reading.

____________________ **8.** The artist _________ his name in the corner of his creation.

____________________ **9.** Susan felt _________ run through her when she saw the strange shadow under the trees.

____________________ **10.** Roberta made friends easily. She was definitely not _________ around new people.

Write a Poem

On a separate sheet of paper, write a poem about your favorite season during the year. Use as many vocabulary words as you can.

Home Activity Your child identified and used vocabulary words from *The Stranger.* Write your own short story together. Try to use all of the vocabulary words in the story.

Name ______________________________

Vocabulary • Context Clues

- When you are reading and see a word that has more than one meaning, you can use **context clues,** or words around the multiple-meaning word, to figure out its meaning.

Directions Read the following passage. Then answer the questions below.

Fall is a season with many different kinds of weather. Sometimes it can be warm and sunny. Sometimes it can be very rainy. But a lot of the time, fall days can feel like winter.

On fall mornings, we often see icy frost covering the ground and bushes in front of our house. When we go back inside, we have to remember to shut the windows and doors carefully. Otherwise, a cold draft moves through the house. Our house has an old-fashioned parlor where we can sit by the fire and tell stories. My sister likes stories that take place in the warmth of spring or summer. But I am most fascinated by the stories about people who work together and are able to survive a cold winter.

1. What does *frost* mean in this passage? What clues helped you figure this out?

____

____

2. What is another meaning for *frost?*

____

3. What does *draft* mean in this passage? What clues helped you figure this out?

____

4. What is another meaning for *draft?*

____

5. *Fall* can mean "a season of the year between summer and winter" or "to drop down." How is it used in the passage? How can you tell?

____

____

Home Activity Your child identified and used context clues to understand words that have multiple meanings. With your child, write a list of words that have multiple meanings. Take turns using the word in sentences. Be sure to make a sentence that uses each meaning.

Name ___________________________

Compare and Contrast

Directions Read the following passage. Then answer the questions below.

Alejandra was lying in her bed trying to sleep. She heard a howling noise outside that frightened her. Even though she knew it was probably just the wind, she could not calm herself down. She became so upset that she leaped out of bed and ran down the hall.

She burst into the front parlor and saw her mother sitting next to the fire writing a letter. Her mother looked up and smiled. "Would you like to help write this letter to your grandpa? Maybe you can think of something interesting for me to add," she said in a soothing voice. Alejandra could still hear the wind, but she felt safe and happy. She made up a funny story about a little girl who was frightened by the howl of the wind. Her mother added the story to the letter and said, "Your grandpa will say that reminds him of me when I was little!" After they finished, Alejandra hugged her mother and walked to her room. She was certain she would sleep happily for the rest of the night.

1. Which room is Alejandra in at the beginning of the passage?

____

2. How does she feel when she is in this room? Why does she feel this way?

____

____

3. Which room does Alejandra run to at the end of the first paragraph?

____

4. How does she feel when she gets there? Why do you think she feels this way?

____

____

5. How does Alejandra feel when she returns to her room? Why?

____

____

Home Activity Your child read a short passage and made comparisons and contrasts. Read two short stories or articles with your child. The stories should have some similarities without being too similar. Help your child to compare and contrast the details in the stories.

Name ______________________________

Cause and Effect

- A **cause** is why something happens. An **effect** is what happens.
- Sometimes clue words such as *because, so,* and *since* signal causes and effects. Other times you must figure out the causes and effects for yourself.

Directions Read the following passage. Then answer the questions below.

Every fall, the Stevensons celebrate a tradition they call Fall Day. Fall Day starts with yard work. Mom and Dad rake the leaves into big piles. Alicia and Paul are in charge of getting the leaves into the yard waste bags. After the leaves are picked up, they all go inside for hot apple cider.

After drinking the cider, they drive to the pumpkin farm. Alicia and Paul pick out pumpkins to take home and carve. That night, they will light candles inside the pumpkins and set them on the porch, because they like to look at the pumpkins' glowing faces. Fall Day is tiring, but it is always fun.

1. Why do Mom and Dad rake the leaves into piles?

____

____

2. Why do the Stevensons drive to the pumpkin farm?

____

3. Why do Alicia and Paul light candles in their pumpkins?

____

4. Why do the Stevensons call this day Fall Day?

____

____

5. What is a tradition you observe every year? What is the cause of this tradition?

____

____

Home Activity Your child identified causes and effects in a short passage. Talk to your child about something your family does as a tradition. Ask your child to write down what the tradition is and why it is done.

Name ______________________________

Cause and Effect

- A **cause** is what makes something happen. An **effect** is what happens.
- Sometimes clue words such as *because, so,* and *since* signal causes and effects. Other times you must figure out the causes and effects for yourself.

Directions Read the following passage. Then complete the diagram to show causes and effects.

The score was 20 to 20. It was the last few seconds in the game. Daniel and Mario tried to remain calm. They played this game each summer. Volleyball on the beach was their favorite sport, and they were a great team. The ball was served. The return tipped the net, so Mario dove for the ball and hit it straight up into the air. Sand splashed in his face. He looked up to see Daniel hit the ball over the net. The ball sailed toward the line. The other team couldn't reach it, and it fell to the sand. Mario jumped up, because Daniel had made the winning play.

Cause		Effect
The ball tipped the net.	→	**1. Mario** ______________________________
2. Daniel hit ______________________________	→	**3. The ball** ______________________________
4. Daniel ______________________________	→	**5. Mario** ______________________________

Home Activity Your child identified causes and effects in a brief passage. Write down three different decisions you and your child have made recently. Talk about what caused you to make those decisions and what effect those decisions have had.

Name ______________________________

Almanac

An **almanac** is a book that is published every year. It contains calendars, weather information, and dates of holidays. It also contains charts and tables of current information about subjects such as city population and recent prize winners in science, literature, or sports.

Directions Review this information from an almanac.

Fall Facts

- Fall usually lasts from September 22 (or 23) to December 21 (or 22).
- September 22 (or 23) has equal hours during the day and night.
- December 21 (or 22) is the shortest day of the year.
- Fall, also called autumn, is a time for harvesting crops.
- Fall is a popular time for festivals celebrating crops.

Fall Holidays

Holiday	Date	Common Image
Columbus Day	second Monday in October	ship
Halloween	October 31	pumpkin
Thanksgiving	fourth Thursday in November	turkey

Fall Leaves

- Some trees have leaves that turn yellow (instead of orange or red) each autumn. Examples include birch, tulip poplar, hickory, and redbud trees.
- During the fall in the United States, the most brilliant leaf colors appear in New England states.

Peak Times To See Colorful Leaves

State	Time
Maryland	September and early October
North Carolina	mid-September to mid-October
New York	mid-September to early November
Maine	end of September to mid-October
West Virginia	early October to end of November
Georgia	late October
Kentucky	October and most of November

Name ________________________________

Directions Use the information from the almanac to answer the following questions.

1. Which section gives information about trees and leaf colors?

____

2. What are the three holidays listed in this part of the almanac?

____

3. What is the shortest day of the year?

____

4. An image of a ship is often used to indicate which holiday?

____

5. How is the table labeled "Peak Times to See Colorful Leaves" arranged?

____

6. In which states can people best view leaves changing color on Thanksgiving?

____

7. Give two examples of trees whose leaves change only to yellow.

____

8. About how long is autumn, according to the information given in the almanac?

____

9. Which is more likely to be useful when planning a vacation: an almanac or an encyclopedia?

____

10. For what reasons might you choose an almanac over a dictionary to find information about autumn?

____

____

Home Activity Your child studied an almanac and answered questions about its use. With your child, look at the almanacs in a library's reference section. Choose a topic and find out what kinds of information on this topic can be found in an almanac.

Name

Family Times

Summary

Adelina's Whales

Adelina Mayoral lives in La Laguna, Mexico. Each January, the gray whales arrive in the lagoon near La Laguna and stay for three months before migrating farther north for the summer. Whale-watchers, scientists, and photographers visit La Laguna from all over the world to observe and interact with the whales.

Activity

Silly Sentences Create silly sentences about unusual pets. Try to make each sentence sillier than the one before. If someone says, "If I had a pet whale, I'd walk it on a leash every day," you might say, "If I had a pet whale, I'd sleep inside its mouth underwater."

Comprehension Skill

Fact and Opinion

A **statement of fact** can be proved true or false. You can use a reference book or your own knowledge, or ask an expert, to prove it true or false. A **statement of opinion** cannot be proved true or false. It is a belief or judgment.

Activity

Not Just the Facts Together, with a family member, read a short newspaper editorial. Identify sentences that are statements of fact, statements of opinion, or both. Talk about what clues made you decide to categorize the sentences the way you did.

Lesson Vocabulary

Words to Know

Knowing the meanings of these words is important to reading *Adelina's Whales*. Practice using these words.

Vocabulary Words

biologist a scientist who studies living things

bluff a high, steep slope or cliff

lagoon a pond or small lake, especially one connected with a larger body of water.

massive big and heavy; bulky

rumbling making a deep, heavy, continuous sound

tropical of or like the regions 23.45 degrees north and south of the equator, where the sun can shine directly overhead

Grammar

Main and Helping Verbs

The **main verb** shows the action in a sentence. The **helping verb** works with the main verb, helping to show whether the action in the sentence is in the past, present, or future. *Am, is, are, was,* and *were* can be helping verbs. *For example: I am talking to Mother.* "Talking" is the *main verb* and "am" is the *helping verb.*

Activity

When Is It Happening? Make a list together of several action verbs. Then see if you can write three sentences for each one of them, each one using a helping verb to show action happening in the past, present, and future. *For example: We were cooking dinner. We are cooking dinner. Soon, we will be cooking dinner.*

Practice Tested Spelling Words

________	________	________	________
________	________	________	________
________	________	________	________
________	________	________	________
________	________	________	________

Name ______________________________

Fact and Opinion

- **A statement of fact** might be proved true or false by doing research.
- A **statement of opinion** cannot be proved true or false. It is a belief or a judgment. It often contains a word of judgment, such as *best, should,* or *beautiful.* It may begin with the words *in my opinion* or *I believe.*

Directions Read the following passage. Then complete the table. Read each statement and answer the questions at the top of each column.

People and their pets have special relationships. Many people believe that their pets are a part of their families. Some people dress their animals in colorful clothes and buy expensive food for them to eat.

Pets also help people in many ways. For instance, pets can cheer up people who are sick or living alone. Barking dogs protect people and their homes. In addition, seeing-eye dogs guide their blind owners. These dogs are trained to stop walking if they sense a dangerous situation and to avoid low branches and other obstacles. Whether the animals are companions or trained partners, animal experts feel that it's important to treat them kindly.

Statement	Does it state a fact or an opinion?	If an opinion, what are the clue words? If a fact, how could you prove it?
Seeing-eye dogs guide their blind owners.	1.	2.
Many people believe that their pets are a part of their family.	3.	4.

5. Write a statement of fact from the passage. How could you prove it?

____

____

Home Activity Your child identified statements of fact and statements of opinion in a short passage. Read an article or story about nature with your child. Ask your child to identify the facts and opinions in the article or story.

Name ______________________________

Vocabulary

Directions Choose the word from the box that best completes each sentence. Write the word on the line.

Check the Words You Know

- ___biologist
- ___bluff
- ___lagoon
- ___massive
- ___rumbling
- ___tropical

Joan Ferguson looked out over the blue **1.** ___________. She viewed the whales shooting air out of their blowholes. As the mist covered the air above the water, a low **2.** ___________ sound echoed across the valley. Joan felt small as she observed the **3.** ___________ mammals. She was a **4.** ___________ or a scientist who studied animals. Joan came to the same **5.** ___________ location every year.

Directions Circle the word or words with the same or nearly the same meaning as the first word in the group.

6.	**rumbling**	deep sound	squeaky sound	sharp sound	silent
7.	**bluff**	lake	creek	cliff	island
8.	**massive**	tiny	bulky	salty	long
9.	**biologist**	nurse	doctor	teacher	scientist
10.	**lagoon**	pond	bluff	island	ocean

Write a Newspaper Article

On a separate sheet of paper write a newspaper article about an animal that returns to the same place every year. Remember to include a title, and use as many vocabulary words as you can.

Home Activity Your child identified and used vocabulary words from *Adelina's Whales.* Read a story about animals with your child. Point out unfamiliar words in the story. Challenge your child to find the meanings by looking at nearby words.

Name ______________________________

Vocabulary • Context Clues

- When you read, you may come to a word whose meaning you know, but that meaning does not make sense in the sentence. Use **context clues** to find the meaning.
- **Homonyms** are words that are spelled the same but have different meanings.

Directions Read the following passage. Then answer the questions below.

The tropical island nation of Jamaica is wonderful to visit. Its weather is warm and sunny, although brief rain showers fall almost every day. The sound of thunder rumbling through the sky gives everyone time to take cover. Since it is sunny so much, it is a lovely place to go swimming. There are many waterfalls and warm-water lagoons on the island. Some of the lagoons are hidden behind a bluff or a cluster of hills. At the beach, you might sit on the sand, read a book, and watch for the flukes of a passing whale.

1. What does the word *bluff* mean in this passage? What clues can help you determine the correct definition?

____

2. *Sand* can mean "tiny grains of stone and shell" or "what you do to make wood smooth." How is it used in the passage? How can you tell?

____

3. *Beach* can mean "the sand at the ocean's edge" or "to wash up on the shore." Which meaning does it have above? How do you know?

____

4. *Flukes* can mean "parts of an animal" or "strokes of luck." How is it used in the passage? How can you tell?

____

5. Why are context clues useful when you encounter homonyms?

____

____

Home Activity Your child identified and used context clues to understand homonyms used in a passage. Work with your child to identify other words that are spelled the same but have different meanings. Make a list of of the words and take turns using them in sentences that employ both the words' meanings.

Name ________________________________

Generalize

Directions Read the article. Then answer the questions below.

Many birds migrate, or move from one place to another at specific times of the year. For example, birds such as geese and sparrows fly south for the winter. It is warmer in the south, and there is more to eat there. Some birds will fly the same exact path year after year. Some scientists say that birds don't get lost because they use the stars at night to guide them. When some birds migrate, they form different patterns in the sky. One of the most common is the V formation. Geese migrate in a V formation. Each goose takes turns as the lead bird. The other geese follow in the shape of a V. The lead bird must fly directly into the wind and block the wind for the other birds. By taking turns as lead bird, no goose becomes too tired during the journey. Seeing the birds fly south is always a sign that winter is on its way.

1. Write an example of a generalization in the passage.

____

2. How did you know that this was a generalization?

____

____

3. Write another example of a generalization in the passage.

____

4. How did you know that this was a generalization?

____

____

5. Write a generalization of your own that relates to the passage. Use a clue word like *most, many, usually, sometimes, few, seldom, all,* or *generally.*

____

____

Home Activity Your child has read information about the migration of birds and generalized statements about the information. Challenge your child to find two examples of generalizations from a magazine article.

Name ______________________________

Fact and Opinion

- A **statement of fact** might be proved true or false by doing research.
- A **statement of opinion** cannot be proved true or false. It is a belief or a judgment. It often contains a word of judgment, such as *best, should,* or *beautiful.* It may begin with the words *in my opinion* or *I believe.*

Directions Read the following passage. Then answer the questions below.

Patrick ran to the edge of the stairs and looked at the large chalkboard next to them. It had information about the ocean's tides and the day's weather. Patrick loved knowing what time the tide was going to come in. He knew the tides were caused by the sun and moon pulling the water. Knowing this helped him decide when he would go swimming. The size of the waves always showed how fast the winds were blowing. Patrick knew if the winds were strong, then the waves would be high. He also knew that the winds might bring colder water to the shore. It looked like the ocean was going to be calm today.

Patrick ran down the stairs to the beach and looked around. The beach was already busy. He saw his friends and headed toward them. Patrick knew it was going to be a great day.

1. Give one example of a fact from the passage.

____

____

2. How do you know this is a fact and not an opinion?

____

3. Give one example of an opinion from the passage.

____

4. How do you know this is an opinion and not a fact?

____

5. On a separate sheet of paper, create a graphic organizer showing which sentences from the above passage are facts and which are opinions.

Home Activity Your child identified facts and opinions in a short passage. Read the promotional material from a book or video to your child. Work together to identify the facts and opinions in the promotion.

Fact and Opinion

- A **statement of fact** can be proved true or false by doing research.
- A **statement of opinion** cannot be proved true or false. It is a belief or a judgment. It often contains a word of judgment, such as *best, should,* or *beautiful.* It may begin with the words *in my opinion* or *I believe.*

Directions Read the following passage. Then complete the table. Read each statement and answer the questions at the top of each column.

In my opinion, dolphins and whales are the best communicators in the animal world. Dolphins and whales make sounds that travel underwater. These sounds are beautiful, almost like music. Animals also communicate in other ways. They use body language or make faces. But I think the sounds animals make are by far the best way that animals communicate. The next time you hear the special sounds of whales or dolphins, try to imagine what they are saying.

Statement	Does it state a fact or an opinion?	If an opinion, what are the clue words? If a fact, how could you prove it?
In my opinion, dolphins and whales are the best communicators in the world.	**1.** ______________	**2.** Best, ______________ ______________
Dolphins and whales make sounds that travel underwater.	**3.** ______________	**4.** Do research about ______________ ______________

5. Write a statement of opinion from the passage. How do you know it is an opinion?

____

____

Home Activity Your child identified statements of fact and statements of opinion in a short passage. Talk with your child about places you can research facts to prove they are correct. Give your child two facts to look up. Challenge your child to write a paragraph with the information.

Name ________________________________

The *Readers' Guide to Periodical Literature*

The ***Readers' Guide to Periodical Literature*** is a set of books that is an index of articles published in periodicals. Each volume lists articles published in a specific year. Within each volume, articles are listed alphabetically by author and subject. The introductory pages of each volume explain how to use the *Readers' Guide.*

Directions Look at the volumes of the *Readers' Guide to Periodical Literature* illustrated below. Then answer the questions that follow.

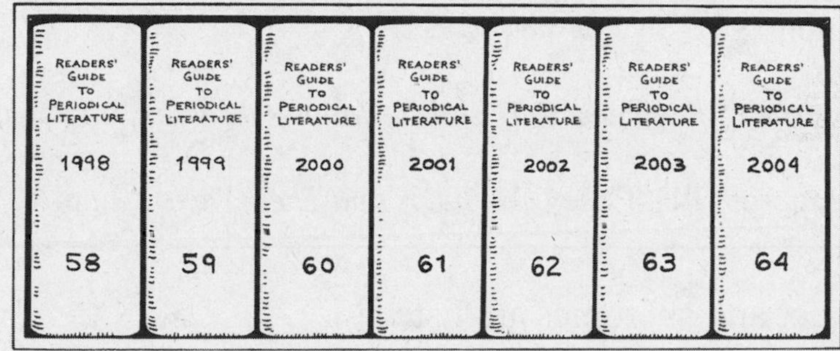

1. What order are volumes organized in? What volume will be published for 2005?

____

2. If you were looking to read more about some whales that were saved in 2002, which volume would you look in?

____

3. How would you use the *Readers' Guide* to find the most up-to-date information about whales?

____

4. If you wanted to read articles about whales written by the biologist Dr. Joan Brady, why do you think you would check several volumes?

____

____

5. How are the *Readers' Guides* important for research today?

____

____

Name ____

Directions The entry below is similar to what you might see in the *Readers' Guide.* Read it, then answer the questions that follow.

WHALES
COMMUNICATION
See also
Animal behavior
Marine animals
Sharing information. K. Kleeman. il *Animal Quarterly* v.45 pp. 98–101 O '03
Whales' habits. S. Romberg. il *The Animal Sanctuary* v.20 pp. 22–26 Mr '04
ENDANGERED *See* Endangered species
MIGRATION PATTERNS
See also
Animal migration
Marine animals
The dangerous journey for whales. K.T. Smith. *Nature Observers* v.150 pp. 210–222 N '03
Whales' yearly patterns. T.H. Finley. il *Whales and Their Ways* v.2 pp. 101–123 S '04

1. What main subject and subtopics are listed?

____

____

2. Name the magazine and article about how whales share information.

____

3. Where would you find more information about whale communication?

____

4. Which magazine has an article titled *Whales' Yearly Patterns*?

____

5. Are there any listings about whales that are endangered? Where would you find them?

____

Home Activity Your child answered questions about the *Readers' Guide to Periodical Literature.* With your child, go to the library and look for articles about something that your child is interested in.

Name ______________________________

Family Times

Summary

How Night Came from the Sea: A Story from Brazil

Why do we have day and night? A Brazilian legend says there was always daylight on Earth until the African goddess Iemanja's daughter left her ocean home to marry a land dweller. When Iemanja's daughter became homesick for the cool, shadowy world under the sea, her mother sent some of the darkness up to her, and now we have night on land as well as day.

Activity

Pourquoi Tales The word *pourquoi* means *why* in French. Create your own *pourquoi* tale, a story about why a familiar pattern in nature exists. Answer a question about night and day, such as *Why does the sun rise and fall in the sky?*

Comprehension Skill

Generalize

When you **generalize,** you make a broad statement or rule that applies to many examples, such as *All oceans contain salt water.* Words such as *all*, *most*, *always*, *usually*, or *generally* help you to find generalizations. If a generalization is supported by facts or details, it is valid (logical). If it is not supported by facts and details, it is faulty (false).

Activity

Valid or Faulty? Make up your own generalizations and write them down. Then ask a family member to write whether they are valid or faulty. Switch roles and repeat the activity.

Lesson Vocabulary

Words to Know

Knowing the meanings of these words is important to reading *How Night Came from the Sea*. Practice using these words.

Vocabulary Words

brilliant shining brightly; sparkling

chorus anything spoken or sung all at the same time

coward person who lacks courage or is easily made afraid; person who runs from danger, trouble, etc.

gleamed flashed or beamed with light

shimmering gleaming or shining faintly

Grammar

Subject-Verb Agreement

The **subject** and **verb** in a sentence must **agree.** In other words, if the subject is a singular noun or pronoun, the verb must also be in its singular form. If the subject is plural, the verb must also be plural. *For example: She eats lunch every day. The children eat at the table.* The singular "she" *agrees* with the singular "eats," and the plural "children" *agree* with the plural "eat."

Activity

Disagree to Agree Take turns writing simple sentences in which the subject and verb do not agree. Have family members correct each sentence in two ways, first by changing the subject and second by changing the verb. For example, if someone writes *The dog bark*, make the sentence correct by saying both *The dogs barks* and *The dogs bark*.

Practice Tested Spelling Words

Name____

Generalize

- A **generalization** is a broad statement or rule that applies to many examples.
- Clue words such as *all, most, always, usually,* or *generally* signal generalizations.

Directions Read the following passage. Then complete the diagram by writing down generalizations and their clue words from the passage.

Tom and Jim always had fun when they went camping. They planned the fun things they would do on their trip for days. They liked to plan their camping trips for summer because the weather was usually good. Tom planned their daily hikes. He packed a light breakfast, some water, and a compass. Then he and Jim would usually hike an hour or two in the morning before the sun rose. They often found themselves on top of a hill where they could watch the sunrise and eat breakfast. Jim was responsible for building their campfires. He gathered sticks and wood and made sure that the fire pit was safe. Jim's campfires were built so well, they often burned late into the night. Usually they talked after dinner until the fire faded away. Tom and Jim's camping trips were always full of great memories.

Generalization	Clue Word?
Tom and Jim always had fun when they went camping.	always
1.	usually
2.	**3.**
4.	**5.**

Home Activity Your child identified generalizations and their clue words in a short passage. Have your child write a paragraph generalizing a topic. Challenge him or her to use the clue words from this passage in their paragraph.

Name ______________________________

Vocabulary

Directions Choose the word from the box that best matches each clue. Write the word on the line.

Check the Words You Know

- ___brilliant
- ___chorus
- ___coward
- ___gleamed
- ___shimmering

______________ **1.** flashed or beamed with light

______________ **2.** shining brightly; sparkling

______________ **3.** a person who lacks courage or is easily made afraid

______________ **4.** gleaming faintly

______________ **5.** anything spoken or sung all at the same time

Directions Choose the word from the box that best completes each sentence below. Write the word on the line shown to the left.

______________ **6.** The queen's necklace was set with _______ gems.

______________ **7.** He looked into the well and saw the water ________ in the moonlight.

______________ **8.** "I'm no _______," said Beatriz, as she climbed the ladder to the diving board.

______________ **9.** The shiny guitar ________ in the store window.

______________ **10.** Carolyn sat at the window and listened to the ________ of frogs greeting the sunset.

Write a Description

On a separate sheet of paper, write a description about the sky at night. Remember to include details about what you see. Use as many vocabulary words as you can.

Home Activity Your child identified and used vocabulary words from *How Night Came from the Sea: A Story from Brazil.* Read another story about day and night. Write poems with your child about the sky either during the day or at night.

Name ____________________

Vocabulary • Context Clues

- When you are reading and see an unfamiliar word, you can use **context clues,** or words around the unfamiliar word, to figure out its meaning.

Directions Read the following passage and look for context clues as you read. Then answer the questions below.

Wearing her mask and fins, Joy walked into the ocean. Joy had heard about the reef in the ocean, and she was excited to be visiting it. As she swam out to the reef, she could no longer hear the chorus of waves crashing on the beach. She looked under the water and saw different kinds of fish swimming around her. She was a bit afraid of the bigger fish, but Joy was not a coward! As she reached the edge of the reef, she saw something shimmering ahead. She swam closer to the coral and saw a fish shining with brilliant colors. Joy caught a quick movement to the side. A school of fish gleamed, their scales reflecting light like a million tiny mirrors. Joy knew she would never forget this day. She pulled out her camera and took a picture so she could share her journey with her friends.

1. Explain how you can use context clues to help determine the meaning of *chorus*.

____

____

2. What does *coward* mean? What clue helped you to determine the meaning?

____

3. What does *shimmering* mean? What clues help you to determine the meaning?

____

4. What does *gleamed* mean? What clues help you to determine the meaning?

____

5. Write one word you did not know from the passage. What clues helped you determine the meaning?

____

Home Activity Your child identified and used context clues to understand new words in a passage. Read a story about the ocean or about taking a journey. Work with your child to identify unfamiliar words in the story and the context clues to help understand those words.

Name ______________________________

Cause and Effect

Directions Read the article. Then answer the questions below.

One night, two frogs were on a journey from the river to the pond when they found themselves at the dairy. They saw something shimmering in a tall bucket. Neither frog was a coward, so they hopped their way toward the bucket to check it out. It wasn't easy balancing on the edge of the bucket, but they were determined. They leaned forward to gaze into the white liquid that gleamed in the moonlight. But they leaned too far and slipped right into the bucket, which was full of milk. At first, they both tried to leap out of the bucket, but the sides were high and slippery, so they fell back in. The frogs kept swimming round and round in circles. They swam so long that it became more difficult. The milk was turning to cream. They kept on swimming in circles. By the time the weary frogs saw the first brilliant light of morning, the cream had turned to butter. The two frogs were able to stand on the butter and finally hop out of the bucket to safety.

1. What caused the frogs to fall into the bucket of milk?

____

____

2. Why did the frogs fall back into the milk after they tried to drop out?

____

____

3. What may have caused the milk to turn to cream, and then to butter?

____

____

4. How were the frogs finally able to get out of the bucket?

____

____

5. What do you think the moral of this fable is?

____

Home Activity Your child has read a short passage and answered questions about cause and effect. Make up a short story with your child. Talk about causes and effects of the story you wrote.

Name ______________________________

Generalize

- A **generalization** is a broad statement or rule that applies to many examples.
- Clue words such as *all, most, always, usually,* or *generally* signal generalizations.

Directions Read the following passage. Then answer the questions below.

Sun and Moon were disagreeing again. It was always the same argument. Sun spent too much time in the sky, and Moon didn't have enough time to herself. Sun told Moon he stayed longer because that was what people and animals wanted. In fact, Sun was sure that they wished he would stay around longer. That was why, every day, Sun shone in the sky, even when it was time for Moon to take over. Usually, Sun remained in the sky for an hour after his day was finished, creating all different kinds of beautiful colors. Moon wished Sun would just go away at the same time every day. But he never did. Sun seldom listened to Moon. Many times, Sun and Moon would be in the sky at the same time. Moon would try to outshine Sun, but it never worked. Sun was just too bright. It seemed Sun and Moon would never solve this problem.

1. Write a generalization from the passage.

____

2. How did you know that this was a generalization?

____

3. Write another generalization from the passage.

____

4. How did you know that this was a generalization?

____

5. On a separate sheet of paper, write a short description of what you visualized while you read the passage.

Home Activity Your child identified generalizations in a short passage. Read a magazine article together. Ask your child to underline some generalizations. Talk about why he or she knows they are generalizations.

Name ______________________________

Generalize

- A **generalization** is a broad statement or rule that applies to many examples.
- Clue words such as *all, most, always, usually,* or *generally* signal generalizations.

Directions Read the following passage. Then complete the diagram by writing down generalizations and their clue words from the passage.

Mother Bear was busy preparing. Winter was on its way. She gathered her cubs and explained that soon it would be darker during the daytime. "In the winter," she said, "bears usually sleep all day and all night. It is very helpful that it is dark so much." The cubs didn't understand. They were generally awake during the daytime. They wanted to play out by the river.

Mother Bear said, "It will be too cold to play outside, and the river will be frozen." As the cubs gathered in the cave, Mother Bear told them, "Go to sleep, and I will wake you up when it is time to play again. Everyone settled in for a long slumber. The cubs had been wrong. In winter, all bears sleep during the day.

Generalization	Clue Word
In the winter, bears usually sleep all day and all night.	usually
1. ______________________ during the daytime.	**2.** ______________________
3. ______________________ ______________________	Everyone
4. ____________ bears sleep during the day.	**5.** ______________________

Home Activity Your child identified generalizations and their clue words in a short passage. Read a fairy tale or a tall tale with your child. Ask your child to find several generalizations and their clue words.

Name ______________________________

Textbook/Trade Book

- A **textbook** teaches about a particular subject. These books are organized to help you find information quickly. Textbooks contain tables of contents, chapter titles, headings, subheadings, illustrations with captions, and vocabulary words.
- A **trade book** is any book that is not a textbook, periodical, or reference book. The skills you use for understanding trade books are a lot like those for textbooks.

Directions Use the following sample of a textbook to answer the questions below.

Earth Science Unit 3

Chapter 4 The Sun

Lesson 2: Patterns of Day and Night

Vocabulary rotates, terminator

The Terminator The Earth **rotates,** or turns, from day to night on a twenty-four hour basis. Night and day occur on a line called the **terminator.** The terminator is an imaginary vertical line that divides the Earth into night and day. The terminator's shape changes during the year as the length of days and nights changes.

The sun can be seen rising on one part of the terminator and setting at another place. When the sun is rising, it is lit on the right side of the Earth; when it is setting, it is lit on the left side of the Earth. At times, the sun can been seen "skimming" the northern or southern hemisphere.

1. Why are the words *rotates* and *terminator* printed in **boldfaced type?**

____

2. What type of textbook is this? What is the title of this chapter?

____

3. Does the passage help you learn about day and night? Why or why not?

____

____

4. What is the subject of this section of the lesson? How can you tell?

____

5. Why do textbooks divide information into units, chapters, lessons, and sections?

____

Name ______________________________

Directions Use the following section of a trade book to answer the questions below.

Every night Karamo looked up and saw a twinkling light. It was in the same place in the sky every night, and Karamo wondered how it got there. Was it special? Why was it so bright? Karamo walked through the forest to his village. He found his grandfather sitting near the river's edge. He sat next to his grandfather and asked him about the star. Karamo's grandfather smiled and nodded his head. He knew which star Karamo was talking about. It was a special star. The story of how the star took its place in the sky is a famous story that many people know. Grandfather took a deep breath and began to tell the story of the star.

Long ago there was a happy smiling boy called Moth, who lived in a village much like the one Karamo lived in. Moth became well known for his wisdom. As the boy grew older, the village's crops were in danger, and the boy went off to search for other places in the forest to move the village. When he found a good place, he sent a huge white moth to flutter over his head. His friends and neighbors walked toward the moth until they reached the spot Moth had found. That spot was the village Karamo now lived in, and the twinkling star was the moth, still fluttering over their heads.

6. What is the subject of this story?

____

7. According to the grandfather, what do people believe about the twinkling star?

____

8. Do you think this passage comes from a trade book or a science textbook? Why?

____

____

9. How would you describe the author's purpose?

____

____

10. On a separate piece of paper, create your own legend about something in nature.

Home Activity Your child learned about textbooks and trade books and applied their knowledge to two sample passages. Together, browse through a textbook and discuss different parts of the book. Have your child identify titles and headings that show the book's organization. Invite him or her to explain the importance of different elements in a textbook.

Name ____________________

Family Times

Summary

Eye of the Storm: Chasing Storms with Warren Faidley

Storm Hunter In spring, summer, and fall, weather patterns produce thunderstorms, tornadoes, and hurricanes in the United States. Most people take cover from storms, but photographer Warren Faidley travels around the country to take pictures of them. In August of 1992, Faidley went to Miami, Florida, to take pictures of Hurricane Andrew.

Activity

Storm Stories Share stories about storms you remember. What time of year did the storm strike? Did you know the storm was coming, and if so, how? How did the storm affect you and your family?

Comprehension Skill

Graphic Sources

Graphic sources help explain written information using visual material such as photographs, drawings, diagrams, maps, tables, and time lines.

Activity

Mapping Andrew Use the table to trace Hurricane Andrew's route on a world map or globe.

mid-August	A tropical wave forms off the western coast of Africa.
August 21	Tropical Storm Andrew heads west towards the Bahamas.
August 23	Hurricane Andrew reaches Eleuthera, an island in the Bahamas.
August 24	Andrew crosses the southern tip of Florida.
August 25	Andrew crosses the Gulf of Mexico, reaches Louisiana.

Lesson Vocabulary

Words to Know

Knowing the meanings of these words is important to reading *Eye of the Storm.* Practice using these words.

Vocabulary Words

destruction great damage; ruin

expected thought something would probably come or happen

forecasts statements of what is coming; predictions

inland in or toward the interior; the land away from the border of a coast

shatter to break into pieces suddenly

surge a swelling motion; sweep or rush, especially of waves

Grammar

Past, Present, and Future Tenses

Verbs have different **tenses** to show when something is happening in time. **Past tense** verbs tell about actions that have already happened. *For example: We heard about a storm coming.* "Heard" is in the *past tense.* **Present tense** verbs tell what is happening now. *For example: We are putting things in the car.* "Are putting" is in the *present tense*. **Future tense** verbs tell what will or might happen. *For example: We will drive away from the coast.* "Will drive" is in the *future tense.*

Activity

Sentence Hunt Read an article in a newspaper or magazine, a story, or a chapter in a book with a family member. Find examples of sentences that use past, present, and future tense.

Practice Tested Spelling Words

______	______	______	______
______	______	______	______
______	______	______	______
______	______	______	______
______	______	______	______

Name ____________________

Graphic Sources

- A **graphic source** shows or explains information in the text. Pictures, maps, charts, time lines, and diagrams are all graphic sources.

Directions Study the following table. Then answer the questions below.

Major Hurricanes, 1900–2000*

Name/Date of Hurricane	Location	Category / Damage Description
unnamed (1935)	Florida	5 / catastrophic
Camille (1969)	Mississippi, Louisiana, Alabama, Virginia	5 / catastrophic
Andrew (1992)	Florida, Louisiana	5 / catastrophic
unnamed (1919)	Florida, Texas	4 / extreme

*Hurricanes are rated in a range from a category 1 (minimal) to category 5 (catastrophic).

1. What does this table show?

____

____

2. What term is used to describe the force of a category 5 hurricane?

____

3. How many years passed between the most recent and the least recent category 5 hurricanes listed in the table?

____

4. Why are all of the major hurricanes in the table either category 4 or 5?

____

5. What other graphic source could effectively show this information? Explain.

____

____

Home Activity Your child identified information from a graphic source. Work with him or her to identify other graphic sources in magazines. Together, take information from a magazine article and create a graph to show it.

Name ______________________________

Vocabulary

Directions Choose the word from the box that best matches each definition. Write the word on the line.

Check the Words You Know

- ___destruction
- ___expected
- ___forecasts
- ___inland
- ___shatter
- ___surge

_______________ **1.** a swelling motion

_______________ **2.** in or toward the interior

_______________ **3.** statements of what is coming; predictions

_______________ **4.** great damage; ruin

Directions Solve the following puzzle by writing the word that matches each definition. The circled letters will spell a secret word.

5. the land away from the border of a coast ___ ◯ ___ ___ ___ ___

6. to break into pieces suddenly ___ ___ ◯ ___ ___ ___ ___

7. devastation ___ ___ ___ ◯ ___ ___ ___ ___ ___ ___ ___

8. sweep or rush, especially of waves ___ ◯ ___ ___ ___

9. descriptions of the future ___ ___ ◯ ___ ___ ___ ___ ___ ___

10. thought something would probably come or happen ◯ ___ ___ ___ ___ ___ ___ ___

Write a Business Letter

On a separate sheet of paper, write a business letter asking for aid after a hurricane. Decide to whom you would write this letter and what you would say. Use as many vocabulary words as you can.

Home Activity Your child identified and used vocabulary words from *Eye of the Storm.* Together, read an encyclopedia entry about hurricanes. Then have your child write a few descriptive sentences about hurricanes, using the vocabulary words.

Name ______________________________

Vocabulary • Word Structure

- An **ending** is a letter or letters added to the end of a base word.
- The ending *-ed* is added to a verb to make it past tense. The ending *-ing* is added to a verb to make it tell about present or ongoing actions. The endings *-s* and *-es* can be added to nouns to make them mean more than one.

Directions Read the following passage. Then answer the questions below.

Nom Hee stood at the window. The winds were stronger than expected, and she was getting nervous. Weather forecasts on radio and television called for a major rainstorm. Her aunt should have come home from work by now, and Nom Hee wondered where she was.

Suddenly, the lights grew very bright and then went out. Nom Hee knew that was what happens when power surges through the wires of a house. She began searching in the dark for a flashlight. After she found it, she picked up the phone. The telephone was not working.

Just then the front door opened. It was her aunt. She had just seen a window shatter from the strong winds. Wow, this was going to be some storm!

1. How does the ending of *expected* change its base word's meaning?

____

2. What does *forecasts* mean? If you removed the ending, how would the word's meaning change?

____

____

3. Change the word ending to make the verb *surge* show an ongoing action.

____

4. What do the words *expected, called, wondered,* and *walked* have in common?

____

5. Write a sentence using an *-ed* and an *-s* or *-es* word.

____

Home Activity Your child identified and used word endings to understand new words in a passage. Work with him or her to identify new words and their meanings in a news article. Have your child change the word endings on a few words and note the changes in meaning.

Name ____________________

Cause and Effect

Directions Read the following article. Then answer the questions below.

Tornadoes often form near thunderstorms. In fact, a tornado and a severe thunderstorm are caused by the same conditions—that is, high humidity, unstable air near the ground, and winds. Tornadoes formed along with thunderstorms are usually accompanied by rain and wind.

The effects of tornadoes can be dramatic and extremely harmful. Tornadoes tear through parts of the United States each year, their high winds causing injuries, taking lives, and causing damage to property in towns and cities. Much of the damage and many of the injuries caused by tornadoes relate to flying debris.

Sometimes experts can predict a tornado, but other times a tornado forms by surprise. In certain conditions, many tornadoes form at one time. The United States has a warning system to inform citizens of possible tornadoes. Because people have heeded tornado warnings and taken cover, many lives have been saved over the past years.

1. What conditions cause a tornado?

____

____

2. What are two effects of a tornado?

____

____

3. What is responsible for many of the injuries and much of the damage in a tornado?

____

4. What has been an effect of the tornado warning system used in the United States?

____

5. On a separate sheet of paper, explain why a tornado drill at school might contribute to saving human lives.

Home Activity Your child has read information about the causes and effects of tornadoes. Discuss a type of storm that occurs in your region. Together, discuss how people remain safe during such a storm.

Name ______________________________

Graphic Sources

- A **graphic source** shows or explains information in the text. Pictures, maps, charts, time lines, and diagrams are all graphic sources.
- As you read, use graphic sources to help you understand information. Compare information in the text with information in the graphic sources.

Directions Study the following text and diagram. Then answer the questions below.

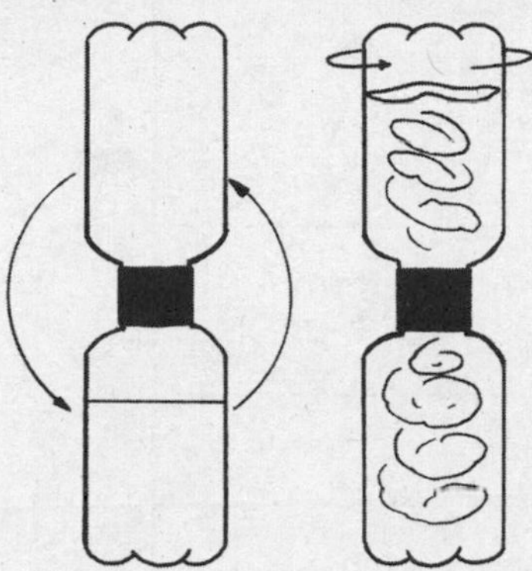

Materials needed: 2-liter soda bottles, water, food coloring, duct tape

How to create a tornado: Fill one bottle with water and some food coloring. Connect the two bottles with duct tape. One tube will be upside down, the other right side up (see diagram). Turn the water-filled bottle to the top, twist the bottles, and watch the tornado move from top to bottom.

1. What are the materials needed to complete this activity?

____

2. What is the first step in creating this tornado?

____

3. What is another step in this activity?

____

4. What is an example of how the diagram might help a person complete the activity?

____

____

5. On a separate sheet of paper, make a prediction about whether or not the experiment will work. List all the reasons you think it might work or not.

Home Activity Your child used a graphic source along with text to obtain information. Together, read about and complete another science experiment that employs diagrams or other graphic sources.

Name ______________________

Graphic Sources

- A **graphic source** shows or explains information in the text. Pictures, maps, charts, time lines, and diagrams are all graphic sources.

Directions Read the following chart and answer the questions below.

Disasters and Their Causes

Type of Disaster	Causes
flood	heavy rains, melting snow, ocean waves coming on shore
hurricane	low air pressure, energy obtained from contact with warm ocean water
wildfire	lightning, human accidents
winter storm	cold temperatures, moisture, winds

1. What tells you the topic of this graphic source?

____

2. Which disaster is not directly related to water?

Checking the chart's second column shows that ______________________

____

3. How are the four types of disasters arranged in this chart?

Studying the chart's first column shows that ______________________

____

4. Which types of disasters are never caused by human beings?

Disasters not caused by people are ______________________

5. How would you alter this chart to add information about the effects of disasters?

____

Home Activity Your child used a graphic source to analyze information about disasters. Together, use graphic sources you find in reference books or on the Internet to learn more about natural disasters.

Name ______________________________

Online Telephone Directory

- An **online telephone directory** lists phone numbers and addresses for individual people and businesses.
- The white pages lists entries for individuals and businesses in alphabetical order.
- The yellow pages lists entries for businesses (as well as advertisements) by category, or type of business.

Directions Examine the online yellow pages screen. For each of the five businesses listed below, write words that define the category of business you wish to search.

Yellow Pages
Powered by Software Source

Hotels Restaurants Movies About Us

Quick Search–The quickest way to find the business you're looking for. Either type in the business name or enter the category of business you would like to find.

Business name or type

Insurance companies

○ Business name ______ city

◉ Category of business ______ state

Search!

______________ **1.** a business that sells raincoats

______________ **2.** a business that sells storm shutters for windows

______________ **3.** a business that sells hurricane safety kits

______________ **4.** a business that sells homeowners' insurance

______________ **5.** a business that repairs storm-damaged roofs

Name ______________________________

Directions Use the online yellow pages screen to answer the following questions.

6. Why is it important to include the city and state for the business you are searching for online?

____

____

7. If you knew the type—but not the name—of a business, would it best to use the white pages or yellow pages to find it? Why?

____

____

8. What might be the result if your search keywords were spelled incorrectly?

____

____

9. If you remembered only part of the name of a local business, how would you search for its telephone number?

____

____

____

10. Why might a person choose to use an online telephone directory instead of a regular telephone book?

____

____

Home Activity Your child learned about locating and collecting information using various sources, including an online telephone directory. Together, search for three businesses using the white and yellow pages of an online directory and of a print telephone book.

Name

Family Times

Summary

The Great Kapok Tree

A man treks into the Amazon rain forest to chop down a great kapok tree but ends up napping instead. As he sleeps, the creatures that live in the kapok tree whisper in his ear, asking him not to destroy their home. When the man wakes, he looks at the animals gathered around him and decides not to cut down the tree after all.

Activity

Connect with Nature Think about your favorite natural place, such as a park, forest, or along a river or lake. Name the creatures that live in the habitat and discuss how their lives and your lives would change if this place were to disappear.

Comprehension Skill

Generalize

When you **generalize,** you make a broad statement based on several examples. Clue words like *generally*, *usually*, *always*, *all*, and *most* tell you that an author is making a generalization. A generalization can be valid (logical) or faulty (wrong). Sometimes you can tell when a generalization is faulty, and other times you must do research to find out.

Activity

Find the Generalizations Read a short newspaper or magazine article with a family member. When you encounter a generalization, list examples suggested by the statement, then decide if the statement is valid or faulty.

Lesson Vocabulary

Words to Know

Knowing the meanings of these words is important to reading *The Great Kapok Tree.* Practice using these words.

Vocabulary Words

canopy the uppermost layer of branches in forest trees

dangle to hang and swing loosely

dappled marked with spots

fragrant having or giving off a pleasing odor; sweet-smelling

pollen a fine, yellowish powder released from the anthers of flowers. Grains of pollen carried by insects, wind, etc., to the pistils of flowers fertilize them.

pollinate to carry pollen from anthers to pistils; bring pollen to. Flowers are pollinated by bees, bats, wind, etc.

slithered moved with a sliding motion

wondrous wonderful

Grammar

Irregular Verbs

Some verbs use a new spelling to form the past tense *(wrote, ate, ran)* and a different spelling to form the past tense with *has* or *have (has written, have eaten, had run)*. These are called **irregular verbs.** *For example: to go/went/had gone; to drink/drank/had drunk; to lie/lay/had lain; to break/broke/had broken; to feel/felt/had felt.* Because the spelling changes in irregular verbs do not follow any simple pattern, each irregular verb's forms must be memorized one at a time.

Activity

Irregular Sentences Use the irregular verbs listed above to write eight sentences following this pattern: *He (writed/wrote) this book.* In the parentheses, list two verb forms– one correct and one incorrect. Have a family member read each sentence aloud, then circle the correct form. When you are done, trade roles.

Practice Tested Spelling Words

____	____	____	____
____	____	____	____
____	____	____	____
____	____	____	____
____	____	____	____

Name ______________________

Generalize

- A **generalization** is a type of conclusion in which a broad statement is made based on several examples.
- Clue words such as *all, most, always, usually,* or *generally* signal generalizations.
- A generalization can be valid (logical) or faulty (wrong) depending on the number of examples on which it is based and how logical the thinking is.

Directions Read the following passage. Then complete the diagram below by finding a generalization and its support.

For the animals in the rain forest, it was a typical day. The squirrel monkeys were swinging above the trees, gathering juicy fruit for their babies to eat. The snakes were slithering into the river to cool off from the hot sun. The birds were gathering twigs and leaves from the forest floor to build their nests way above in the mighty branches. Not a single animal lacked something to do, except maybe the sloth. The sloth just hung lazily from a shady tree.

Generalization
5.

Support from Text
1.

Support from Text
2.

Support from Text
3.

Support from Text
4.

Home Activity Your child used a graphic organizer to find a generalization and support for it. Together, read a short passage from a fiction or nonfiction text. Have your child make two generalizations about the events in the story—one valid and one faulty. Have him or her explain the difference between the two.

Name ____________________

Vocabulary

Directions Choose the word from the box that best matches each definition. Write the word on the line.

Check the Words You Know
___canopy
___dangle
___dappled
___fragrant
___pollen
___pollinate
___slithered
___wondrous

____________ **1.** having or giving off a pleasing odor

____________ **2.** to bring pollen to

____________ **3.** moved with a sliding motion

____________ **4.** a fine, yellowish powder released from the anthers of flowers

____________ **5.** the uppermost layer of branches in forest trees

Directions Choose the word from the box that best replaces the underlined word or words. Write the word on the line.

____________ **6.** The birds flew above the highest branches of the trees.

____________ **7.** When she lifted the rock, dozens of worms slid around looking for shelter.

____________ **8.** The view of the sunset on the horizon was marvelous.

____________ **9.** Aaron ran alongside the spotted horse, trying to catch his reins.

____________ **10.** Christopher liked to hang and swing from the swing set after school.

Write a Narrative

On a separate sheet of paper, write a narrative in which animals do things they might not do in real life. Use as many vocabulary words as you can.

Home Activity Your child identified and used vocabulary words from *The Great Kapok Tree.* Together, think about other animals and the types of personality traits they might exhibit in a fable.

Name ________________________________

Vocabulary • Word Structure

- A **suffix** is a syllable added to the end of a base word to change its meaning or the way it is used in a sentence. For example, the suffix *-ous* can make a word mean "full of ____." The suffix *-ate* means "to make or do _____."

Directions Read the following passage. Then answer the questions below.

As Lee walked through the forest preserve, she took in the trees' rich scent. She sat down on a bench and looked around. Lee couldn't help but find nature amazing. There was the wondrous sunset, the dappled chipmunk running by her feet, and the shade coming from the canopy above her. She watched a bee pollinate one last flower before its day ended. As Lee looked at the flowers, she noticed some trash on the ground. Lee threw the trash into the garbage and sat back down. The forest was a marvelous place, and she didn't want its fragile state to be ruined.

1. What is the suffix in the word *wondrous*?

____

2. How does this suffix help you understand the meaning of *wondrous*?

____

____

3. What does *pollinate* mean? How do you know?

____

____

4. How does the suffix in *marvelous* help you figure out the meaning of the word?

____

____

5. Write two other words that use the suffixes *-ous* or *-ate.*

____

Home Activity Your child identified and used suffixes to understand new words in a passage. Work together to identify meanings of words with *-ous* and *-ate* suffixes in an article. Help your child come up with a way to remember the meanings of these suffixes.

Name ______________________________

Author's Purpose

Directions Read the following passage. Then answer the questions below.

Rain forests are an important part of all our lives, and they need help from all of us. Rain forests should be protected for many reasons. For instance, rain forests provide people with many foods and medicines. Of course, rain forests are important to the lives of many animals and plants. In fact, rain forests are home to about fifty percent of our plant and animal population! Isn't that amazing?

Unfortunately, rain forests are in danger every day. Many rain forests are being cut down to make room for crops and cattle. Yet you can do something to protect our rain forests from further damage. Begin by writing a letter to one of the people who represents your state in the U.S. Congress. In your letter, tell him or her about your belief in the importance of saving rain forests from future harm.

1. What is the topic of this passage?

____

2. What is the author's main purpose?

____

3. What might be a secondary purpose of the author?

____

____

4. Do you think the author meets his or her main purpose? Why or why not?

____

____

5. On a separate sheet of paper, choose a topic you feel is important. Decide on a purpose, and then write a paragraph about this topic.

Home Activity Your child identified the author's purpose in an article. Together, find another article about an interesting aspect of nature. After reading the article, discuss the author's purpose.

Name ________________________________

Generalize

- A **generalization** is a type of conclusion in which a broad statement is made based on several examples.
- A generalization can be valid (logical) or faulty (wrong) depending on the number of examples on which it is based and how logical the thinking is.

Directions Read the following passage. Then answer the questions below.

Morris the mole thought that none of the animals in the forest was worth getting to know. *They are always so busy, and they never seem to care for anyone but themselves,* Morris thought. What Morris didn't realize was that the animals didn't get a chance to have a conversation with him. Why? Because he rarely peaked his head out of his burrow.

One day, Morris came out of his burrow to look for food. He hurried along, paying no attention to where he was going. Suddenly, Morris realized that he was lost. Just then, Susie the squirrel came along.

"Do you need help?" she asked.

"Yes," said Morris shyly. Susie showed him back to the main part of the forest.

"Hope to see you around more often." Susie said.

1. What generalization does Morris make first?

____

2. Why does Morris make this generalization?

____

3. Is Morris's generalization valid or faulty? Why?

____

4. What clue words in the passage help you identify Morris's generalization?

____

5. What is the central problem in this story? What happens in the resolution?

____

____

Home Activity Your child identified and analyzed a generalization, as well as elements of a story's structure. Read a fairy tale together, and have your child point out generalizations made by a character or by the author.

Name ___________________________________

Generalize

- A **generalization** is a type of conclusion in which a broad statement is made based on several examples.
- Clue words such as *all, most, always, usually,* or *generally* signal generalizations.
- A generalization can be valid (logical) or faulty (wrong) depending on the number of examples on which it is based and how logical the thinking is.

Directions Read the following passage. Then complete the diagram below by finding a generalization and its support.

Jack the chipmunk did not want to ask Billy for help. He was afraid that Billy—the largest bear Jack had ever seen—would refuse to help him. Moreover, he feared that Billy would be angry with him for asking.

Billy would be the fourth bear that Jack tried to talk to that day. Arnold, the first bear, paid absolutely no attention to Jack. He didn't even stop fishing in the stream to listen. The second bear, Donovan, roared loudly when Jack appeared before him. Then Penny rose up on her hind legs and took a big swat at him with her massive paw. Now Jack was faced with the challenge of his next encounter with a bear.

Generalization

5. Jack had good reasons for ___________________________________

____

Support from Text

1. Arnold ___________

Support from Text

2. Donovan ___________

Support from Text

3. ___________

Support from Text

4. Billy is the ___________

Home Activity Your child used a graphic organizer to find a generalization and support. Have your child make a generalization about his or her present life. Together, find facts to support this generalization.

Name ______________________________

Schedule

- A **schedule** is a special chart that lists events and when they take place, side by side.
- Bus, train, and other travel schedules often present information in boxes. They usually contain both rows and columns, each of which may have a label or heading.

Directions Use this cruise ship schedule to answer the questions below.

Cruise Ship	Depart Miami, Florida	Arrive Belém, Brazil	Guided Tour on Amazon River	Arrive Miami
Amazon Princess	June 1	June 5	June 8–10	June 15
Forest Explorer	June 11	June 15	June 18–20	June 25
Brasilia Empress	July 4	July 8	July 11–13	July 18
Amazon Princess	July 31	August 4	August 7–9	August 14
Forest Explorer	August 8	August 23	August 15–17	August 22
Brasilia Empress	August 30	September 3	September 6–8	September 13

1. How many days is each cruise? How can you tell?

____

____

2. How many ships travel this route? How can you tell?

____

3. If you traveled on the second sailing of the *Forest Explorer,* during which days would you tour the Amazon River?

____

4. If you wished to spend your August 6 birthday in Brazil, on which ship would you need to travel?

____

5. If you wanted to sail on the *Brasilia Empress,* what would be your choice of departure dates from Miami?

____

Name ______________________________

Directions Use the schedule of shipboard events to answer the questions below.

Schedule of Activities for June 20							
Activity	**7–9 A.M.**	**9–11 A.M.**	**11 A.M.– 1 P.M.**	**1–3 P.M.**	**3–5 P.M.**	**5–7 P.M.**	**7–9 P.M.**
Bird Watching	+	+	+				
Ship Walk	+	+	+	+	+	+	
Dolphin Watching	+	+	+	+	+		
Shuffleboard			+	+	+		
Midday Movie			+				
Tropical Fish Viewing	+	+	+	+	+	+	
Ping-Pong Tournament					+	+	+
Talent Show						+	
Photography Class		+		+			+
+ = Activity is available.							

6. What do the plus signs on the schedule represent? How do you know?

____

____

7. Between which hours might you be able to look for tropical fish?

____

8. Which activities occur at the same time as the talent show?

____

____

9. If you watched the Midday Movie Feature, which activities would you be missing?

____

____

10. How does the schedule assist passengers in planning their day?

____

____

____

Home Activity Your child learned about reading a schedule. Together, look at the schedule for a sporting event or for another form of travel. Have your child read and explain the schedule to you.

Name

Family Times

Summary

The Houdini Box

Young Victor wants to be a magician like his hero, famed escape artist Harry Houdini, but his attempts at escape end up as disasters. One Halloween night, he receives a wooden box at Houdini's house. Victor opens it many years later and discovers Houdini's secrets.

Activity

It's Magic Do you know any magic tricks you can perform for you family? Write down the directions for performing a magic trick, and practice, practice, practice. If you don't know any, find a book on magic tricks and learn one. Watch how your family is amazed when you perform for them!

Comprehension Skill

Compare and Contrast

When you **compare and contrast,** you tell how things are alike and different. Words such as *similar, as, unlike*, and *instead* signal a comparison and contrast.

Activity

My Hero Who are your heroes? Ask a family member to choose one of his or her own heroes, and choose one of your own. Discuss your heroes, making comparisons and contrasts between the two people. How are they alike? How are they different?

Lesson Vocabulary

Words to Know

Knowing the meanings of these words is important to reading *The Houdini Box*. Practice using these words.

Vocabulary Words

appeared came into sight, was seen

bustling being noisily busy and in a hurry

crumbled fell into pieces; decayed

escape to get out and away, get free

magician person who entertains by creating illusions

monument something set up to honor a person or an event

vanished disappeared, especially suddenly

Grammar

Plural Pronouns

A **pronoun** is a word that replaces a noun. Pronouns can be used as the subject of a sentence or in its predicate. *For example: Alice Bennett gave the book of magic tricks to her cousin John Bennett. She gave it to him.* In the second sentence, "she" is a *pronoun* that stands in for "Alice Bennett," "it" stands in for "the book of magic tricks," and "him" replaces "her cousin John Bennett." *We*, *you*, *they*, *us*, and *them* are **plural pronouns.** The pronoun *you* can be singular or plural. Be sure to match the correct pronoun to the noun it replaces.

Activity

Pronoun Parade Make a chart of the people in your family (pets, too) and the singular and plural pronouns you'd use to talk about them. Then add to your chart groups such as your school, your community, and your neighbors. List the singular and plural pronouns you'd use in place of these nouns.

Practice Tested Spelling Words

______	______	______	______
______	______	______	______
______	______	______	______
______	______	______	______
______	______	______	______

Name ___________________________

Compare and Contrast

- To **compare and contrast** means to tell how two or more things are alike and different.
- Clue words such as *like* and *as* can show similarities. Clue words such as *however* and *instead* can show differences.

Directions Read the following passage. Then complete the diagram by comparing and contrasting magic tricks with special effects.

Have you seen strange creatures and amazing superheroes in movies? Today's special effects are like the stage magic performed for years and years, but they're even harder to figure out. For years, magicians have used quick hands and distraction to make something seem to appear or disappear. In a similar way, special effects make you think you're seeing something that doesn't really exist. To create movie magic, special-effects artists use computers to create moving pictures that fool the eye. When you see them unfolding in front of you, both magic tricks and special effects seem real. They both work because of the hard work of people who love to entertain us.

Special Effects and Magic Tricks	
Alike	**Different**
Both seem real.	**3.**
1.	**4.**
2.	**5.**

Home Activity Your child compared and contrasted two kinds of illusions in a nonfiction passage. Take turns with your child pointing out similarities and differences between two pieces of furniture.

Name ____

Vocabulary

Directions Choose the word from the box that best matches each definition. Write the word on the line.

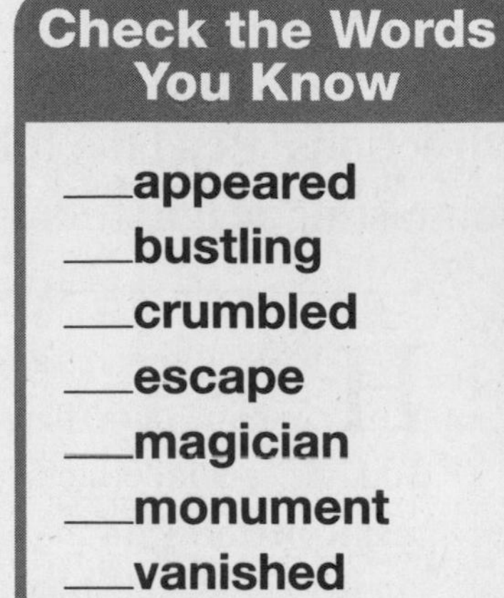

____________________ **1.** something set up to honor a person or an event

____________________ **2.** was seen

____________________ **3.** disappeared suddenly

____________________ **4.** being noisily busy

____________________ **5.** fell to pieces

Directions To solve this puzzle, write the word that matches each definition. The circled letters will spell a secret word.

6. ___ ___ ___ (___) ___ ___ ___ ___

7. (___) ___ ___ ___ ___ ___ ___ ___

8. ___ ___ ___ ___ ___ ___ ___ (___)

9. ___ ___ ___ (___) ___ ___ ___ ___

10. ___ ___ (___) ___ ___ ___

6. broke into bits
7. went suddenly from sight
8. loud and in a hurry
9. a performer skilled in illusions
10. to get away or get out

Write a Note

Think of something mysterious that happened to you. On a separate sheet of paper, write a note to a friend describing it. Be sure to tell why it puzzled you. Use as many vocabulary words as you can.

Home Activity Your child identified and used vocabulary words from *The Houdini Box.* With your child, take turns telling a story incorporating the vocabulary words. Alternate adding sentences, each sentence containing at least one vocabulary word, until all vocabulary words are included.

Name ___

Vocabulary • Context Clues

- When you see an unfamiliar word in your reading, use **context clues**, or words around the unfamiliar word. They can help you figure out the word's meaning.
- **Synonyms** are words that mean almost the same things.
- **Antonyms** are words with opposite meanings.

Directions Read the following passage about a magician. Then answer the questions below. Look for context clues as you read.

Hundreds of people streamed through the crowded, noisy streets of the bustling market. In the shadow of an old monument, a crowd gathered. All the people were orderly as a man waved his hands over a small boy's head. Then they burst into raucous cheering. The man, a street magician, pulled coins and scarves and white birds from behind the wide-eyed boy's ears. The clever performer took a bow and gave a sly smile to the child's mother. The crowd laughed as a fruit-seller's apples vanished from her basket. They roared when the apples appeared again, one by one, from a policeman's pockets. Even the usually dour blacksmith could not help feeling joyful at the magician's tricks.

1. What does *bustling* mean? What clues help you to determine the meaning?

___

2. What antonym for *vanished* helps you determine its meaning? What does it mean?

___

3. What antonym for *raucous* helps you find its meaning? What does it mean?

___

4. What does *sly* mean? What words help you determine its meaning?

___

5. What type of context clue helps you to determine the meaning of *dour?* What does *dour* mean?

___

Home Activity Your child used synonyms and antonyms as clues to understanding new words in a passage. Choose a newspaper or magazine article with your child and take turns naming synonyms and antonyms for words you find in the article.

Name ______________________________

Plot and Character

Directions Read the following story. Then answer the questions below.

It was Daniel's tenth birthday—November 11, 1854. He and his brother went to see Jean Eugène Robert-Houdin, the greatest magician in the world. In one astounding moment, Robert-Houdin asked people in the audience to lift some weights. Not even the strongest person could lift them. But Robert-Houdin could, with only one finger. "How in the world did he do that?" Daniel wondered. After the show, Daniel sneaked into the bustling backstage area and peeked at the weights. They were held down by giant electric magnets. When the magician switched off the current, he could lift them easily. "Now I know the secret!" Daniel told his brother. "But I won't tell. I don't want to spoil the fun."

1. How would you describe Daniel's attitude toward the magician?

____

____

2. What are two main events of the story?

____

____

3. Explain what makes Daniel sneak backstage after the show.

____

____

4. What plot event is the climax of the story?

____

____

5. On a separate sheet of paper, explain why Daniel told his brother, "Now I know the secret! But I won't tell."

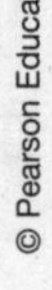

Home Activity Your child analyzed the plot events and character in a fictional passage. Discuss the plot of a favorite book or movie with your child. Have your child tell you about the main character and why he or she makes the decisions he or she does in the story.

Name ______________________________

Compare and Contrast

- To **compare and contrast** means to tell how two or more things are alike and different.
- Clue words such as *like* and *as* can show similarities. Clue words such as *however* and *instead* can show differences.

Directions Read the following passage. Then answer the questions below.

Is the hand quicker than the eye? Sometimes. A magician may use quick, careful hand movements to make you think you have seen or heard something you haven't. Magicians also use optical illusions, images that fool the eye. These illusions often use mirrors, painted backdrops, or special lighting.

Optical illusions make you think you see something on the stage that is not there. Magicians also use illusions of sound to confuse an audience. You may hear someone's voice sounding like it comes from a box that is actually empty. You may hear the sound of a coin hitting the floor even if no coin has been dropped. Illusions like these make magic seem real.

1. How are the hand movements and optical illusions used by magicians similar?

____

2. How are these two kinds of visual tricks used by magicians different?

____

____

3. How does the sound of a voice contrast with the use of hand movements?

____

4. Name one other comparison or contrast you could make using this passage.

____

5. On a separate sheet of paper, predict how a magician might be able to fool one of our other senses, such as the sense of touch or smell.

Home Activity Your child compared and contrasted ideas in a passage and also used these ideas to make a prediction. Have your child compare and contrast two performers or entertainers. Then ask your child to predict other ways two entertainers could be alike and different.

Name ______________________________

Compare and Contrast

- To **compare and contrast** means to tell how two or more things are alike and different.
- Clue words such as *like* and *as* can show similarities. Clue words such as *however* and *instead* can show differences.

Directions Read the following passage. Then complete the diagram by comparing and contrasting.

Yesterday, when Kim performed her magic act for her family, she was calm and skillful. But today Kim was nervous. She was doing the same magic tricks for all her friends. Everything started well, as her vanishing coin trick worked perfectly. But with her second trick, things started to go wrong. Kim was trying to guess the card a friend had picked. Kim lost count of the cards in her hand and didn't get it right. Then her deck of cards showered to the floor. Maybe, Kim thought, she should stick to family shows!

First Show and Second Show	
Alike	**Different**
1. Kim performed ______________ each time.	**3.** Kim felt ______________ the first time, but ______________ the second time.
	4. During the second show, the second trick ______________.
2. ______________ worked in both shows.	**5.** The deck of cards ______________ in the second show.

Home Activity Your child compared and contrasted events described in a written passage. Work with your child to compare and contrast two dinners he or she had this week. Then see if your child can predict how the next dinner will be alike and different from those.

Name ______________________

Procedures and Instructions/Manual

- **Procedures and instructions** are directions for using or doing something. Instructions are given in order and often include numbered steps. Read through all the instructions before you begin. Then do what is directed, one step at a time.
- A **manual** usually takes the form of a booklet or handbook. It contains a written set of instructions that help the reader understand, use, or build something. Take note of illustrations, diagrams, headings, labels, and sections (including index and table of contents). Also watch for warnings about special hazards.

Directions Read the following instructions. Then answer the questions below.

The Great Houdini Ring Escape

1. Tie a ring with a "fake knot." Poke a loop of string through a finger ring. Bring the loop all the way back and over the ring. Then pull the ends of the string to make a "knot." Show your audience, but not too closely.
2. Ask someone to hold the two ends of the string. Make sure the string sags.
3. Put a scarf over the ring.
4. Reach under the scarf. Remove the ring by pushing the loop up and back over the ring.
5. Show the ring you're holding to the audience and remove the scarf to reveal the empty string.

1. What is the purpose of these instructions?

____

2. What does the audience see at the end of the first step? The last step?

____

____

3. Which step in this procedure involves an audience member?

____

4. Why is it important that the instructions are followed in order?

____

____

5. What skills are required to perform this procedure successfully?

____

Home Activity Your child analyzed a set of instructions. Find or create a set of simple instructions that tell how to do a household chore. Read over the instructions together, noting the steps to do the procedure.

Name ______________________________

Directions Read over this table of contents for a manual of magic tricks. Then answer the questions below.

MANUAL of AMAZING MAGIC TRICKS
by Charlie Showboat

WARNING Magic tricks require much practice. These tricks must be practiced until you can do them without even thinking.

6. What is the purpose of this manual?

____

7. According to the table of contents, how many sections does this manual contain? Which section might explain the kinds of tricks performed by Houdini?

____

____

8. In which section would you find magic tricks from Japan? Math tricks?

____

9. What page would you turn to for instructions on making a nickel disappear? For definitions of magic terms?

____

10. What message does the warning contain? How do warnings help readers?

____

____

Home Activity Your child analyzed the table of contents of a manual. Together, look through a manual, such as one for a camera or telephone. Invite your child to explain various features of the manual.

Name

Family Times

Summary

Encantado: Pink Dolphin of the Amazon

One of the most mysterious animals on the planet is the amazing pink dolphin of the Amazon. Meet this unique and fascinating creature as you explore the rain forest with your South American guide.

Activity

Oddball Animals With your family, look at lots of pictures of animals and describe the most unusual ones you find. Look at the largest of birds, the ostrich, or the big-footed snowshoe hare, for example. Make a list of your top candidates for "oddest animal."

Long-Beaked Echidna

Comprehension Skill

Compare and Contrast

To **compare and contrast** means to tell how two or more things are alike and different. As you read, you may notice clue words for comparing and contrasting, such as *like*, *similarly*, *however*, and *instead*.

Activity

Alike or Different? With your family, make drawings of crazy creatures. Mix features of one animal with other features of another, such as a rabbit's tail and a camel's hump. Tell how these imaginary creatures compare and contrast with real animals.

Lesson Vocabulary

Words to Know

Knowing the meanings of these words is important to reading *Encantado: Pink Dolphin of the Amazon.* Practice using these words.

Vocabulary Words

aquarium a building used for showing large collections of live fish, water animals, and water plants

dolphins sea mammals related to the whale, but smaller

enchanted delighted greatly; charmed

flexible easily bent; able to change

glimpses short, quick views or looks

pulses regular, measured beats

surface the top of the ground or soil, or of a body of water or liquid

Grammar

Subject and Object Pronouns

Pronouns used as the subject of a sentence are called **subject pronouns.** *I, you, he, she, it, we, you,* and *they* can be subject pronouns. *For example: He went to Brazil in February.* "He" is a *subject pronoun.* Pronouns that can follow action verbs are called **object pronouns.** *Me, you, him, her, it, us, you,* and *them* can be object pronouns. Use the correct pronoun when there is a compound object. *For example: Ted called Jen and me.* "Me" is an *object pronoun.* Be careful not to confuse the two kinds of pronouns in your writing.

Activity

Chart the Part Write sentences that include pronouns, and then draw diagrams to show if the pronouns are subjects or objects. First, circle the subjects. Then draw arrows from the subjects toward the objects. Make sure you use your subject and object pronouns correctly.

Practice Tested Spelling Words

____________	____________	____________	____________
____________	____________	____________	____________
____________	____________	____________	____________
____________	____________	____________	____________
____________	____________	____________	____________

Name ______________________________

Compare and Contrast

- To **compare and contrast** means to tell how two or more things are alike and different.
- Clue words such as *like* and *as* can show similarities. Clue words such as *however* and *instead* can show differences.

Directions Read the following passage and complete the diagram below.

All rain forests have four levels of growth that animals live in, from the forest floor to the emergent trees peaking out above the canopy. Although each rain forest is home to many animals, the animals differ from rain forest to rain forest. In Australia, a bird of paradise soars among the trees, but in South American rain forests, you may spot a scarlet macaw.

You'll notice a colorful cockatoo perching on a branch in Australia. In South America, however, howler monkeys hang out on the limbs. You might be frightened by the frilled lizard lurking in the Australian rain forest. But in South America, you'll have to watch for large animals, such as jaguars, stalking their prey.

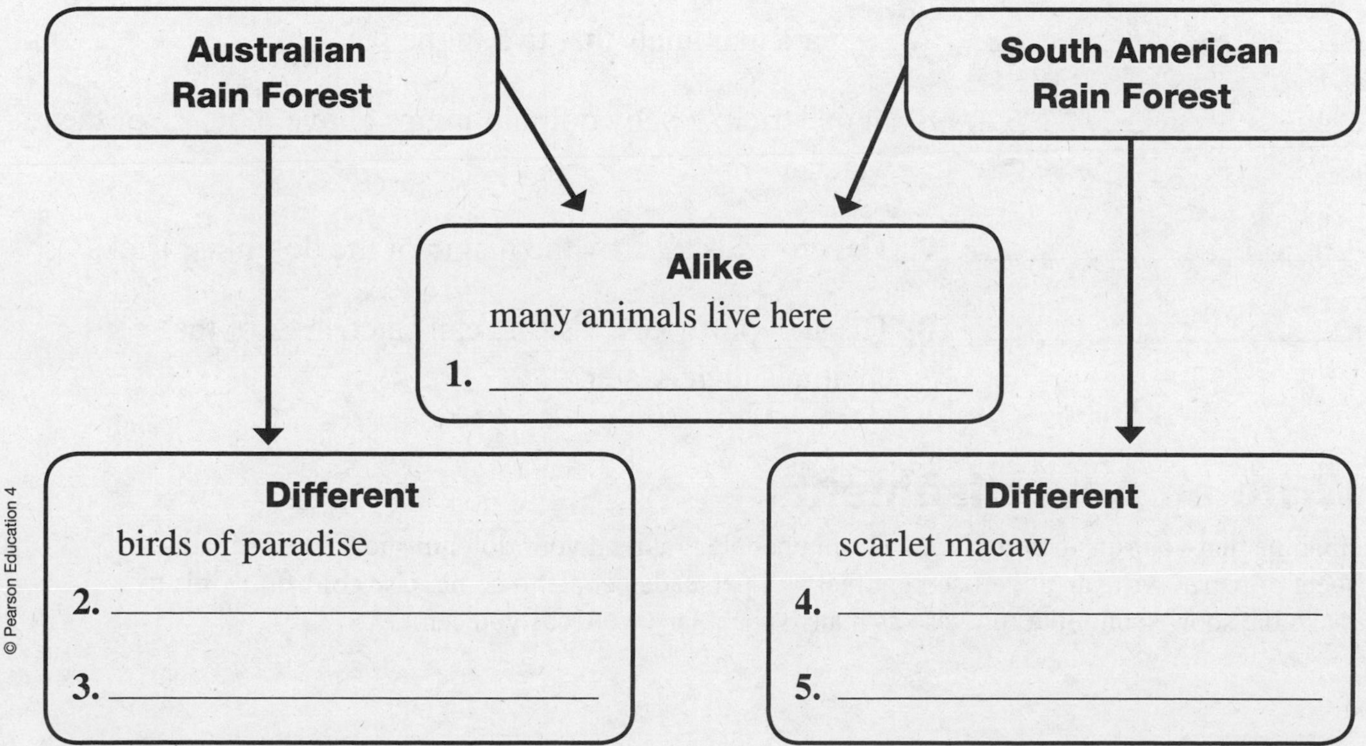

Home Activity Your child compared and contrasted details of a nonfiction passage. Read a book or article about animals and work with your child to find similarities and differences between two animals.

Name ________________________________

Vocabulary

Directions Choose the word from the box that best matches each definition. Write the word on the line.

Check the Words You Know

___aquarium
___dolphins
___enchanted
___flexible
___glimpses
___pulses
___surface

________________ **1.** regular, measured beats

________________ **2.** easily bent

________________ **3.** greatly delighted, charmed

________________ **4.** short, quick views or looks

________________ **5.** the top of the ground or soil, or of a body of water

Directions Choose the word from the box that best completes each sentence. Write the word on the line shown to the left.

________________ **6.** The show at the ___ features dolphins and sharks.

________________ **7.** ___ are mammals that live in the sea.

________________ **8.** In one trick, a baby dolphin jumps above the ___ of the water.

________________ **9.** The crowd is ___ by the magic of the dolphins' tricks.

________________ **10.** Through portholes, visitors can catch ___ of the creatures underwater.

Write an Advertisement

Imagine that you run an aquarium and want people to attend your dolphin show. On a separate sheet of paper, write an advertisement that will persuade people to come. Use colorful words to make the show sound like fun. Use as many vocabulary words as you can.

School + Home

Home Activity Your child identified and used vocabulary words from *Encantado: Pink Dolphin of the Amazon.* Together, write your own short story that takes place at the ocean, a lake, or a river. Try to use all of the vocabulary words in the story.

Name ________________________________

Vocabulary • Context Clues

- Some words have more than one meaning.
- **Context clues,** the words around these multiple-meaning words, can help you decide the correct meaning of the word. If it doesn't make sense in the sentence, try another meaning.

Directions Read the following passage. Then answer the questions below.

Kerry was enchanted by his visit to this delightful place, the rain forest. Just beneath the surface of the water, he saw fish unlike any of those in his aquarium at home. The trees grew so large that their branches reached out into the water, like flexible arms bending out to his boat. He was surprised when he caught glimpses of dolphins making their way down the long river. Kerry knew he would not have enough time to absorb everything that he saw. He knew he would return to learn more about this amazing world so different from where he lives.

1. Which context clues tell you that *enchanted* means "greatly delighted, charmed"?

____

2. *Glimpses* can mean "sees" or "short views." How is it used in the passage? How can you tell?

____

3. *Surface* can mean "the outside or top of anything" or "to rise up." How is it used in the passage? How can you tell?

____

4. Which context clues tell you that *flexible* means "easily bent"?

____

5. *Absorb* can mean "to soak up" or "to learn." How is it used in the passage? How can you tell?

____

Home Activity Your child identified and used context clues to understand words that have multiple meanings. Read a story or nonfiction article with your child. Find words that have more than one meaning and figure out which meaning goes with each word.

Name ______________________________

Generalize

Directions Read the following passage. Then answer the questions below.

If you hear a squeak, whistle, or click, you may be lucky enough to catch a glimpse of a dolphin. Everything about dolphins is appealing. They wear a smile at all times, and they make funny, happy sounds. Dolphins are playful too. They like to jump out of the water and slap the surface with their flexible tails. They are famous for being friendly and even have been known to pull people along in the water. Not only are dolphins playful, but also they are intelligent. Their brains are large, about the size of a dog's. Like a dog, they can be trained to perform tricks. In addition, their sense of hearing and eyesight are excellent. There are different kinds of dolphins, including pilot whales and orcas, and all are delightful creatures.

1. Write the first sentence where the writer generalizes about dolphins. How well is this generalization supported?

____

____

2. Give two good reasons to support the generalization that dolphins are very playful.

____

____

3. What generalization ends the paragraph?

____

4. Why did the author include the facts about the size of dolphins' brains and their hearing and sight?

____

____

5. On a separate sheet of paper, write a paragraph about another animal that lives in the water. Include at least one generalization that is supported by facts.

Home Activity Your child has made generalizations after reading a short passage. Read a factual article about snakes or sharks with your child. Ask your child to make a generalization based on facts from the article.

Name ________________________________

Compare and Contrast

- To **compare and contrast** means to tell how two or more things are alike and different.
- Clue words such as *like* and *as* can show similarities. Clue words such as *however* and *instead* can show differences.

Directions Read the following passage. Then answer the questions below.

When Sir Henry Johnston went to the Congo rain forest in 1899, he found a mysterious animal. Its legs and back end were black-and-white striped, like a zebra's. Its body looked something like a donkey's, but with dark brown fur that felt like velvet. And its neck was long, like a giraffe's. What could this animal be? This unusual animal is the okapi. Unlike most other mammals, it has only one home, the rain forest of the Congo. At first, explorers thought the okapi was related to the horse. However, they were surprised to find out that instead it is a member of the giraffe family. If you see this strange animal at a zoo, you may be surprised too.

1. What is the author trying to compare and contrast? Which words show comparison and contrast?

____

____

2. How is the okapi similar to other animals?

____

3. How is it different from other animals?

____

4. How is the okapi different from what explorers expected?

____

5. Which three phrases in the passage help you to visualize this animal?

____

____

Home Activity Your child compared and contrasted details of a nonfiction passage. Read a newspaper article with your child about a strange or unusual event. Ask your child to compare and contrast the unusual event with more ordinary events. Have your child pick out details that help him or her visualize the event.

Compare and Contrast

- To **compare and contrast** means to tell how two or more things are alike and different.
- Clue words such as *like* and *as* can show similarities. Clue words such as *however* and *instead* can show differences.

Directions Read the following passage and complete the diagram below.

Some people think butterflies are beautiful, while bats are scary. But both of these flying creatures use their senses in puzzling ways. In the dark, bats can "see" with their ears. When bats squeak, they are sending out sounds. From the echoes of their squeaks, they can tell where things are. Butterflies use their senses in strange ways too. When they land on flowers, their feet "taste" for nectar. If a flower is sweet, they unroll a long feeding tube. Bats see by hearing, and butterflies taste by feeling. Both have unexpected ways to experience the world.

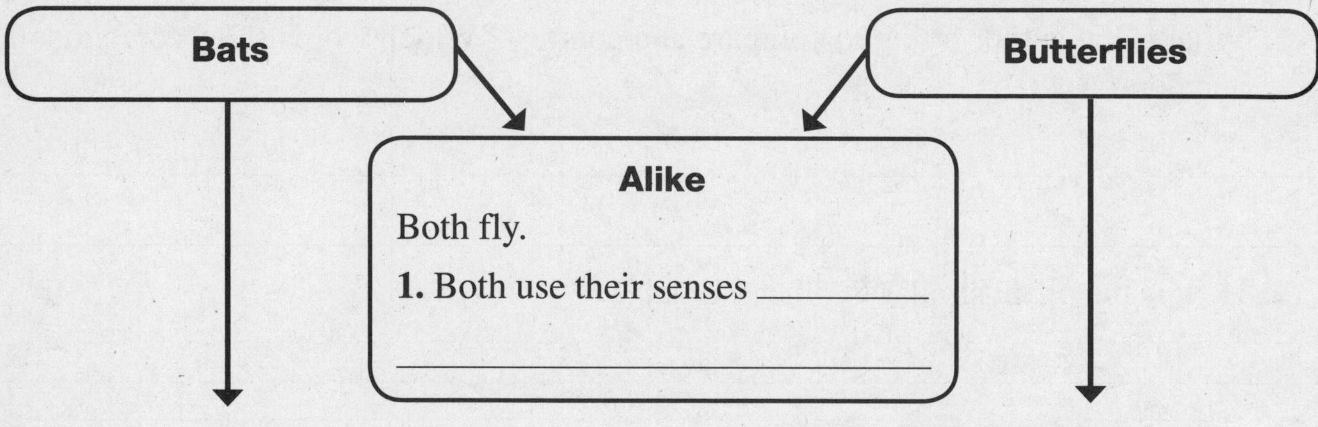

Different

2. Bats are considered ______________
____

3. Bats "see" ______________
____

Different

4. Butterflies are considered
____

5. Butterflies "taste" ______________
____

Home Activity Your child compared and contrasted details of a nonfiction passage. Look at a picture of an unusual fish or bird with your child. Work with your child to compare and contrast how this creature is similar to and different from other fish or birds.

Name ______________________________

Poster/Announcement

- A **poster** is an **announcement** for an event. Posters are large in size. Usually they use color and large type to attract attention.
- Posters answer these questions about an event: Who? What? When? Where? How? Why?

Directions Read this poster. Then complete the chart by telling how the poster answers the questions.

See the Top Trainers in America!

All–New Dolphin Show

Springfield City Aquarium

Saturday, March 8

11:00 A.M.

Only $1 per person

Proceeds Benefit the Red Cross

Who?	top trainers in America
What?	**1.**
When?	**2.**
Where?	**3.**
Why?	**4.**

5. On a large sheet of paper, make a colorful poster for a school event. Choose the most important information. Make sure your poster tells who, what, when, why, how, and where.

Name ___________________________________

Directions Read over this announcement. Then answer the questions below.

> **HELP SAVE THE RAIN FOREST!**
>
> Come hear
>
> Manuel Ortega,
>
> Costa Rican Biologist
>
> **"What Kids Can Do to Save the Rain Forest"**
>
> Don't miss this multimedia presentation for children ages 8–11. Enjoy activities, animals, and rain forest snacks. Bring your questions.
>
> **January 12, 5 P.M.**
>
> Santa Fe Public Library
>
> 2100 S. Rio Grande Way

6. What is the purpose of this announcement?

____

7. What is the event? Who is featured?

____

____

8. When and where is the event taking place?

____

9. Why do you think the event is taking place?

____

10. What does this announcement emphasize? How?

____

____

Home Activity Your child learned about announcements. With your child, think of a school or community activity that is coming up. Work with your child to write an announcement to post. Make sure your child includes answers to these questions: who, what, when, why, how, and where?

Name

Family Times

Summary

The King in the Kitchen

A peasant wants to marry a princess, but first he must guess what the king is cooking. He realizes that the king has made a wonderful glue that will make a fortune!

Activity

How Inventive! Imagine how everyday things might have been invented. Share your ideas with your family members as you make up your own wacky stories. Make a list of things you'd like to see invented, as well.

Comprehension Skill

Character and Setting

A **character** is a person in a story. You can learn about characters from what they do, what they say, and what others say about them. The **setting** of the story is the place and time the story occurs. Setting may or may not be important to a story.

Activity

Keeping in Character With family members, pretend to be selected characters from a book or real life. Show what each character is like by what you say and do. What happens when you change the settings in which your characters live? How do they respond to their new surroundings?

Lesson Vocabulary

Words to Know

Knowing the meanings of these words is important to reading *The King in the Kitchen.* Practice using these words.

Vocabulary Words

duke a nobleman of the highest title, ranking just below prince

dungeon a dark underground room or cell to keep prisoners in

furiously with unrestrained energy, speed, etc.

genius a person having very great natural power of mind

majesty title used in speaking to or of a king, queen, emperor, etc.

noble high or great by birth, rank, or title

peasant a farmer of the working class in Europe, Asia, and Latin America

porridge food made of oatmeal or other grain boiled in water or milk until it thickens

Grammar

Pronouns and Antecedents

A **pronoun** is a word that can replace nouns or groups of nouns. The **antecedent** is the noun or nouns to which the pronoun refers. *For example: The king said he was hungry.* "He" is the *pronoun*, and "king" is the *antecedent.* Pronouns may be singular or plural. If the antecedent is plural, then the pronoun that refers to it is plural. *For example: The boys say they are ready.* "Boys" is plural, so the pronoun that refers to it must also be plural (*they*).

Activity

A Perfect Match Look at pictures in a magazine with your family, and use pronouns and antecedents as you describe each picture. For example, you might point out, *Those singers are great, and they have a new hit.* Make sure your pronouns and antecedents go together!

Practice Tested Spelling Words

____________	____________	____________	____________
____________	____________	____________	____________
____________	____________	____________	____________
____________	____________	____________	____________
____________	____________	____________	____________

Name ___________________________

Character and Setting

- **Characters** are people in a story. You can learn what characters are like by noticing what they say and do and how they interact with other characters.
- **Setting** is the time and place in which the story occurs.

Directions Read the following passage and complete the diagram below.

Long ago and in a faraway place, a royal family lived in a castle. Princess Lil was a lovely girl, but she was clumsy. The king and queen called a duchess to the castle. "How do you do?" said Princess Lil, knocking over a spinning wheel. The duchess gave the princess twenty lessons in grace and balance. "I think I am getting better," Princess Lil said as she tripped over her royal throne.

The duchess came to love Lil for her kind sweetness. Lil never blamed anyone else for her clumsiness, and she always tried to help pick up what she knocked over. These were very rare things for a princess to do. Princess Lil offered other people so much more than grace and balance. Did Princess Lil learn to be graceful? No, but the duchess learned a lesson in kindness.

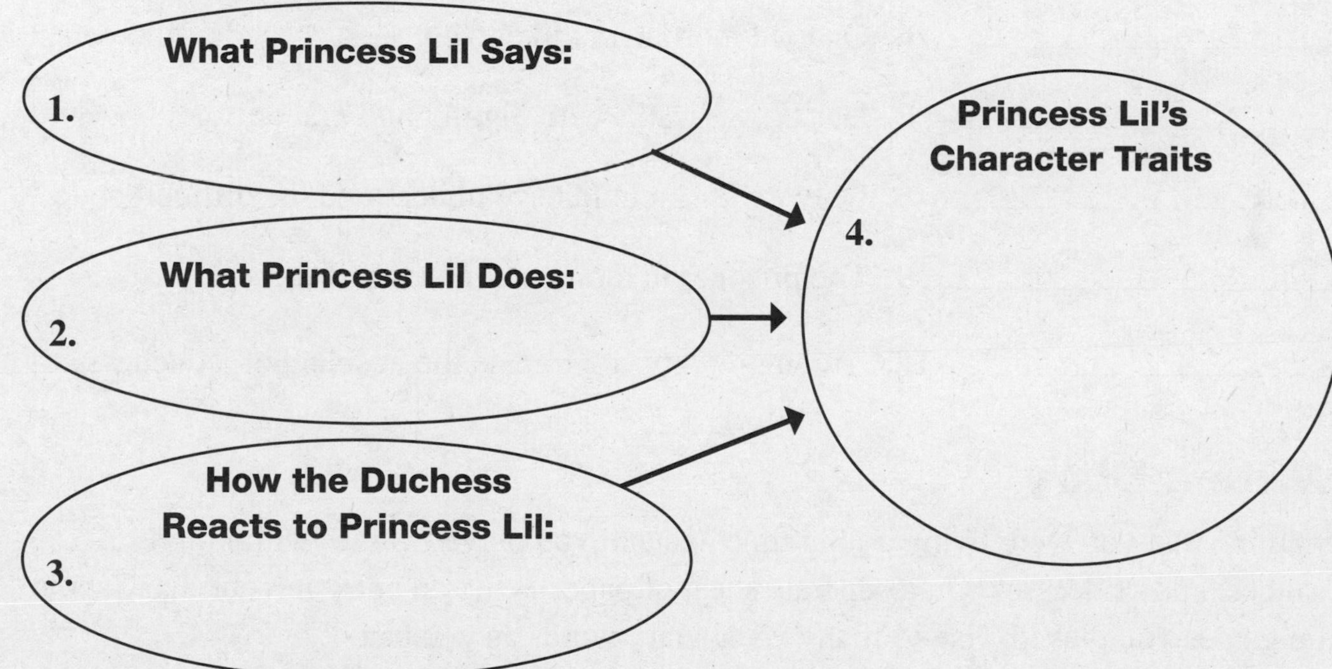

5. Write a sentence to describe the setting of this story.

____

Home Activity Your child read a short story and analyzed one of the characters and the setting. Read a fairy tale with your child. Work with your child to identify the setting and the traits of the main character.

Name ______________________________

Vocabulary

Directions Choose the word from the box that best matches each definition. Write the word on the line.

Check the Words You Know
___duke
___dungeon
___furiously
___genius
___majesty
___noble
___peasant
___porridge

________________ **1.** with unrestrained energy

________________ **2.** high and great by birth, rank, or title

________________ **3.** title used in speaking to or of a king, queen, emperor, etc.

________________ **4.** one who has great natural power of mind

________________ **5.** a farmer of the working class

Directions Choose the word from the box that fits best in each sentence. Write the word on the line shown to the left.

________________ **6.** On cold mornings, I like to eat _____ made from oats.

________________ **7.** Her _____ walks with dignity and grace.

________________ **8.** Only a _____ could have understood the difficult code.

________________ **9.** The prisoner in the _____ never saw the sun.

________________ **10.** Among royalty, a _____ is the husband of a duchess.

Write a Diary

Imagine that you were living a long time ago and you played games with knights, princes, and princesses. On a separate sheet of paper, write an entry in your diary about the games you played. Use as many vocabulary words as you can.

Home Activity Your child identified and used vocabulary words from *The King in the Kitchen.* Play a vocabulary game with your child where you give clues to the vocabulary words and your child tries to guess the word.

Name ____________________

Vocabulary • Dictionary/Glossary

- **Dictionaries** and **glossaries** provide alphabetical lists of words and their meanings. A dictionary is its own book, but a glossary is part of a book.
- Sometimes using context clues won't help you figure out the meaning of an unfamiliar word. When this happens, you can use a dictionary or glossary to find the word's meaning.

Directions Read the following passage. Look for context clues as you read to help you define each word in the table. Use a dictionary or glossary if necessary.

One cold night, the royal cook was furiously fixing porridge for the servants. He threw some oats into a pot. Then he tossed in some dried-up apples and crumbly pieces of nuts. He flung in the last of the honey from the honey jar. He splashed in water and let the ingredients boil. To his surprise, the king entered the kitchen and wanted to eat what he was cooking. "Your Majesty, it's for the servants. I'll make you a noble feast instead," he said. The king replied, "That's not necessary. Besides, I'm famished." After he tasted the porridge, he began to gulp more and more. "You're a genius, Cook!" he said. "And it's good for a chilly morning. It's perfect for our royal breakfast."

Word	Definition
furiously	**1.**
Majesty	**2.**
porridge	**3.**
genius	**4.**

5. Use a dictionary or glossary to find the definition for *famished*.

____

Home Activity Your child learned to understand unfamiliar words after looking them up in a dictionary or glossary. Work with your child to identify unfamiliar words in a story. Have him or her look them up in a dictionary and see which meaning fits best in the sentence.

Name ________________________________

Graphic Sources

Directions Read the play. Then answer the questions below.

DUKE: I need something to eat. What can I have?

DUCHESS: Here's a recipe. Good luck cooking! *(reads the recipe aloud):*

PEAS PORRIDGE
(serves 2)

2 cups peas

2 tablespoons oil

2 teaspoons salt

1/4 cup water

1. Place all ingredients into a bowl.
2. Mash together until smooth. Serve.

DUCHESS: I can't wait to try this!

DUKE *(after mixing furiously):* I'll bet this will be good on bread. Here, have a taste.

DUCHESS: This doesn't taste like porridge made from peas.

DUKE: Peas? Oops, I thought you said peanuts!

DUCHESS: Oh, well. It tastes good anyway.

1. What is the main ingredient in the recipe? How do you know this?

____

____

2. Explain how the ingredients in the recipe differ from the ingredients the duke used.

____

3. What is the first step in the process for making peas porridge?

____

4. In which step should the duke have realized that he had made a mistake? Why?

____

5. On a separate sheet of paper, write a surprising recipe of your own that may turn out to be a favorite. Write down the ingredients and the steps to follow.

Home Activity Your child has read a recipe. Help your child to find a recipe for a good snack. Ask him or her questions about the ingredients and the process. Challenge him or her to follow the steps in making the recipe.

Name ________________________________

Character and Setting

- **Characters** are people in a story. You can learn what characters are like by noticing what they say and do and how they interact with other characters.
- **Setting** is the time and place in which the story occurs.

Directions Read the following passage. Then answer the questions below.

One snowy morning, Jorie was doing something she wasn't supposed to do. She went out of her backyard and climbed boldly onto the top of a big hill covered with ice and snow. From there she could see the hills of Utah all around, white and rolling. "I dare you to come up here too!" she called to her brother below. "You're going to get in trouble again!" he replied. As Jorie stood and waved at him, she lost her balance. Plop! She landed on a patch of ice and began to slip down the hill. "Whoop! Out of the way!" she howled with glee as she whizzed past. "That was so much fun!" she told her brother with a big smile. "*You* try it!" Jorie and her brother spent the whole day sliding down the snowy hill.

1. When Jorie climbs onto the icy hill, what do her actions tell you about her?

____

2. "I dare you to come up here," Jorie says. What tone of voice do you think she was using? What do these words show you about her?

____

3. What does Jorie's brother's reaction to Jorie's dare tell you about her?

____

4. What is the setting of the story? How is the setting important?

____

____

5. Look back in the story and find words that show Jorie's expressions and feelings. Write these down. What do these words tell you about Jorie?

____

Home Activity Your child described the character and setting of a story. Read a seasonal story with your child. Work together to identify the setting and the traits of the main character.

Name ______________________________

Character and Setting

- **Characters** are people in a story. You can learn what characters are like by noticing what they say and do and how they interact with other characters.
- **Setting** is the time and place in which the story occurs.

Directions Read the following passage. Then complete the diagram.

Jake's father was the greatest inventor in the Moon Colony. He invented a low-gravity fishbowl and a space-pod that couldn't crash. Jake wished he had a good idea for an invention. He wanted everyone to be proud of him. Jake told his father, "I'm going to work very hard." He thought and thought. He worked and worked over many months. One day by mistake Jake knocked over two bottles his father had set out. The liquids mixed together. He noticed that the substance bubbled up and cleaned the counter. And that's how Jake invented a new kind of soap that washes dishes by itself. "I'm proud of all your effort," his dad said.

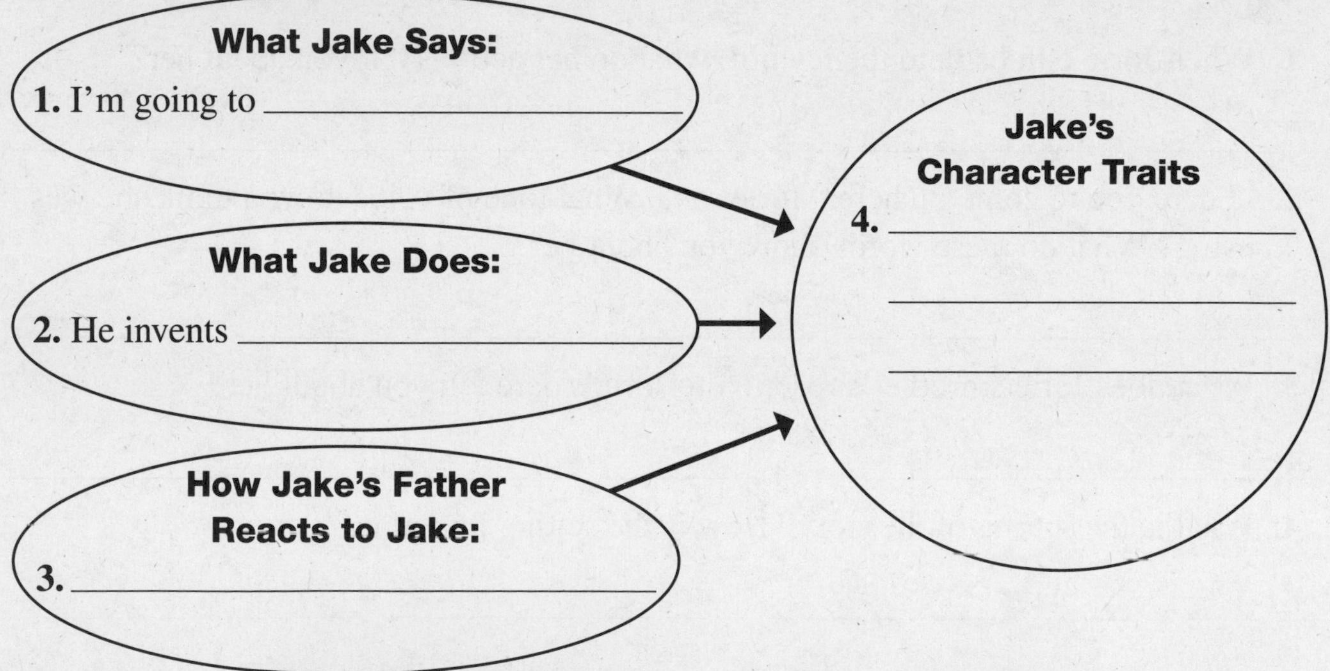

5. Reread and review the story to look for details. Write a sentence to describe the setting of this story. Include words that suggest time.

____

Home Activity Your child analyzed the main character and the setting in a story. Read a tall tale with your child. Then work with him or her to explain the characters and setting.

Name ___________________________________

Follow and Clarify Directions

- **Follow directions,** or instructions, in order. Directions are usually numbered.
- Read through all the directions before you begin. Then do what is instructed, one step at a time.
- Try to visualize the end result of the directions to see where you are headed.

Directions Read the directions in this recipe. Then answer the questions below.

Ants on a Log
(two servings)

This is a healthy snack for camping.

INGREDIENTS
2 large celery stalks
1/3 cup peanut butter
1/4 cup raisins

PREPARATION
1. Wash and dry two celery stalks.
2. Cut off the leafy tops with a kitchen knife. Cut each celery stalk into four parts.
3. Spread peanut butter into the groove on the celery pieces. Now they look like logs.
4. Press raisins onto the "logs" for "ants."
5. Enjoy!

1. What is the end result of this recipe?

____

2. What is the first step in the directions?

____

3. Which other steps are completed before spreading the peanut butter?

____

____

4. Why can't step 4 be done before step 3?

____

____

5. Why do you think this snack is called "Ants on a Log"? Explain what helps you to visualize it.

____

____

Name ______________________________

Directions Read over these directions. Then answer the questions below.

You may have seen sand castles on the beach or watched the results of a sand castle building contest live or on television. Here's the best way to build your own sand castle.

1. Choose sand that is moist enough to stick together. Fine, flat-grained sand is best. This sand is often found near the high-water line.
2. Start by making a pile of sand about 1 foot to 1 1/2 feet high. Its height and width will depend on what you want your castle to look like. Work from the top down to the base for the best results.
3. Pack the sand-pile down and make a smooth, flat top.
4. Use a shovel edge or ruler to carve the castle's tower and walls. You can also use pails, shovels, cans, spoons, melon-ballers, and so on.
5. Move down the pile in a stairstep fashion. Be creative, creating towers and walls.
6. Remember that sand castles have a very short life. Don't spend a long time trying to make a single perfect window on one tower. Instead, have fun and remember what you might try differently on your next attempt.

6. What is the purpose of these directions?

____

7. How high should your pile of sand be?

____

8. Should you work from the bottom up or from the top down?

____

9. Name some items you might use in building your sand castle.

____

____

10. Why shouldn't you worry much about your first attempt at building a sand castle?

____

____

____

Home Activity Your child learned about following directions. With your child, read the directions for a card or board game. Try to follow them, step by step. Help your child to clarify each step in the directions.

Name

Family Times

Summary

Seeker of Knowledge

No one could figure out old Egyptian writing until a young Frenchman solved the mystery. An ancient stone provided the clues, and Jean-François Champollion provided the solution.

Activity

Crack the Code Make up a "family code" that's a secret all your own. It might be saying the last syllable of a word first or starting every word with a certain letter of the alphabet. Try out your code—and make others wonder!

Comprehension Skill

Graphic Sources

Use **graphic sources** to help you understand what you read. Graphic sources include maps, charts, and time lines. A graphic source organizes information in a way that is easy to see. It can add to what you learn when you read.

Activity

See It, Say It Look at a map with family members. Close your eyes and point to a place on the map. Work together to figure out everything you can about this place using information found on the map.

Lesson Vocabulary

Words to Know

Knowing the meanings of these words is important to reading *Seeker of Knowledge*. Practice using these words.

Vocabulary Words

ancient of times long past

link anything that joins or connects, as a loop of a chain does

scholars learned people; people having much knowledge

seeker one who searches or tries to find

temple a building used for the service or worship of a god or gods

translate to change from one language into another

triumph victory; success

uncover to make known; reveal; expose

Grammar

Possessive Pronouns

Possessive pronouns may be used in place of possessive nouns. Like possessive nouns, they show who or what owns something. Remember never to use an apostrophe with possessive pronouns.

Pronoun	Possessive Pronoun
I	my/mine
you	your/yours
he	his
she	her/hers
it	its
we	our/ours
they	their/theirs

Activity

Pronoun Poetry Write each of the personal pronouns on a card: *I, you, he, she, it, we, they.* On the other side of each card, write the pronoun's possessive form. Work with a family member to make up poems that help you remember possessive pronouns: "These are its mitts, / The mitts are its, / Those are their chairs, / The chairs are theirs."

Practice Tested Spelling Words

________	________	________	________
________	________	________	________
________	________	________	________
________	________	________	________
________	________	________	________

Name ______________________________

Graphic Sources

- A **graphic source,** such as a picture, a map, a time line, or a chart, organizes information and makes it easy to see.

Directions Study the map and the caption below it. Answer the questions that follow.

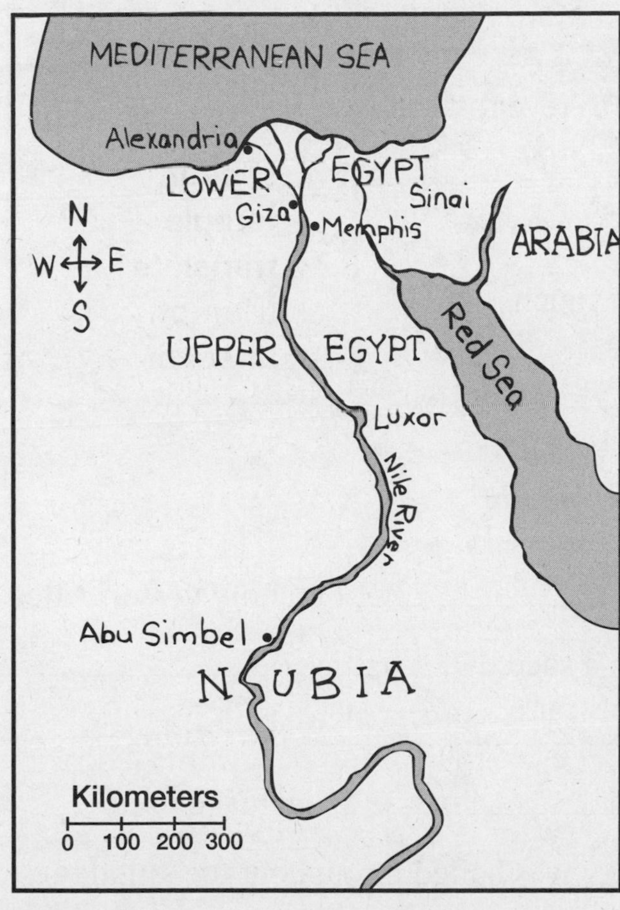

Egyptian history dates back eight thousand years to about 6000 B.C. Ancient Egypt consisted of two parts: Lower Egypt and Upper Egypt. The southern boundary of modern Egypt is about 50 kilometers south of Abu Simbel.

1. What does this map show?

____

____

2. Where is Alexandria located? In what part of Egypt is it?

____

____

____

3. How close were the cities of ancient Egypt to the Nile River?

____

____

4. About how far is Alexandria from Giza, the home of the pyramids?

____

5. How does this map help you better understand ancient Egypt?

____

____

____

Home Activity Your child used information on a map to answer questions. Look at a map with your child. Talk about the information you can learn from the map, such as key locations and distances between the places shown.

Name ______________________________

Vocabulary

Directions Choose the word from the box that best matches each definition. Write the word on the line.

Check the Words You Know
___ancient
___link
___scholars
___seeker
___temple
___translate
___triumph
___uncover

________________ **1.** anything that joins or connects

________________ **2.** victory, success

________________ **3.** to make known; to reveal

________________ **4.** of times long past

________________ **5.** people who have much knowledge

Directions Choose the word from the box that best fits in each sentence. Write the word on the line.

Always on a quest, the knight was a **6.** ________________ of a holy vessel. After many years, he found the object of his search in a sacred **7.** ________________. After his discovery, his next task was to **8.** ________________ the writing inscribed on it. The writing was in an **9.** ________________ language used thousands of years earlier. The knight's discovery was hailed throughout the kingdom as a **10.** ________________.

Write a News Report

On a separate sheet of paper, write a news report announcing the discovery of a new language. You will need research to help you tell how, when, where, and by whom the discovery was made. Use as many vocabulary words as possible.

Home Activity Your child identified and used vocabulary words from *Seeker of Knowledge*. Have your child create a story about finding a secret treasure. Ask your child to use the vocabulary from the lesson in the story.

Name ______________________________

Vocabulary • Word Structure

- When you see an unknown word, you can use what you know about **Greek and Latin roots** to help you figure out the word's meaning.
- The Latin word *ante* means "before," as in the word *antechamber.* The word *scholarly* comes from the Latin word *scholaris,* meaning "of a school." The word *celebrity* comes from the Latin word *celebrare,* which means "to honor."

Directions Read the following passage. Look for Latin roots as you read. Then answer the questions below.

Since ancient times, breaking an enemy's code has been very important. During World War II, Allied code-breakers worked hard to uncover the secrets found in German codes. From 1939 to 1945, these scholars used their knowledge of math and technology to crack the codes of German communications. If code breakers could translate a message, spies might be caught and lives could be saved. Breaking a code was a triumph to celebrate!

1. How is the meaning of *ancient* similar to the meaning of the Latin word *ante*?

____

2. How is the meaning of *scholars* related to the meaning of the Latin word *scholaris*?

____

3. *Translate* comes from the Latin word *translatus,* meaning "carried across or transferred." How is the meaning of *translate* similar to the meaning of *translatus*?

____

____

4. Which word above comes from the Latin word *triumphus,* meaning "victory"?

____

5. How does knowing the meaning of the Latin word *celebrare* help you understand the meaning of *celebrate?*

____

Home Activity Your child identified and used Latin roots to understand unfamiliar words. Work with your child to identify words with Latin or Greek roots in an article. Use a dictionary to confirm meanings.

Name ______________________________

Main Idea and Details

Directions Read the following passage. Then answer the questions below.

During World War II, the U.S. military needed a code to send messages about troop movements and plans. The code also had to be impossible to crack. Everyone searched and searched. Then Philip Johnston came up with an idea. He thought about using the Navajo language as a secret code.

The complex Navajo language had no alphabet, was never written, and was spoken only in the American Southwest. Outside of the Navajo people, only a handful of others understood it.

Johnston persuaded the Marines that the Navajo language would make an ideal military code.

The first Navajo "code talkers" developed code words and ways of using Navajo to spell out messages. From 1942 to 1945, about four hundred Navajos served as code talkers for the Marines. They sent messages with great speed over phones and radios. And their code was never cracked by the Japanese. Navajo code talkers were recently honored by the U.S. government for their skill and bravery.

1. What is the main idea of this passage?

____

____

2. What is a detail that supports that main idea?

____

____

3. What is another detail that supports the main idea of the passage?

____

____

4. Write a two-word title that can suggest the main idea of this passage.

____

5. On a separate sheet of paper, write a summary of this passage.

Home Activity Your child has identified the main idea and supporting details of a nonfiction passage. Read a short article to your child. Challenge your child to state the main idea and find supporting details.

Graphic Sources

- A **graphic source,** such as a picture, a map, a time line, or a chart, organizes information and makes it easy to see.

Directions Study the following time line to answer the questions below.

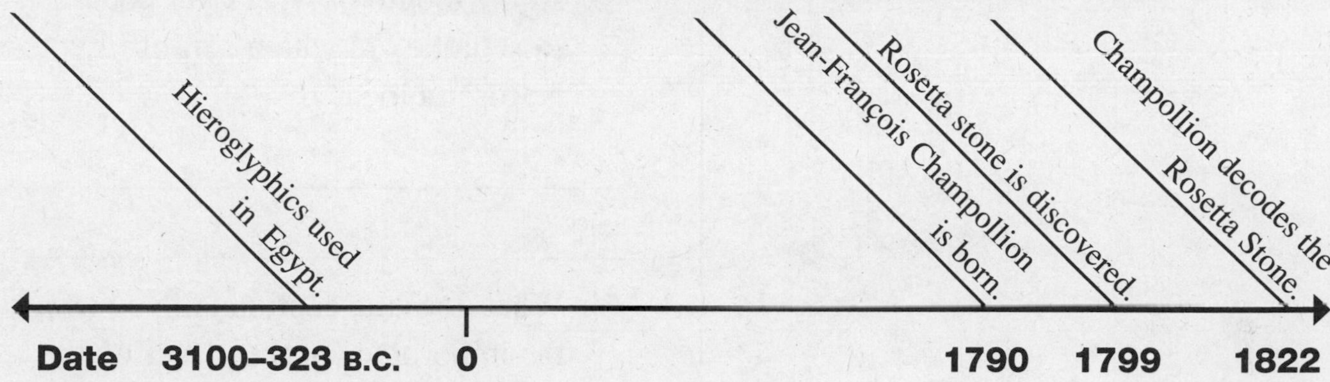

Hieroglyphics, the written language of ancient Egypt, puzzled scholars for many years. Understanding the Rosetta Stone was the key to understanding hieroglyphics.

1. What does the time line show?

____

2. About how long ago were hieroglyphics first used? How long after its discovery was the Rosetta Stone decoded?

____

3. How does the caption help to link the events on the time line?

____

____

4. Why is Jean-François Champollion included on the time line?

____

5. How is getting information from a time line different from reading it in a sentence?

____

Home Activity Your child used a time line to learn about the history of hieroglyphics. Read a magazine article about an ancient culture together. Create a time line of important events from that culture.

Name ____

Graphic Sources

- A **graphic source,** such as a picture, a map, a time line, or a chart, organizes information and makes it easy to see.

Directions Study the map below, which shows locations in *Seeker of Knowledge.* Answer the questions that follow.

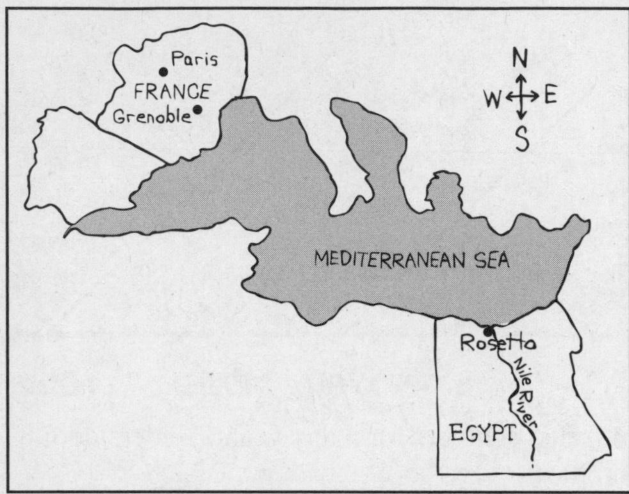

Jean-François Champollion of Grenoble, France, decoded the Rosetta Stone, which was found in Rosetta, Egypt.

1. Paris is where scholars studied the Rosetta Stone. In which direction did the Rosetta Stone travel to reach Paris?

____

____

2. What separates France from Rosetta, Egypt, where the Rosetta Stone was found?

____

3. At the mouth of what river does Rosetta lie? In which part of Egypt is Rosetta located?

____

____

4. What does the caption tell you about the importance of the places on the map?

____

____

____

____

5. On a separate sheet of paper, write what you learned from the map. What does the map show you?

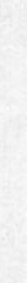

School + Home **Home Activity** Your child answered questions about locations on a map. Ask your child to draw a map from your home to a familiar location. Be sure to include specific landmarks on the map.

Thesaurus

- A **thesaurus** is a kind of dictionary that lists **synonyms** (words with the same or similar meanings), **antonyms** (words with opposite meanings), and other related words. Parts of speech are listed to show how a word is used. If a word has multiple meanings, synonyms for each meaning are given.
- You can use a thesaurus to help you find new and interesting words so you don't repeat the same words too often in your writing.

Directions If you opened a page in a student thesaurus, you might find these listings. Use them to answer the questions below.

soundless (adj) still, mute, quiet. See SILENT.

spark (n) **1. flash:** flicker, flare, sparkle, glow, glint, glimmer; **2. stimulus:** goad, spur, motivation, inspiration.

spark (v) **1. flash:** flicker, flare, sparkle, glint; **2. stimulate:** goad, spur, motivate, inspire, ignite, start, activate. (ant) extinguish, douse.

sparkle (v) **1. with light:** glitter, shine, flicker, glint, glimmer, glow, dazzle, shimmer: *The silver ornaments sparkle in the firelight.* **2. with intelligence:** be lively, be vivacious, be the life of the party, shine, dazzle: *Her stories sparkle with clever humor.*

sparse (adj) scanty, meager, slight, scarce, thin, poor, spare, skimpy, few and far between. (ant) thick, abundant, plentiful.

1. How many synonyms are there for *sparse* on this thesaurus page? What part of speech are they?

____

2. Which numbered list of synonyms would you use for *sparkle* as it is used in this sentence: "The crystal candlesticks sparkle brightly on the mantle." Why?

____

3. Look at this sentence: "A spark of understanding appeared in Jeff's eyes as he read the explanation." Would you look at the entries for the noun or the verb *spark* to replace *spark* with a synonym?

____

____

4. Rewrite the following sentence using a synonym for the verb *spark.* "The teacher's goal was to *spark* the students' interest in chemistry."

___

___

5. Give an antonym for *sparse.*

___

6. Use an antonym for the verb *spark* in this sentence: "A thick, dull-looking textbook will probably ______ a student's interest in any subject."

___

7. Give three synonyms for *soundless.* Do they have exactly the same meaning?

___

___

8. Where does the entry for *soundless* indicate you might find more synonyms for the word?

___

___

9. How are the two meanings for the verb *spark* like the two meanings for the noun *spark*? How do they differ?

___

___

___

10. Why would you use a thesaurus when you write? Explain your answer.

___

___

Home Activity Your child learned about using a thesaurus as a resource. Ask your child to use a thesaurus to find synonyms for a word picked at random from a newspaper article.

Name ______________________________

Family Times

Summary

Encyclopedia Brown and the Case of the Slippery Salamander

A salamander has been stolen from the Den of Darkness in the town aquarium. Encyclopedia Brown, the police chief's son, solves the mystery that has his dad stumped.

Activity

Puzzle Me Look in the newspaper or books for brainteasers and word games. Work with a family member to see how many of the answers you can find.

1.									
2. S	A	L	A	M	A	N	D	E	R

1. Something not known
2. Amphibian

Comprehension Skill

Plot

The **plot** is the story line or series of events that show characters in action. After presenting some background, the story starts when a character has a problem. During the **rising action** the problem builds, and at the **climax** problems are met directly. Then during the **resolution,** the problem is usually solved and the story ends.

Activity

Joke Jam Share with family members a joke that has a plot. Riddles and knock-knocks are out—funny stories are in! If you don't know any jokes, look in a joke book. Ask your family to tell you some jokes in return.

Lesson Vocabulary

Words to Know

Knowing the meanings of these words is important to reading *Encyclopedia Brown*. Practice using these words.

Vocabulary Words

amphibians cold-blooded animals with backbones and moist skin

crime a violation of law

exhibit thing or things shown publicly

lizards any of many reptiles with long bodies and tails and movable eyelids

reference something used for information or help

reptiles cold-blooded animals with backbones and lungs

salamanders any of numerous animals shaped like lizards, but related to frogs

stumped puzzled

Grammar

Contractions

A **contraction** is a word made by putting two words together. In a contraction, one or more letters are left out. An apostrophe is used in place of the missing letter or letters. Some contractions are formed by joining a pronoun and a verb. *For example: it + is = it's, we + are = we're, I + am = I'm, they + will = they'll.* Other contractions are formed by joining a verb and *not. For example: was + not = wasn't, did + not = didn't, have + not = haven't, are + not = aren't.* Be careful not to confuse the contraction *it's* with the possessive pronoun *its.*

Activity

Cut It Short Play a game with family members to see who can spot contractions around you, then tell what words they combine. Look for these shortcuts on signs, such as "Don't Walk," and in newspapers and magazines.

Practice Tested Spelling Words

Name ______________________________

Literary Elements • Plot

- A **plot,** or underlying story structure, is found only in fiction.
- A plot begins when a character has a problem or **conflict.** The problem builds up during the **rising action,** is met directly at the **climax,** and comes to an end, with the action winding down, during the **resolution.**

Directions Read the following passage. Then complete the diagram below.

Cory was trying out for a dance group that performed at city festivals. After waiting for four hours, it was finally her chance to dance. She had practiced so much, she did not think about individual steps. As Cory moved to the music, she focused on the rhythm and her feet knew what to do. When she'd finished, she knew she had danced her best. Cory had to wait again to find out if she had made it. Finally, a dance coach found her. "Welcome to Junior Jazz," the coach said. "Hooray!" shouted Cory.

Problem ↓	1.
Rising Action ↓	**Cory waited for her turn.**
Rising Action ↓	2.
Climax ↓	3.
Resolution	4.

5. What do you know about tryouts that helps you to understand the plot events?

____

____

Home Activity Your child read a short passage and identified its plot structure. Read a story with your child, and work with him or her to identify the problem, rising action, climax, and resolution of the plot.

Name ____________________

Vocabulary

Directions Choose the word from the box that best matches each definition. Write the word on the line.

Check the Words You Know
___amphibians
___crime
___exhibit
___lizards
___reference
___reptiles
___salamanders
___stumped

____________ **1.** cold-blooded animals with backbones and moist skins

____________ **2.** confused because something is hard to understand or solve

____________ **3.** a source used for information

____________ **4.** reptiles with long bodies and tails and movable eyelids

____________ **5.** animals shaped like lizards but related to frogs and toads

Directions Choose the word from the box that best completes each sentence. Write the word on the line.

David raced over to the new **6.** ____________ at the zoo. Nothing was there! He was baffled and **7.** ____________. Had there been a **8.** ____________ in which the animals were stolen? Had they escaped? He checked the sign as a **9.** ____________ about the animals that should be in the new exhibit. Suddenly he noticed where all of the rattlesnakes and other **10.** ____________ were hiding! The large sign had hidden them from view.

Write a Description

On a separate sheet of paper, write a description of an imaginary animal. Use as many vocabulary words as you can.

Home Activity Your child identified and used vocabulary words from *Encyclopedia Brown and the Case of the Slippery Salamander.* Read an encyclopedia article with your child. Have your child point out unfamiliar words. Work together to try to define each word by using the synonyms or antonyms around it.

Name ___________________________

Vocabulary • Context Clues

- **Synonyms** are words with the same or almost the same meaning.
- **Antonyms** are words with opposite meanings.
- When you read, you may come across a word you don't know. Look for synonyms or antonyms as clues to the unknown word's meaning.

Directions Read the following passage. Then answer the questions below.

Tamika's science fair exhibit, or display, featuring rattlesnakes was amazing. She presented a rattlesnake's skin and explained that unlike amphibians, reptiles have scales. Tamika also included pictures of the rattlesnake's diet, which included rabbits, rats, and squirrels.

Her best friend, Ty, was stumped and confused. He asked, "How can a snake eat animals that are larger than itself?" Tamika had been baffled by this herself, but now she was enlightened. She showed Ty her encyclopedia. Together, they looked at pictures of the snake's jaws expanding.

1. What does *exhibit* mean? What synonym helps you determine its meaning?

____

2. Explain why *reptile* and *amphibian* are not antonyms.

____

____

3. What does *baffled* mean? What synonym helps you determine its meaning?

____

4. What does *enlightened* mean? What antonym helps you determine its meaning?

____

5. Write a sentence using a word from the passage and its synonym or antonym.

____

____

Home Activity Your child identified vocabulary words using synonyms and antonyms in context. With your child, read an article about an animal and ask your child to identify unfamiliar words. Encourage your child to figure out the meanings using context clues such as synonyms and antonyms.

Name ______________________________

Compare and Contrast

Directions Read this story. Then answer the questions below.

Kara and her family were stumped by the mystery of the dripping water. Sometimes, water dripped from the ceiling in Kara's room. But in her brother Bill's room next door, the ceiling never dripped. "Let's study both rooms," said Kara's dad. Soon the family noticed similarities and differences. Neither ceiling had any cracks, and both rooms were warm. In Bill's room the ceiling was warm too. In Kara's room, however, the ceiling was very cold because there was no attic above it.

After a little thought, Kara said, "I think my class is studying this in science. It's called *condensation*. Water in the air turns into liquid when it touches something cold—like the drops of water on the outside of a cold glass. My room has a cold ceiling, so the warm air turns into water there and drips."

Her dad looked pleased and announced, "Mystery solved!"

1. Why does Kara's family compare and contrast the two rooms?

____

____

2. What is one way the two rooms are similar?

____

3. What is another way the two rooms are similar?

____

4. What is one way Kara's room is different from Bill's room?

____

5. On a separate sheet of paper, explain how comparing and contrasting the two rooms helped Kara solve the mystery.

Home Activity Your child has read a short passage and used comparison and contrast to analyze it. Read your child short articles about two different parts of the world. Challenge him or her to identify similarities and differences between the two places.

Name ______________________________

Literary Elements • Plot

- A **plot,** or underlying story structure, is found only in fiction.
- A plot begins when a character has a problem or **conflict.** The problem builds up during the **rising action,** is met directly at the **climax,** and comes to an end, with the action winding down, during the **resolution.**

Directions Read the following passage. Then answer the questions below.

The Bahamas is home to exotic wildlife. Many species of lizards and other reptiles live there. One summer, three men arrived at the islands. They said they were studying animals at a college in Europe. Local residents became suspicious when they noticed one of the men. He looked like someone who had stolen animals from the island many years earlier. Could it be the same person? After some debate, the residents contacted the police.

The three men were stopped at the airport, and their luggage was inspected. Five hundred live lizards were hidden in their luggage! The men had planned to take the lizards to Germany and sell them. Instead, the men were arrested, and the lizards were returned home alive.

1. In this story, what is the problem?

____

2. What is one event in the rising action?

____

3. What event is the climax of the plot?

____

4. What is the resolution?

____

5. What did you already know about the Bahamas that helped you understand this passage?

____

____

Home Activity Your child read a short passage and identified its plot structure. Read a story with your child. Work together to identify the problem, rising action, climax, and resolution of the plot.

Name ____________________

Literary Elements • Plot

- A **plot,** or underlying story structure, is found only in fiction.
- A plot begins when a character has a problem or **conflict.** The problem builds up during the **rising action,** is met directly at the **climax,** and comes to an end, with the action winding down, during the **resolution.**

Directions Read the following passage. Then complete the diagram below.

Brett, Tyrelle, and Jon were racing imaginary cars. Their "cars" were really water bottles, and the "track," thc slide in Tyrelle's backyard. After a few races, the boys were puzzled. Brett won every race. What was Brett's secret?

When Ted came over, Tyrelle and Jon asked Ted if he could solve the mystery.

"I know!" Ted said. "Brett's bottle is empty. Tyrelle's and Jon's still have some water in them. The heavier bottles create more friction, which slows them down. Brett's bottle weighs less and creates less friction. That's why he wins." Brett admitted his secret was out.

Problem ↓	**1.** The boys couldn't understand ____________________
Rising Action ↓	Brett wouldn't tell his secret.
Rising Action ↓	**2.** The boys asked ____________________
Climax ↓	**3.** Ted ____________________
Resolution	**4.** Brett ____________________

5. Explain how the problem in this story is solved.

____

____

Home Activity Your child read a short passage and identified its plot structure. With your child, read a story about someone who solves a problem. Ask your child to identify the problem, rising action, climax, and resolution in the story.

Name ____________________

Card Catalog/Library Database

Card catalogs and **library databases** provide information you need to find a book in the library. The card catalog has drawers with cards in them. The cards provide information about a book including its **author, title, subject,** and **call number.** You can search a card catalog by author, title, or subject. A library database is the online version of a card catalog.

Directions Use this card from a card catalog to answer the questions below.

J597.9 PA

Reptiles and Amphibians
Kel, Serge, 1960–

Through its descriptions and breathtaking photographs, this book provides readers a safe, up-close look at the fascinating world of crocodiles, caimans, salamanders, caecilians, and others.

Publisher: Reptile Universe Press
Pub date: c2003.
Pages: 96

ISBN: 0739842434

1. The call number for this book is in the upper left corner. What is its call number?

____

2. The title of this book is in boldface type. What is its title?

____

3. The author's name is underneath the title. Who is the author? When was he born?

____

4. When was the book published? How many pages does it have?

____

5. How would you search the card catalog to find more books on the subject of reptiles and amphibians?

____

____

Name ______________________________

Directions Look at the search results from a library database. Then answer the questions below.

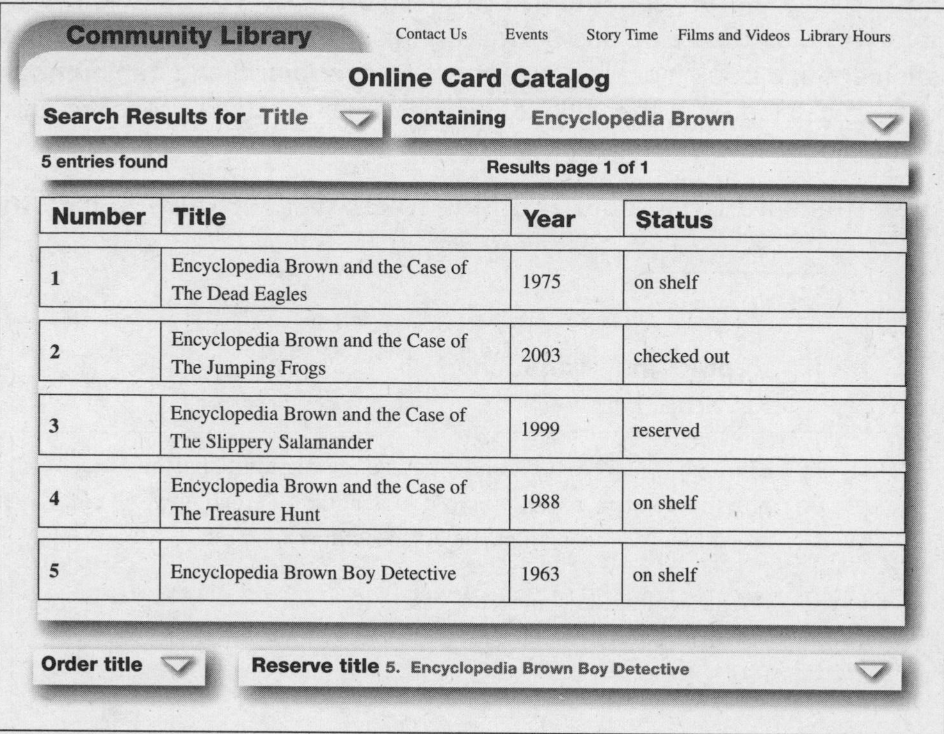

Community Library — Contact Us | Events | Story Time | Films and Videos | Library Hours

Online Card Catalog

Search Results for Title containing Encyclopedia Brown

5 entries found — Results page 1 of 1

Number	Title	Year	Status
1	Encyclopedia Brown and the Case of The Dead Eagles	1975	on shelf
2	Encyclopedia Brown and the Case of The Jumping Frogs	2003	checked out
3	Encyclopedia Brown and the Case of The Slippery Salamander	1999	reserved
4	Encyclopedia Brown and the Case of The Treasure Hunt	1988	on shelf
5	Encyclopedia Brown Boy Detective	1963	on shelf

Order title — Reserve title 5. Encyclopedia Brown Boy Detective

6. These results are from a search for titles containing *Encyclopedia Brown.* How can you tell?

____

7. How many entries were found for this search? How many are shown on the screen?

____

8. How many of these books could you check out today? How can you tell?

____

____

9. Which book is the newest? When was it published?

____

10. Which book is the oldest? When was it published?

____

Home Activity Your child learned about using a card catalog and library database to locate books. Go to the library or check online for a library database. Practice finding books together using the card catalog or the library database.

Name

Family Times

Summary

Sailing Home: A Story of a Childhood at Sea

Can you imagine eating, sleeping, playing, and going to school all at sea? That's exactly what the Madsen family children did aboard their father's cargo ship, the *John Ena*. The Madsen family shared many memorable events on the ship, from surviving frightening storms to celebrating the holidays.

Activity

Sea Vocabulary Together, investigate the vocabulary words used to describe the parts of a ship (such as *galley*, *bow*, and *mast*). Find the words on the Internet or in a reference book. Imagine your family is aboard a ship. Using the vocabulary words, pretend to have a conversation at sea.

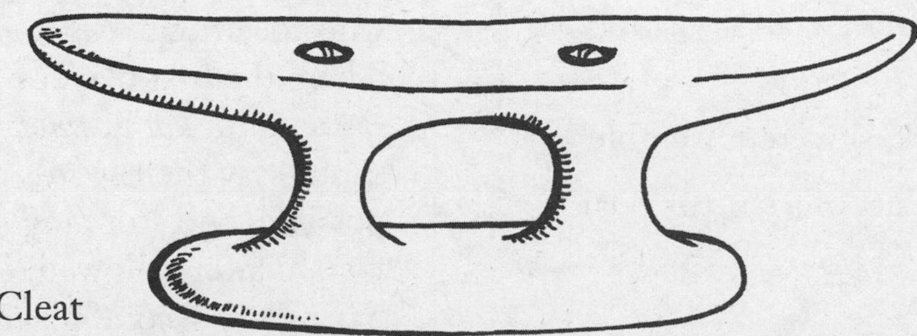

Cleat

Comprehension Skill

Author's Purpose

The **author's purpose** is the reason or reasons the author has for writing. An author may write to persuade, to inform, to entertain, or to express ideas and feelings.

Activity

My Magazine Think about a type of magazine you would like to create. Determine the main purpose of the magazine. With that purpose in mind, discuss what kinds of articles, pictures, and features your magazine would include in order to carry out that purpose.

Lesson Vocabulary

Words to Know

Knowing the meanings of these words is important to reading *Sailing Home: A Story of a Childhood at Sea*. Practice using these words.

Vocabulary Words

bow the forward part of a ship, boat, or aircraft

cargo load of goods carried by a ship, plane, or truck

celestial of the sky or outer space

conducted directed; managed

dignified having dignity; noble; stately

navigation skill or process of finding a ship's or aircraft's position and course

quivered shook; shivered; trembled

stern the rear part of a ship or boat

Grammar

Adjectives and Articles

Adjectives are words that describe persons, places, or things. *For example: blue; many; long.* **Proper adjectives** are adjectives made from proper nouns. They are always capitalized. *For example: French, Antarctic, English.* **Articles** are special adjectives like *a*, *an*, and *the*. Articles come before nouns, and sometimes before adjectives, too.

Activity

Article, Adjective, Noun Play this game with a family member. Start by having one player name an article. *For example: an.* The next player must quickly name an adjective that agrees with the article. *For example: easy.* Then, the first player must quickly say a noun. *For example: game.* Players should say their words as quickly as possible—no stopping to think about your answers allowed! Start again by having the second player name an article. Play several rounds.

Practice Tested Spelling Words

____	____	____	____
____	____	____	____
____	____	____	____
____	____	____	____
____	____	____	____

Name ______________________________

Author's Purpose

- The **author's purpose** is the reason or reasons the author has for writing.
- An author might have more than one reason for writing. Four common reasons are to persuade, to inform, to express ideas or feelings, and to entertain.

Directions Before you read the passage below, predict the author's purpose and write it in the diagram. Then read the passage and complete the rest of the diagram.

Ship's Crew Needed Immediately

The *Flora* will be leaving San Francisco on Tuesday, May 2, and a crew is needed before departure. The *Flora* is a cargo ship that will be carrying lumber to several cities along the coast of South America. It is a four-masted ship with plenty of living spacc. What better way is there to see the world than aboard a beauty like the *Flora?* Of course, you will also be paid standard wages for your service on our ship. If you are interested, please come by the transportation office and ask for Mr. Selvingson.

Before Reading		After Reading
Prediction of Author's Purpose or Purposes	**Reasons for Prediction**	**Author's Actual Purpose or Purposes**
1.	**2.** **3.**	**4.**

5. Do you think the author met his or her purpose? Why or why not?

____

____

Home Activity Your child used a graphic organizer to predict and then to confirm the author's purpose in a text. Together, look at one section of a book or an article in a magazine. Make predictions about the author's purpose. Then read the section or article to learn whether or not your prediction was correct.

Name ____

Vocabulary

Directions Choose a word from the box that best replaces the underlined word or words. Write the word on the line.

Check the Words You Know

- ___bow
- ___cargo
- ___celestial
- ___conducted
- ___dignified
- ___navigation
- ___quivered
- ___stern

____________________ **1.** The captain of the ship looked very noble, as if he were a king.

____________________ **2.** The children trembled as the mighty ship approached.

____________________ **3.** I ran to the rear part of the ship to wave good-bye.

____________________ **4.** Using the heavenly patterns, she charted our location.

____________________ **5.** The captain directed the unloading of goods.

____________________ **6.** Don't forget to mop the forward part of the ship.

Directions Choose the word from the box that best matches each clue. Write the word in the puzzle.

Across

7. load of goods

8. shivered

Down

9. skill of finding a ship's position

10. managed

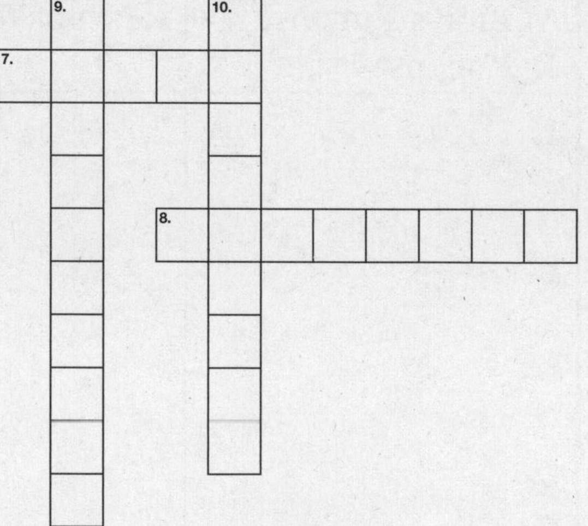

Write a Friendly Letter

Pretend you have been living aboard a cargo ship for several weeks. Write a letter to a friend describing your experience. Use as many vocabulary words as you can.

Home Activity Your child identified and used vocabulary words from *Sailing Home*. Together, make up a poem about sailing a ship. Use several of the vocabulary words.

Name ________________________________

Vocabulary • Context Clues

- **Homonyms** are words that are spelled and pronounced the same but have different meanings. **Homographs** are words that are spelled the same but have different meanings and pronunciations.
- Use **context clues** to help you figure out the meaning of homonyms and homographs.

Directions Read the following letter. Then answer the questions below.

Dear Suzanne,

I am writing you this letter as I lean on the railing on the bow of the ship. Whether you are at the bow or the stern, you have an excellent view of the sky above. So far, life at sea has been very exciting. After we have unloaded the cargo at a port, we have free time to explore.

Last week we stopped on the coast of France, and I took a canoe out and rowed up the coast to a little village. There you have it. I'm doing fine! So don't cry another tear for me!

Sincerely,

James

1. How do you know that the word *stern* does not mean "firm" in this letter?

____

2. Which words from the passage tell you whether the homonym *lean* means "thin" or "to rest on something or someone for support"?

____

3. What context clue helps you know the meaning of *tear* in this letter?

____

____

4. How is the word *bow* a homonym?

____

5. Are the words *days* and *daze* homographs? Why or why not?

____

Home Activity Your child identified the meanings of homographs and homonyms by using context clues. Make a list of all the homographs and homonyms that you can think of. After each word, draw a picture that shows the different meanings of each word.

Name ______________________________

Sequence

Directions Read the following passage. Then answer the questions below.

On the first day aboard the ship, our dog Sammy caused a lot of trouble. After Mother said that Sammy could join us, we were so excited. By the end of the day, however, he was not our favorite friend anymore. First, Sammy jumped on the lap of Captain Howard, who is very stern and formal. The captain was not pleased and scowled at us. Later, Sammy knocked over the bucket of soapy water that the cabin boy was using to mop the deck. Water splashed everywhere. We tried to call Sammy over to us, but he wouldn't listen. In fact, he was in such a frenzy that he slipped on the soapy water and slid right down the stairs below deck. At first we heard nothing. Then Sammy howled so loudly that we had to cover our ears. Apparently Sammy had sprained his leg. I guess he had to learn his lesson the hard way!

1. What is the last event in the story?

____

____

2. When were the children excited?

____

____

3. What was the second thing that Sammy did to make everyone upset?

____

4. What clue words in the passage help you to figure out the order of events?

____

____

5. On a separate sheet of paper, write the main events in this story on a time line.

Home Activity Your child identified the sequence of events in a story. Together, share one or more funny family stories. Invite your child to write down one of the stories using clue words to signal the order of events.

Name ___________________________

Author's Purpose

- The **author's purpose** is the reason or reasons the author has for writing.
- An author might have more than one reason for writing. Four common reasons are to persuade, to inform, to express ideas or feelings, and to entertain.

Directions Make a prediction about the author's purpose for the following article. Then read the article and answer the questions below.

A Ship of Ghosts?

There are many mysteries about the fates of some of the world's most famous ships. One such mystery surrounds a ship called the *Mary Celeste*. One day in December of 1872, a ship named the *Dei Gratia* was sailing in the middle of the Atlantic Ocean. The crew noticed another ship, which made no response to the *Dei Gratia's* greeting.

Some of the crew of the *Dei Gratia* went aboard the other ship, which was named the *Mary Celeste,* to find out more. When these men returned to the *Dei Gratia*, they reported that no one was on the ship. Nobody has ever found out what happened to the people aboard the *Mary Celeste.*

1. Before reading, what did you predict was the author's purpose?

____

2. Why did you think this was the author's purpose?

____

3. After reading, what do you think was the author's purpose or purposes?

____

4. Was the author successful in achieving this purpose or purposes? Why or why not?

____

____

5. If this article were rewritten and given the new title "Why I Am Spooked by the *Mary Celeste*," what would you predict the author's purpose to be?

____

Home Activity Your child predicted and identified an author's purpose in an article. Before reading a nonfiction article together, predict the author's purpose. Then discuss how the two of you can use an appropriate reading pace to fit the author's purpose. For example, you might read an informative article more slowly than you would an article meant to entertain.

Name ______________________________

Author's Purpose

- The **author's purpose** is the reason or reasons the author has for writing.
- An author might have more than one reason for writing. Four common reasons are to persuade, to inform, to express ideas or feelings, and to entertain.

Directions Predict the author's purpose before you read and record it in the diagram. Then read the passage and complete the rest of the diagram.

My First Storm at Sea

The storm was like nothing I had seen before. The waves were the size of buildings, and they came crashing down on our deck as if they were angry. The rain came down in thick sheets. It made it hard to see from one end of the ship to the other. Luckily, the captain had sailed through many storms like this during his life. Instead of acting out of panic, he acted calmly and with great concentration. Within the hour, he managed to steer us through the worst of the storm. I was never happier to see a storm end in my life!

Before Reading		After Reading
Prediction of Author's Purpose or Purposes	**Reasons for Prediction**	**Author's Actual Purpose or Purposes**
1.	The article's title **2.** **3.**	**4.**

5. Do you think the author met his or her purpose? Why or why not?

____

____

____

Home Activity Your child used a graphic organizer to predict and confirm the author's purpose in a text. Invite your child to teach you how to look for signs that indicate an author's purpose before reading.

Name ______________________________

Parts of a Book

- Learning the **parts of a book** helps you locate information. At the front of a book, the **title page** gives its title, author, and publisher. Then the **copyright page** tells the year a book was published. Finally, the **table of contents** lists titles and page numbers of chapters and sections. At the back of a book, an **appendix** contains graphs and charts. A **bibliography** lists books that an author used to research or write his or her own book. An **index** lists the page numbers where important words or ideas can be found. A **glossary** gives definitions of important words.
- A **chapter title** is the name of a chapter. A **section heading** is the name of a section within a chapter. **Captions** explain graphic sources and usually appear above or below them. Numbered **footnotes** appear at the bottom of pages or at the back of a book. They provide additional information about a subject.

Directions Study the table of contents for the book *The World of Ships* below.

TABLE OF CONTENTS

Name ___________________________

Directions Use the table of contents to answer the questions below.

1. Would you find the title of this book before or after the table of contents?

____

2. The words in bold print are examples of which part of a book?

____

3. "Ship Vocabulary" is an example of what part of a book?

____

4. On what page can you begin to read about Captain Crane?

____

5. Where in this book might you find a definition for the word *stern*?

____

6. Given the topic of this book, what might you expect to find in the appendix?

____

7. Would this be a good source for a report on oceans? Why or why not?

____

____

8. If you wanted to read about ghost ships, where in this book might you look?

____

9. How would it help you to study this table of contents before reading this book?

____

____

10. If you wanted to know whether this book was more up-to-date than another book on ships, which part of the book would you consult?

____

Home Activity Your child learned about parts of a book and answered questions about how to use various parts. Together, open a reference book to any page. Take note of the section headings, graphic sources, and any captions. Name as many parts of a book you can find on several different pages.

Name

Family Times

Summary

Lost City: The Discovery of Machu Picchu

Professor Hiram Bingham goes on a journey to Peru to find the lost city of Vilcapampa. With the help of a farmer named Arteaga and a Quechua boy, Bingham finds something unexpected—the beautiful and mysterious city of Machu Picchu sitting among the clouds.

Activity

Journal of Discovery Bingham recorded his experiences in Peru in a journal. Pretend you have uncovered the ruins of a city. Together with a family member, write a journal entry that describes the ruins and how you feel upon discovering them. Use drawings to enhance your journal entry.

Comprehension Skill

Compare and Contrast

To **compare and contrast** is to tell how two or more things are alike and different. Words such as *similar*, *as*, *unlike*, and *instead* signal a comparison and contrast.

Activity

Tell Me What I See Choose two items in the room. Compare and contrast the qualities of the two items without staring at them or naming what they are (you can call them item A and item B). Have a family member guess what items you are describing. Switch roles, and repeat the activity.

Lesson Vocabulary

Words to Know

Knowing the meanings of these words is important to reading *Lost City: The Discovery of Machu Picchu.* Practice using these words.

Vocabulary Words

curiosity an eager desire to know

glorious magnificent; splendid

granite a very hard gray or pink rock that is formed when lava cools slowly underground

ruins what is left after a building, wall, etc., has fallen to pieces

terraced formed into flat, level land with steep sides

thickets bushes or small trees growing close together

torrent a violent, rushing stream of water

Grammar

Comparative and Superlative Adjectives

A **comparative adjective** is used to compare two people, places, things, or groups. Add *–er* to most adjectives to make them comparative. *For example: softer.* A **superlative adjective** is used to compare three or more people, places, things, or groups. Add *–est* to most adjectives to make them superlative. *For example: hardest.* Remember that there is no need to combine the words *more* or *most* with comparative or superlative adjectives in your writing.

Activity

Big, Bigger, Biggest From magazines or newspapers, cut out pictures of three things or people that have qualities that you could compare. Glue them to a sheet of paper. Write the appropriate adjective beneath each picture. For example, if you had a picture of a bicycle, a car, and an airplane, you might caption them as *big*, *bigger* and *biggest*. Repeat the activity with new pictures.

Practice Tested Spelling Words

____________	____________	____________	____________
____________	____________	____________	____________
____________	____________	____________	____________
____________	____________	____________	____________
____________	____________	____________	____________

Name ______________________________

Compare and Contrast

- To **compare and contrast** means to tell how two or more things are alike and different.
- Clue words such as *like* and *as* can show similarities. Clue words such as *however* and *instead* can show differences.

Directions Read the following passage. Then complete the diagram below.

The ancient Greek and Roman cultures seem very similar on the surface. For instance, in both cultures, the people lived in areas with warm climates and wore similar clothing. Both societies also produced great poets and artists. However, they do have some major differences.

Greece was a series of small city-states. Rome, on the other hand, was a huge empire, ruled by an emperor. Greek buildings and Roman buildings were both grand, but Rome's were built using more advanced methods.

Greek and Roman Cultures	
Similarities	**Differences**
1.	**3.**
2.	**4.**

5. What did you visualize when you read the passage?

____

____

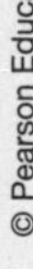

Home Activity Your child read a short passage and used a graphic organizer to compare and contrast two cultures. Have your child compare and contrast two people you both know well. Ask your child to be specific in naming their similarities and differences.

Name ______________________________

Vocabulary

Directions Choose the word from the box that best matches each definition. Write the word on the line.

Check the Words You Know

- ___curiosity
- ___glorious
- ___granite
- ___ruins
- ___terraced
- ___thickets
- ___torrent

________________ **1.** a violent, rushing stream of water

________________ **2.** magnificent; splendid

________________ **3.** formed into flat, level land with steep sides

________________ **4.** what is left after a building has fallen to pieces

________________ **5.** an eager desire to know or learn

Directions Choose the word from the box that best completes each sentence. Write the word on the line shown to the left.

________________ **6.** The ___ walls of the cave were cool to the touch.

________________ **7.** The carvings were covered by overgrown ____ of berry bushes.

________________ **8.** The ___ hill was planted with crops.

________________ **9.** The archaeologists were thrilled to discover the ___ of an ancient city.

________________ **10.** The ___ sunshine made the lake sparkle.

Write a Description

Pretend you are an archaeologist who has just discovered some ancient ruins. Write a description about what you have found. Use as many vocabulary words as you can.

Home Activity Your child identified and used vocabulary words from *Lost City: The Discovery of Machu Picchu.* With your child, make up a story about an ancient civilization. Use the vocabulary words from the selection.

Name ________________________________

Vocabulary • Word Structure

- When you see an unknown word, you can use what you know about **Greek and Latin roots** to help you figure out the word's meaning.
- The Latin word *terra,* meaning "earth, land," is in the words *terrain* and *territory.* The Latin word *gloria* means "praise," as in the word *glorify.*

Directions Read the following passage. Then answer the questions below.

The curiosity was getting the better of me. I had to know what was at the end of this path. We had been hiking on rugged terrain for hours. We had to change direction twice to avoid a very powerful torrent that could have knocked us to our feet if we had tried to cross it. At least it was a glorious day. The sun was shining bright and the sky was a beautiful light blue. Finally, we saw a terraced hill before us. Once we were completely out of the trees, I could see the top of the hill. There was a huge granite structure in all its glory.

1. What is the Latin root in *terraced?* How does the root help you understand the meaning of the word?

____

2. How does the root in *glorious* help you understand its meaning?

____

3. What do you think *terrain* means? How does the root help you understand the word's meaning?

____

4. It does not make sense to substitute the meaning of the Latin root for *glory* in the passage. How is the meaning of *glory* related to the meaning of the Latin root?

____

5. Write a sentence using a new word with either the root *gloria* or *terra.*

____

Home Activity Your child read a short passage and identified the meanings of unfamiliar words using Latin roots. Look in a dictionary with your child to find other words that use the Latin roots, *gloria* and *terra.*

Name ________________________________

Sequence

Directions Read the article. Then answer the questions below.

Like any scientific researcher, an archaeologist follows a certain process to uncover ancient objects. The first step is research. Archaeologists figure out where they want to dig and gather any information about what could be buried in the ground. Then, at the dig site, they set up a grid system. The grid helps them identify where an object has been discovered. While they dig, archaeologists use special tools, such as trowels, brushes, and dental picks that will not harm the artifact. They are aware of the layers of the soil, which helps them to date the artifact. Next, they take the artifacts to a lab to do further testing.

Archaeologists look at all the information they've gathered and draw conclusions about it. Finally, these conclusions are published in articles for other scientists and the public to read.

1. What is the last step in the process an archaeologist follows?

____

____

2. Why do archaeologists do research first?

____

____

3. When do archaeologists make a grid system?

____

4. What clue words in the passage help you to figure out the order of steps?

____

5. Is the sequence of these steps important to finding objects? Explain.

____

____

Home Activity Your child read a short passage and identified the sequence of events. Together, read about a process with which your child is unfamiliar. After reading, have your child draw a diagram that shows the main steps in the process.

Name ______________________

Compare and Contrast

- To **compare and contrast** means to tell how two or more things are alike and different.
- Clue words such as *like* and *as* can show similarities. Clue words such as *however* and *instead* can show differences.

Directions Read the following article. Then answer the questions below.

Many civilizations have developed their own language and system of writing, including ancient Mayan and Egyptian societies. Both thought highly of writing, using it to record political history and other important events. They also used writing as part of their religions. That is why you can find writing in special places like monuments or temples. Scientists have found the writing of both cultures carved in stone and painted on walls or paper. These cultures used symbols to represent words and numbers. They both put the symbols into columns. However, the Mayan writing was read from left to right, while the Egyptian writing was mostly read right to left. It seems that the Egyptians only used picture or symbol writing on tombs and in temples. They use other forms of writing for other purposes, whereas the Mayans basically used one form.

1. How did both cultures feel about writing?

____

2. What was similar about the types of materials the cultures used for their writing?

____

3. Explain how reading the two forms of writing was different.

____

4. Why do you think Egyptians had two forms of writing instead of one?

____

____

5. Create your own letters using pictures and write your name.

____

Home Activity Your child read a short passage and compared and contrasted details in it. Read an article about an ancient civilization. Visualize the place while reading. Then, draw your visualizations on a piece of paper. Compare and contrast the drawings you and your child made.

Name ______________________________

Compare and Contrast

- To **compare and contrast** means to tell how two or more things are alike and different.
- Clue words such as *like* and *as* can show similarities. Clue words such as *however* and *instead* can show differences.

Directions Read the following passage. Then complete the diagram below.

The archaeologists found shoes made of animal skin. They were worn and rough from water and dirt. They also found a coat made out of thick fur. It was warm and kept out the cold air. A few holes had been cut into it. A type of thick string was threaded through the holes on the front edges of the coat. The strings could be tied together to keep the coat closed. The woman's dress they found was long and made out of animal hide. It had beads on it around the neck. The jewelry was made out of beads and precious stones. There were earrings, necklaces, and bracelets.

Ancient Clothing and Clothing of Today	
Similarities	**Differences**
1. Coats are still ______________ ______________	**3.** Most clothing is not ______________ ______________
2. Earrings, necklaces, ______________ ______________	**4.** Instead of string ______________ ______________

5. On another sheet of paper, draw a picture of how you visualize the clothing described in this passage.

Home Activity Your child has used a graphic organizer to compare and contrast clothing from the past and today. Discuss what people used to do for entertainment in the days before television, movies, and video games. Compare and contrast entertainment in the past with that of the present.

Outline

An **outline** is a plan that shows how a story, article, report or other text is organized. An outline includes a title, main topics, subtopics, and details. You can use an outline to better understand how a text is organized or as a way to organize your own thoughts before you write something of your own.

Directions Read the following outline. Then answer the questions below.

Ancient Civilizations

I. Aztecs
   A. Location and Size
      1. Mexico
      2. made up of hundreds of states
      3. 5 to 6 million people
   B. People
      1. priests and nobles
      2. warriors
      3. serfs or enslaved people

II. Incas
   A. Location and Size
      1. Peru, Ecuador, and Chile
      2. about 12 million people
   B. People
      1. emperor
      2. nobles
      3. farmers

1. What is the title of this outline?

____

2. What two topics are under *Aztecs*?

____

3. What types of Inca people will be included in this report?

____

4. Why do you think the same two subtopics are used under *Aztecs* and *Incas?*

____

____

5. How would an outline help you to organize your thoughts before writing a report?

____

____

Name ______________________________

Directions Read the following article. Then complete the outline below.

Even though the Incas lived long ago, they were highly civilized. Their system of farming was well planned. Their farming allowed them to feed themselves with enough left over to trade. Inca farmers grew cotton, potatoes, corn, and many other crops. Their irrigation system helped them water their crops. Incas kept animals on the farm too. They raised llamas, ducks, and alpacas.

Besides their farming system, the Incas also had buildings and roads. If you were to visit the Inca sites in South America today, you would be able to see the ruins of grand temples, palaces, and military forts. The Inca transportation system was based on two main roads that stretched for hundreds of miles. Minor roads connected the main roads. They also constructed bridges and tunnels.

Directions Complete the outline by writing the correct information on the line shown to the left.

Inca Civilization

6. I. ____________________	I. _____
	A. Crops
	1. cotton
7. I. A. 2. ____________________	2. _____
	3. corn
8. I. B. ____________________	B. _____
	1. llamas
	2. ducks
	3. alpacas
	II. Buildings
	A. Palaces
9. II. B. ____________________	B. _____
	C. Forts
	III. Transportation
	A. Roads
	1. two main roads
10. III. A. 2. ____________________	2. _____
	B. Bridges and Tunnels

Home Activity Your child learned about outlines. Read an article and create an outline together based on the information in the article.

Name

Family Times

Summary

Amelia and Eleanor Go for a Ride

One evening, Eleanor Roosevelt asks her friend Amelia Earhart to dinner. In the middle of the dinner, these two brave and daring friends decide to take a ride in an airplane to see the city lights. Even after their exhilarating flight, they have enough excitement left in them to take a fast spin in Eleanor's new car. It proves to be a memorable evening for the two friends.

Activity

For the Fun of It Amelia and Eleanor took the rides in the plane and the sports car for the fun of it. Discuss with each other what kinds of activities you like to do for the fun of it. Use vivid adjectives to describe how these activities make you feel.

Comprehension Skill

Sequence

Sequence means the order in which things happen. Dates, times, and clue words such as *first*, *then*, *next*, and *last* can help you understand the order of events.

Activity

Five-Year Plan Interview family members about what they would like to accomplish in the next five years. Ask what they would like to do first, next, and last. Would the order of tasks affect how they would be accomplished?

Lesson Vocabulary

Words to Know

Knowing the meanings of these words is important to reading *Amelia and Eleanor Go for a Ride*. Practice using these words.

Vocabulary Words

aviator person who flies an aircraft; pilot

brisk keen; sharp

cockpit the place where the pilot sits in an airplane

daring bold; fearless; courageous

elegant having or showing good taste; gracefully and richly refined; beautifully luxurious

outspoken not reserved; frank

solo without a partner, teacher, etc.; alone

Grammar

Adverbs

An **adverb** tells how, where, or when an action happens. An adverb usually describes a verb. *For example: slept late.* "Late" is an *adverb* that describes the action "slept." An adverb can be written before or after the verb it describes. Adverbs that tell how something happens or happened often end in *–ly. For example: slowly walked.*

Activity

Add Verbs Play this adverb game with a family member. Write down several verbs on squares of paper or note cards and shuffle them. Have Player 1 flip over a verb card, so that Player 2 can think of an appropriate adverb to add to the verb. Once Player 2 has said an adverb that makes sense with the verb on the card, Player 1 should flip over another card. See how many correct responses Player 2 can get in one minute. Switch roles, and repeat the activity, now timing Player 1.

Practice Tested Spelling Words

____________	____________	____________	____________
____________	____________	____________	____________
____________	____________	____________	____________
____________	____________	____________	____________
____________	____________	____________	____________

Name ______________________

Sequence

- **Sequence** is the order in which things happen. Sequence can also mean the steps we follow to do something.
- Look for clue words that signal sequence, such as *first, next, then,* and *last.*
- Pay attention to dates and times the author gives you.
- Some events can happen simultaneously, or at the same time.

Directions Read the following passage. Then complete the diagram below by writing on the diagonal lines events from the passage in sequence.

Emily Howell Warner was not the first woman to fly an airplane. However, she was the first woman to be hired as a pilot by a large airline company in the modern United States.

Emily had gotten excited about flying as a teenager many years earlier. It happened on a flight in 1958, during which she was invited to ride in the cockpit. She loved the experience, and from that day on, Emily had the idea of becoming a pilot. She worked hard to get the proper flight training, putting in 7,000 hours of flight time. In 1961, she began to teach other people how to fly. Still, because she was female, she had trouble getting a job as a commercial pilot. Finally, in 1973, Frontier Airlines hired Emily Warner. Later, she went on to become the first female pilot to reach the rank of captain.

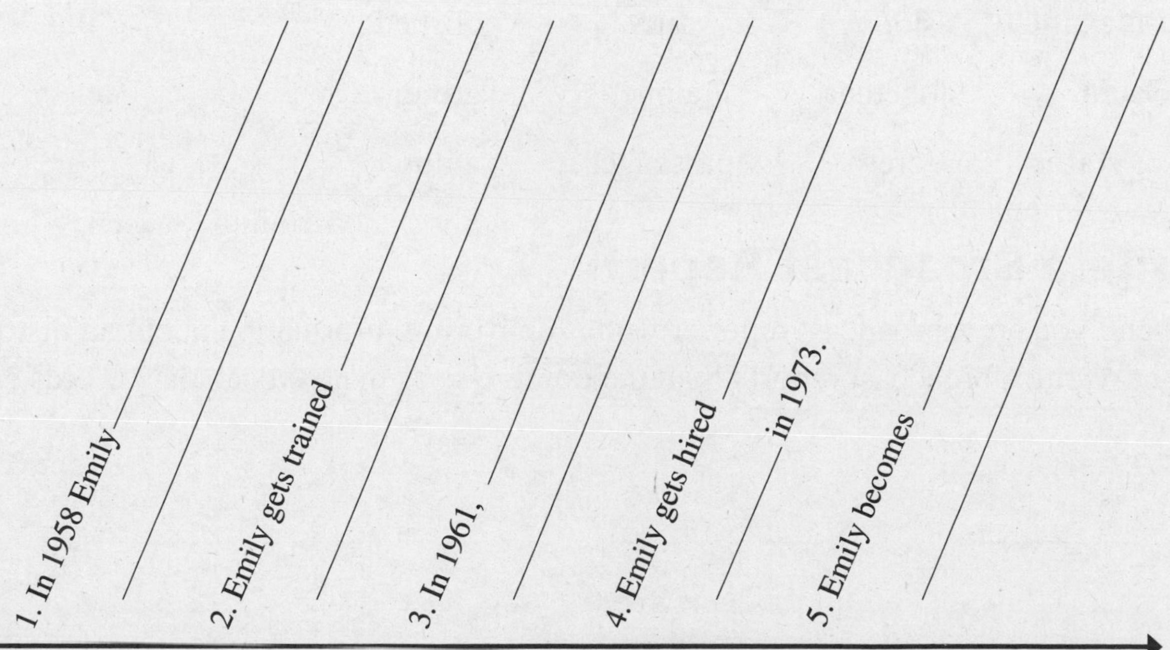

Home Activity Your child used a time line to identify the order of events in a passage. Together, make a simple craft, such as a greeting card or a puppet. Have your child write down the sequence of steps necessary to make the craft.

Name ________________________________

Vocabulary

Directions Choose the word from the box that best matches each definition. Write the word on the line.

Check the Words You Know
___aviator
___brisk
___cockpit
___daring
___elegant
___outspoken
___solo

______________ **1.** having or showing good taste

______________ **2.** without a partner or teacher

______________ **3.** person who flies an aircraft

______________ **4.** not reserved

______________ **5.** place where pilot sits in an airplane

Directions Circle the word that has the same or nearly the same meaning as the first word in each group.

6. brisk	slow	sharp	cloudy
7. daring	fearless	smart	scared
8. elegant	sloppy	dirty	polished
9. solo	together	alone	group
10. aviator	crew	passenger	pilot

Write a Broadcast Report

Pretend you are a broadcast reporter who is delivering information about an historic flight. Write a broadcast report about the event. Use as many vocabulary words as you can.

Home Activity Your child identified and used vocabulary words from *Amelia and Eleanor Go for a Ride.* With your child, read an article about flight or airplanes. Help your child identify the meanings of unfamiliar words in the article.

Name ______________________

Vocabulary • Context Clues

Sometimes you can use **context clues**—the words and sentences around an unknown word—to help you figure out the meaning of the word.

Directions Read the following passage. Then answer the questions below.

Heather came from a daring family. They had no fear and took many risks. Her brother Kyle was a stunt pilot, or aviator. You can see him in the cockpit of planes in a few famous movies. Her mother sailed ships. She once sailed across an ocean all by herself. She loved this solo journey because she was alone with nothing but the sound of the sea. Then there was Heather. She enjoyed acrobatics and gymnastics. Her talents led her to the circus where she became a tightrope walker. Heather would dress up in elegant, or stylish, costumes and walk as light as a feather on the thin rope. When asked why she chose the tightrope, Heather said she was just following in her family's footsteps.

1. What does *daring* mean? How do you know?

____

2. What context clue helps you to figure out the meaning of *aviator?*

____

____

3. What is the *cockpit* of a plane? How do you know?

____

4. Why would sailing *solo* in a ship be a risky decision?

____

5. Find the sentence with the word *elegant.* Rewrite it so you give the context clue in a different way.

____

____

Home Activity Your child identified the meanings of unfamiliar words using context clues. Invent a few new words for common everyday items (for example: a hat could be a *tah*). Give clues as to their meanings in a conversation with your child. Have your child guess the real words. Switch roles and repeat the activity.

Name ________________________________

Draw Conclusions

Directions Read the article. Then answer the questions below.

Nellie Bly, whose name was actually Elizabeth Cochrane, was a spunky journalist ahead of her time. She got her first job in 1885 in a strange way. After she read an article about women being useless creatures, she wrote a very mean letter to the editor. The editor liked her writing and offered her a job. While working for the paper, she went to Mexico and wrote articles about all the problems in the country at the time. The Mexican government was not pleased with her criticisms and kicked her out of the country. She then went to work for the *New York World* newspaper. While working there, Nellie tried to travel around the world in less than eighty days, a record set by characters in a fictional story. She did it in seventy-two days, which made her famous.

1. What conclusion can you draw about Nellie Bly's personality?

____

2. What is one detail or fact that supports this conclusion?

____

____

3. What is a conclusion that you can draw about Nellie's time in Mexico?

____

____

4. What is one detail or fact that supports this conclusion?

____

5. On a separate sheet of paper, draw a conclusion about how women were treated in the 1800s and early 1900s. Write at least three details from your prior knowledge that supports this conclusion.

Home Activity Your child drew a conclusion based on details in an article. Discuss an important woman that you and your child know. Draw a conclusion about what this woman's impact is on other people. Help your child to come up with details to support that conclusion.

Name ________________________________

Sequence

- **Sequence** is the order in which things happen. Sequence can also mean the steps we follow to do something.
- Look for clue words that signal sequence, such as *first, next, then,* and *last.*
- Pay attention to dates and times the author gives you.

Directions Read the article. Then answer the questions.

Clara Barton started her own school in 1852. Soon the student population grew very large. The men in her community said she could not run it any longer by herself. Clara did not want to work under a man at her own school, so she quit. During the Civil War, Clara nursed the wounded and gave supplies out to soldiers. Then, she traveled to Europe where she was introduced to the International Red Cross. After she came back to the United States, she set up her own aid society called the American Association Red Cross. Clara Barton stayed in charge of the Red Cross until 1904. She passed away in 1912.

1. What is the first event described in the passage?

____

2. When did Clara go to Europe?

____

3. How do you know that she didn't start the Red Cross while she was in Europe?

____

____

4. Besides clue words such as *after* and *then,* what other clues tell you the sequence of events in the article?

____

5. Why do you think the author chose to use sequence as the structure of this article?

____

____

Home Activity Your child analyzed the structure of an article to determine the sequence of events. Have your child write a narrative about an event that happened to him or her this week. Help your child use clue words and other ways of signaling when the events occurred in the narrative.

Name ______________________________

Sequence

- **Sequence** is the order in which things happen. Sequence can also mean the steps we follow to do something.
- Look for clue words that signal sequence, such as *first, next, then,* and *last.*
- Pay attention to dates and times the author gives you.
- Some events can happen simultaneously, or at the same time.

Directions Read the passage. Then complete the diagram.

Frannie's great-great-grandmother Harriet fought for women's rights. When Harriet was twenty-two years old, she started a women's organization. As president, Harriet spoke at many conventions and rallies. She told women to stand up for themselves. Later, Harriet went back to college and studied political science. Finally, in 1950, she decided to run for representative in her state. Harriet lost by a few votes. But that doesn't matter to Frannie. Harriet is a hero in her eyes.

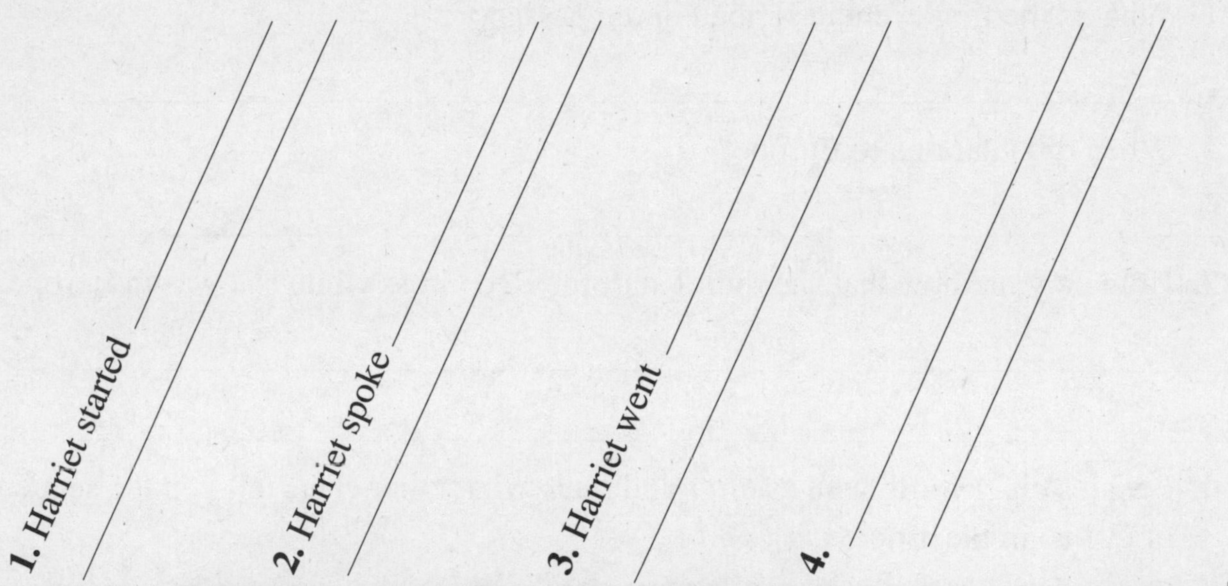

5. Is the sequence of events important to your understanding of this passage?

____

____

Home Activity Your child used a graphic organizer to identify the sequence of events in a passage. Have your child create a time line of the important moments in your life.

Name ________________________________

Diagram/Scale Drawing

- A **diagram** is a special drawing with labels. Usually a diagram shows how something is made, how an object's parts relate to one another, or how something works. Sometimes a diagram must be studied in a certain order to be understood—left to right, top to bottom, or bottom to top. Often diagrams contain text that explains something about the object being illustrated.
- A **scale drawing** is a diagram that uses a mathematical scale. For example, one inch on a scale drawing might be equal to one foot on the actual object in real life.

Directions Study the diagram of an airplane below.

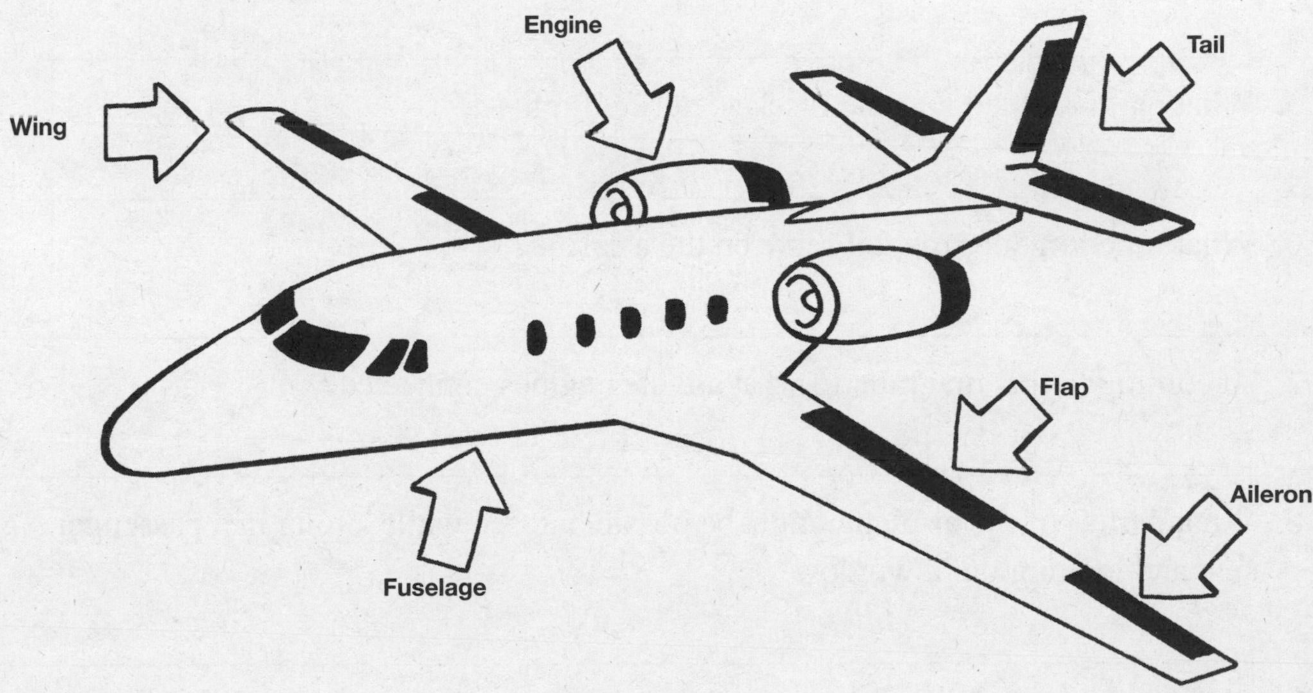

DEFINITIONS

Fuselage: This is the body of the airplane, shaped like a tube. The front landing gear, or wheels, can be folded into the fuselage while the airplane is flying.

Engines: These make the airplane move forward. They are very powerful.

Wings: The wings are designed to provide lift.

Flaps: The flaps are extended to provide additional lift during take-off and put away during the flight to reduce drag.

Ailerons: These are used to turn the plane while flying.

Tail: The three wings on the tail help move the plane up or down, and left or right.

Name ______________________________

Directions Use the diagram to answer the following questions.

1. What does this diagram show?

____

2. What does the caption tell you?

____

3. Where are the ailerons located?

____

4. What part is extended to provide additional lift?

____

5. What part is folded into the fuselage during flight?

____

6. What function does the tail serve on the airplane?

____

7. According to this diagram, to what are the engines connected?

____

8. What part(s) of the airplane might be possible to see while sitting in a passenger seat and looking out a window?

____

9. How does the diagram help you to understand the information in the caption?

____

____

10. What would you have to do to make this diagram into a scale drawing?

____

____

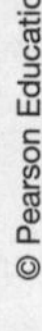

Home Activity Your child learned about diagrams and scale drawings. Together, use the Internet or a reference book to look up the actual measurements of a famous building or structure. Then draw a scale drawing of it.

Name ______________________________

Family Times

Summary

Antarctic Journal: Four Months at the Bottom of the World

Jennifer Owings Dewey is given a wonderful opportunity—the chance to see Antarctica for herself. During her four-month trip, Jennifer witnesses the life cycle of penguins, watches orca whales swim by her boat, experiences life without night, and narrowly escapes a dangerous fall into a glacier crevasse.

Activity

Packing Light Pretend you are going to Antarctica for several months. Besides the necessities you will need in order to survive, you may bring only two personal items. Discuss with your family what those two items would be, and why you would bring them.

Comprehension Skill

Main Idea and Details

The **main idea** makes a point about a topic and has at least one supporting detail. **Details** are smaller pieces of information that tell more about the main idea.

Activity

Finding Support Along with a family member, read a nonfiction article about Antarctica from a reference book or the Internet. What do each of you believe is the main idea of the article? Try to find details in the article that support your main idea.

Lesson Vocabulary

Words to Know

Knowing the meanings of these words is important to reading *Antarctic Journal: Four Months at the Bottom of the World.* Practice using these words.

Vocabulary Words

anticipation act of anticipating; looking forward to; expectation

continent one of the seven great masses of land on Earth; The continents are North America, South America, Europe, Africa, Asia, Australia, and Antarctica.

convergence act or process of meeting at a point

depart to go away; leave

forbidding causing fear or dislike; looking dangerous or unpleasant

heaves rises and falls

icebergs large masses of ice, detached from a glacier and floating in the sea

Grammar

Comparative and Superlative Adverbs

A **comparative adverb** is used to compare two actions. Add *–er* to most adverbs to make them comparative. Use *more* with adverbs that end in *–ly* to make them comparative. *For example: faster, more slowly.* A **superlative adverb** is used to compare three or more actions. Add *–est* to most adverbs to make them superlative. Use *most* with adverbs that end in *–ly* to make them superlative. *For example: fastest, most slowly.*

Activity

Adverb Definitions Make a short dictionary booklet by folding two pieces of paper together in half. In the booklet, list people, animals, machines, or any nouns you know that can perform some sort of action. After each word, write a description of the word that helps to define it by using either comparative adverbs or superlative adverbs.

Practice Tested Spelling Words

____________	____________	____________	____________
____________	____________	____________	____________
____________	____________	____________	____________
____________	____________	____________	____________
____________	____________	____________	____________

Name ______________________________

Main Idea and Details

- The **main idea** tells the most important idea from a paragraph, passage, or article.
- **Details** are small pieces of information that tell more about the main idea.

Directions Read the following article. Then complete the diagram by finding the main idea and the details that support it.

Although Antarctica is far away from the rest of the world, scientists know a great deal about it. They have explored the continent and walked upon its ice. They have discovered mountain ranges and mapped them out. Scientists have even studied hidden features of Antarctica that exist underneath the ice. Now equipment that uses radio-echo sounding technology can determine what these features look like. The knowledge scientists have gained has encouraged tourists to see the continent for themselves.

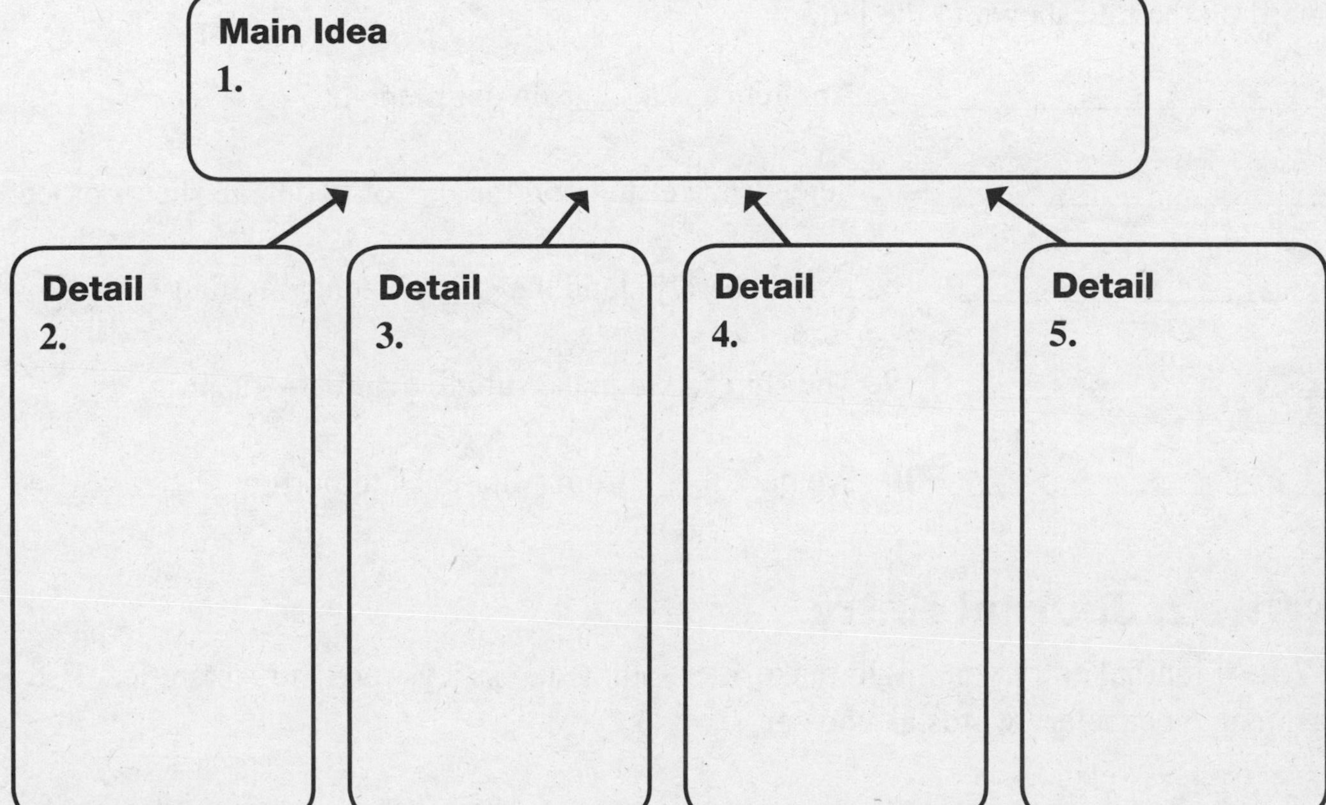

Home Activity Your child used a graphic organizer to determine the main idea and supporting details in an article. Discuss a place your child knows well. Have him or her write a paragraph about the place, including a main idea and details that support it.

Name ______________________________________

Vocabulary

Directions Choose the word from the box that best matches each definition. Write the word on the line.

Check the Words You Know
___anticipation
___continent
___convergence
___depart
___forbidding
___heaves
___icebergs

____________________ **1.** to go away

____________________ **2.** large masses of ice floating in the sea

____________________ **3.** expectation

____________________ **4.** rises and falls alternately

____________________ **5.** causing fear or dislike

Directions Choose the word from the box that best completes each sentence. Write the word on the line shown to the left.

____________________ **6.** Antarctica is a ____ on our planet.

____________________ **7.** Scientists are studying the ___ of two large sheets of ice.

____________________ **8.** I could barely stand the ___ of seeing my first whale.

____________________ **9.** The ship had to make sure to avoid any floating ___.

____________________ **10.** We have to___ from Antarctica tomorrow.

Write a Journal Entry

Write a journal entry you might make after sailing across icy waters to Antarctica. Use as many vocabulary words as you can.

Home Activity Your child identified and used vocabulary words from *Antarctic Journal: Four Months at the Bottom of the World.* Together, create a crossword puzzle using the words from the selection.

Name ______________________________

Vocabulary • Word Structure

- When you see an unknown word, you can use what you know about **Greek and Latin prefixes** to help you figure out the word's meaning.
- The Latin prefix *com-* or *con-* means "with" or "together." The Latin prefix *de-* means "away from." The Latin prefix *anti-* means "against" or "before."

Directions Read the following passage. Then answer the questions below.

Never had the scientists felt such cold. Yesterday, they had departed from Christchurch, New Zealand. During the night, they felt the temperature drop, and their anticipation turned to tough reality. Antarctica, they knew, would show them the convergence between Nature's beauty and its power to threaten life. They would be staying there for several months to compile information about the ecosystem. Something was destroying the natural food chain, and the scientists did not have much time to figure it out.

1. How does the prefix in *depart* help you to figure out its meaning?

____

____

2. What is the meaning of *convergence?*

____

3. Define the word *compile.*

____

4. *De-* and *con-* have nearly opposite meanings. Think about the meaning of *destroying,* and then write a word that means the opposite and uses the prefix *con-*.

____

____

5. What is the meaning of *anticipation?*

____

Home Activity Your child used knowledge about Latin and Greek prefixes to identify the meanings of words. Together, use a dictionary to find other words that use the *con-*, *com-*, *anti-*, or *de-* prefix definitions mentioned above.

Name ______________________________

Draw Conclusions

Directions Read the following article. Then answer the questions below.

Could you imagine wearing winter clothing all year round? You might have to if you lived in Antarctica. The continent of Antarctica wins the prize of being the coldest continent on the planet. The temperature during the Antarctic winter might dip down more than one hundred degrees below zero. Brrr!

However, not all areas of the continent have the same temperature. You may find warmer temperatures if you go to the northern Antarctic Peninsula. Of course, the warmest it usually gets there is about 34°F in the middle of the summer. But this isn't bad, considering that summer temperatures in other parts of the continent are often about –37°F. Now, do you think you will ever complain about the cold again?

1. What conclusion can you draw about the climate in Antarctica?

____

2. What is one detail or fact that supports this conclusion?

____

____

3. What is a conclusion that you can draw from the second paragraph?

____

4. What is one detail or fact that supports this conclusion?

____

____

5. On a separate sheet of paper, write a paragraph describing your idea of the perfect climate. Make sure to include a logical opinion and supporting details in the paragraph.

Home Activity Your child drew a conclusion based on details in an article. Discuss how to go about making a favorite family recipe. Help your child draw a conclusion about what would happen if the recipe were not followed correctly.

Name ______________________________

Main Idea and Details

- The **main idea** tells the most important idea from a paragraph, passage, or article.
- **Details** are small pieces of information that tell more about the main idea.

Directions Read the following article. Then answer the questions below.

Krill: A Favorite Food of Whales

It is strange to imagine large baleen whales making a meal of tiny creatures. Yet that is exactly what happens in the waters around Antarctica. **Krill,** which are sea creatures that look like shrimp, are necessary to the diets of many Antarctic animals. They are tiny organisms compared to the huge whales. Some animals can gather one ton of krill in a single mouthful. Baleen whales catch and eat about 150 million tons of krill in just a few months. Despite their small size, krill are important to supporting life in the waters around Antarctica.

1. What is the topic of this article?

____

2. What is the main idea?

____

3. What is one supporting detail of this main idea?

____

____

4. Do you think "which are sea creatures that look like shrimp" is a supporting detail? Why or why not?

____

5. How does the author structure the main idea and details in this paragraph?

____

____

Home Activity Your child determined the main idea and supporting details in a passage and analyzed its text structure. Together, look through a chapter of a textbook. Have your child point out elements of text structure, such as titles, headings, subheadings, and main ideas and supporting details.

Name ______________________________

Main Idea and Details

- The **main idea** tells the most important idea from a paragraph, passage, or article.
- **Details** are small pieces of information that tell more about the main idea.

Directions Read the following passage. Then complete the diagram below.

The region around Antarctica has become less pure since people began to explore it. One reason for the change is that human beings have brought non-native animals there. For instance, since people settled on the islands near Antarctica, mice, rats, and rabbits now live there as well. Grazing sheep have started to wear away the land. Dogs and cats have killed native birds for food. Of course, human beings have also changed the area around Antarctica by hunting whales and seals and by leaving some areas polluted. Luckily, people have begun to take steps to preserve the natural features of the continent. For example, the Antarctic Treaty was created to protect the land of icy wonder from further harm.

Main Idea

1. The area around Antarctica has become ______________________________

Detail

2. Human beings have brought ______________________________

Detail

3. Grazing sheep have ______________________________

Detail

4. Dogs and cats have ______________________________

Detail

5. ______________________________

School + Home

Home Activity Your child used a graphic organizer to identify the main idea and supporting details in an article. Together, read a short article about another place of natural beauty. Identify the main idea and supporting details in the article.

Name ______________________

SQP3R

- **SQP3R** is a study skill that can help you when reading. Here's what it means:
- **Survey:** Look at the title, author, chapter headings, and illustrations to get an idea of what you are about to read.
- **Question:** Generate questions you want answered when reading the text.
- **Predict:** Try to imagine what the text you're going to read is about.
- **Read:** Read the text, keeping in mind your predictions and questions.
- **Recite:** Recite or write down what you learned from reading the text.
- **Review:** Look back at the text, the predictions you made, the questions you posed, the answers you found in the text, and the information you learned from your reading.

Directions Look at the illustration and read the information below. Follow the SQP3R method.

Glaciers: Wonders in Ice

Three layers make up what are called true glaciers. First, there is a layer of snow on top. The next layer is made of an ice and snow mixture. Finally, solid ice forms the bottom layer. There are also cracks called crevasses that appear while the glacier is moving. Some glaciers move very slowly, so slowly it is hard to tell, while others may move a few hundred feet in a day. It is this movement of the massive ice that makes the unique features of the land. Giant mountain peaks, lakes, and valleys are all results of glaciers that moved and eroded away the land years in the past.

You can visit glaciers but it is not recommended that you walk on them. Deep crevasses may be underneath the snow, making them hard to see. Trained people who have experience with climbing mountains and glaciers, and have special tools, like a rope, crampons, and an ice axe, are better equipped to do this kind of exploring. People who travel on glaciers should never go alone.

Name ________________________________

Directions Use the information to answer the following questions.

1. After surveying the title and illustration, did you think the information would be fiction or nonfiction?

___

2. What are two questions you had before reading?

___

3. Before reading what did you predict the text would be about?

___

4. How far do some glaciers move in a day?

___

5. What is the middle layer in a glacier made up of?

___

6. What makes the unique features of the land?

___

7. Why is walking on a glacier dangerous?

___

8. What did you learn from this text that you did not know before?

___

9. How does making predictions before you read help you?

___

___

10. How does reviewing your questions and information help you?

___

___

Home Activity Your child learned about the SQP3R study method. Choose a fictional story to read. Have your child apply the study method to the story. Ask your child to explain how the study method differed when using it with fiction instead of nonfiction.

Name

Family Times

Summary

"Moonwalk"

While daring each other to jump over rilles, or narrow valleys on the Moon, Gerry and Vern get into trouble. Vern falls and hurts his knee while also knocking his battery, which gives him air to breathe in his spacesuit, loose. Luckily, the boys are able to get to a nearby shelter where Vern is out of danger.

Activity

A Day on the Moon Together, talk about what a day on a space station on the Moon would be like. What would you like to do and see? What would be dangerous? What things would be the same? What things would be different?

Comprehension Skill

Draw Conclusions

Drawing a conclusion is forming an opinion based on what you already know or on the facts and details in a text. Check an author's conclusions or your own conclusions by asking: Is this the only logical choice? Are the facts accurate?

Activity

Correcting Conclusions Read a story with a family member. After reading the first page, draw a conclusion about what the story will be about. Finish reading to find out if you were correct. If so, then go back and point out the details that supported your original conclusion. If not, draw a new conclusion and identify the details that support it.

Lesson Vocabulary

Words to Know

Knowing the meanings of these words is important to reading Moonwalk. Practice using these words.

Vocabulary Words

loomed appeared dimly or vaguely as a large, threatening shape

rille a long, narrow valley on the surface of the moon

runt animal, person, or plant that is smaller than the usual size. If used about a person, *runt* is sometimes considered offensive.

staggered moved or walked unsteadily; wavered

summoning stirring to action; rousing

taunted jeered at; mocked; reproached

trench any ditch; deep furrow

trudged walked wearily or with effort

Grammar

Prepositions and Prepositional Phrases

A **preposition** is a word that shows a relationship between a noun and another word, such as a verb, adjective, or other noun. Prepositions are often used to relate one word to another in space or in time. *For example: during, to, under, across.* A preposition is also the first word in a group of words called a **prepositional phrase.** *For example: out of the box, across the street, for a week.* To avoid confusion, keep prepositional phrases close to the words they modify. The meaning of a sentence can change if the modifier is misplaced.

Activity

Preposition Letters Together with a family member, write a letter to someone using as many prepositional phrases as you can. The letter can be serious or silly. Underline the prepositional phrases.

Practice Tested Spelling Words

____	____	____	____
____	____	____	____
____	____	____	____
____	____	____	____
____	____	____	____

Name ______________________________

Draw Conclusions

Drawing a conclusion is forming a logical, well thought-out opinion based on what you already know or on the facts and details in a text. Facts and details are the small pieces of information in a passage.

Directions Read the following passage. Then complete the diagram below by finding facts and details to help you draw a conclusion about Martin.

On sunny afternoons while his brothers and sisters were outside playing, Martin stayed in his room, buried in a book about planets and stars. The ceiling and walls of Martin's bedroom were covered with stars. Martin made sure the plastic stars were placed in their proper constellations. For the school science fair, Martin spent weeks building a model of the solar system. The teacher said it was the most realistic model she had ever seen. She said it felt as if she were looking at the real planets. Martin told his parents that he wanted above all to become an astronaut when he grew up.

Facts and Details
1.

Facts and Details
2.

Facts and Details
3.

Facts and Details
4.

Conclusion
5.

Home Activity Your child used a graphic organizer to draw a conclusion from a passage. Invite your child to draw a conclusion about a career he or she might like to pursue. Together, write down facts or details about your child interests that support this conclusion.

Name ______________________________

Vocabulary

Directions Choose the word from the box that best replaces the underlined word or words. Write the word on the line.

Check the Words You Know

- ___loomed
- ___rille
- ___runt
- ___staggered
- ___summoning
- ___taunted
- ___trench
- ___trudged

_______________ **1.** The sun shone into the narrow valley on the moon.

_______________ **2.** Justin walked with effort as he grew tired in the hot sun.

_______________ **3.** My brother picked out the unusually small animal as his favorite of the litter.

_______________ **4.** Tina became unsteady when she tried to walk in the space suit.

_______________ **5.** Lisa mocked her brother at the dinner table.

_______________ **6.** The thunder cloud hung threateningly above them.

Directions Choose the word from the box that best matches each clue. Write the word on the line.

_______________ **7.** This is a ditch.

_______________ **8.** You are doing this when you call on your own courage.

_______________ **9.** You might have walked like this when you were tired.

_______________ **10.** You might have walked like this after becoming dizzy.

Write a Story

Write a story about an adventure on the moon. Use as many vocabulary words as you can.

School + Home **Home Activity** Your child identified and used vocabulary words from "Moonwalk." Together, try to act out the meanings of words such as *trudged, staggered, runt,* and *loomed.*

Name ______________________

Vocabulary • Context Clues

- **Synonyms** are words with the same or similar meanings.
- Sometimes an author includes a synonym for an unfamiliar word. In these cases, look for a word set off by commas and preceded by the word *or* or *like.*

Directions Read the following passage. Then answer the questions below.

Kiko and Val were excited about their vacation on the moon. They had heard stories but had never seen such things as a rille, which is like a valley. During the ride they were summoning, or rousing, their courage for their first walk on the moon.

When they finally landed, Kiko staggered, or wavered, as she walked down the portable staircase. She remembered her mother's warning to be careful. Now Kiko could see a deep ditch, or trench, that posed a danger. Kiko gave Val a challenging look, then taunted her for being too scared to leave the spacecraft. Though Val didn't like being mocked by Kiko, she wasn't about to move until she was perfectly ready.

1. What is a synonym for the word *rille?* How do you know?

____

2. How do you know *rousing* is a synonym for *summoning?*

____

3. What is a synonym for *trench?* Why might a trench be dangerous?

____

4. Find the synonym for *taunted.* How do you know that this is the synonym?

____

____

5. After reading the passage, you might describe Val as feeling scared. What is a synonym for *scared?*

____

Home Activity Your child identified the meanings of words using synonyms that appeared as context clues. Call out a word. Then have your child respond with a synonym for that word. Finally, challenge your child to use the word and its synonym in a sentence.

Name ______________________________

Literary Elements • Theme

Directions Read the following story. Then answer the questions below.

The spacecraft was performing strangely. I could hear peculiar noises coming from who knows where. Bleep! Bong! Bop! The same sounds repeated over and over again. I didn't want to alarm Rog in the rear compartment. Perhaps more importantly, I didn't want him to think that I couldn't handle a crisis. I pressed a button to increase the speed of the craft, and the ship jerked into its highest gear. I brought us back to a regular speed by slamming down the brake handle. Then, all of a sudden, the noises stopped.

Rog came through the hatch and into the chamber. "What on Earth are you doing?" he said. "I was sitting in the rear compartment, peacefully listening to my favorite song, 'Bleep! Bong! Bop!' The next thing I know, I'm being tossed all around the room!"

"What was the title of that song?" I asked, feeling embarrassed. Privately, I thought, *Well, that explains that!*

1. What problem is the narrator trying to solve?

____

2. How does the narrator try to solve the problem?

____

3. Why doesn't the narrator ask Rog for help?

____

____

4. What is the theme of this story?

____

____

5. On a separate sheet of paper, write a short story that uses the theme "generosity helps the one who gives as well as the one who receives."

Home Activity Your child identified the theme of a short fiction passage. Read a story together. Work together to identify the theme. Then discuss moments in your own lives where you have seen this theme exhibited.

Name ______________________________

Draw Conclusions

Drawing a conclusion is forming a logical, well thought-out opinion based on what you already know or on the facts and details in a text. Facts and details are the small pieces of information in a passage.

Directions Read the following article. Then answer the questions below.

Several Apollo missions have contributed to our knowledge of the moon. During these missions, astronauts accomplished a number of things. They gathered information and brought back samples, such as moon rocks, for scientists to study. They also took photographs from different sides of the moon, and these images have been helpful to our understanding of this part of our universe.

Although the missions occurred between 1969 and 1972, scientists today still use information collected by Apollo astronauts to help them understand the moon. It may be a very long time before we understand this mysterious place completely, but at least we are on our way.

1. What conclusion can you draw about the Apollo missions?

____

2. What is one fact or detail that supports this conclusion?

____

3. What conclusion can you draw about the challenge of understanding the moon?

____

4. What is one fact or detail that supports this conclusion?

____

5. Reread the passage slowly. Did you understand the passage or any of its details more fully after this second reading? Explain.

____

____

Home Activity Your child drew conclusions from a text and applied a strategy to deepen your child's understanding. Have your child read a nonfiction article. Invite your child to recall as many details as possible. Then your child can reread the article to clarify understanding of the text.

Draw Conclusions

Drawing a conclusion is forming a logical, well thought-out opinion based on what you already know or on the facts and details in a text. Facts and details are the small pieces of information in a passage.

Directions Read the following passage. Then complete the diagram below.

Colin and the other astronauts were curious about the planet Zeeog. They knew from earlier scientific studies that life did exist there. However, they did not know exactly what form this life took. Was it intelligent life?

Colin lowered the spacecraft over Zeeog's surface. Down below, he and the others could see several rows of square structures. The larger structures had markings on them—perhaps some kind of writing? Now the astronauts could see creatures roaming around and moving in and out of the structures. These beings gathered together in groups and pointed upward at the spacecraft. As the craft neared the ground, many of the beings hurried inside. A few others stood outside with their arms outstretched in greeting to the visitors from Earth.

Facts and Details
1. The astronauts could see several ______

Facts and Details
2. The larger structures had ______

Facts and Details
3. The beings gathered ______

Facts and Details
4. ______

Conclusion
5. The beings on Zeeog ______

Home Activity Your child used a graphic organizer to draw a conclusion and support it with details found in a passage. Together, read a news story. Then work to draw a conclusion about the people involved in the story. Try to recall details that support your conclusion.

Name ______________________________

Order Form/Application

Order forms and **applications** are charts with columns and spaces in which you can write or type. An order form is the means by which a person can purchase merchandise by completing a form and e-mailing or sending it to a company. An application is a form by which a person can apply for a job. Application forms ask for identifying information such as name, address, and phone number, and also ask for the person's educational and job history.

Directions Answer the questions below about the following order form.

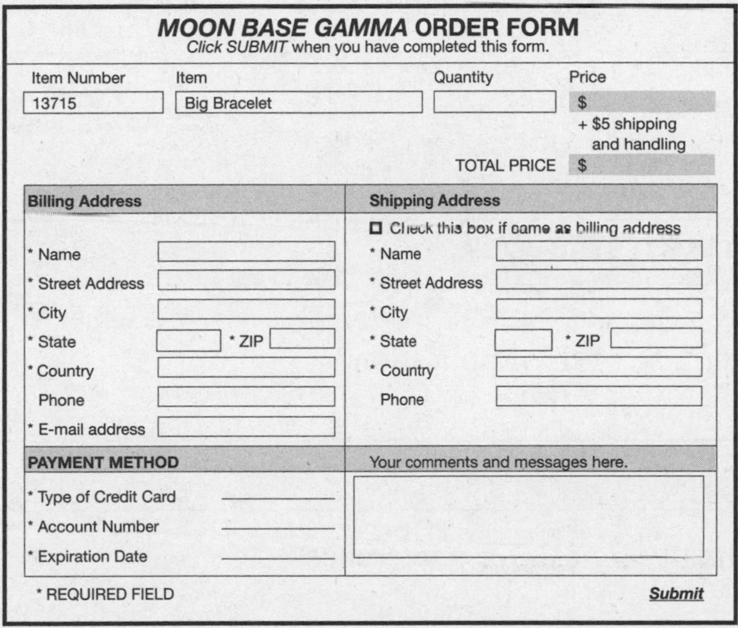

***MOON BASE GAMMA* ORDER FORM**
Click SUBMIT when you have completed this form.

Item Number	Item	Quantity	Price
13715	Big Bracelet		$
			+ $5 shipping and handling
		TOTAL PRICE	$

Billing Address	Shipping Address
	☐ Check this box if same as billing address
* Name	* Name
* Street Address	* Street Address
* City	* City
* State * ZIP	* State * ZIP
* Country	* Country
Phone	Phone
* E-mail address	

PAYMENT METHOD	Your comments and messages here.
* Type of Credit Card ________	
* Account Number ________	
* Expiration Date ________	

* REQUIRED FIELD

Submit

1. What is the difference between the two addresses on the form?

____

2. When would you provide only one address?

____

3. What does *quantity* mean?

____

4. What boxes are you not required to fill in on this form?

____

5. What do you do when you are finished filling out the form?

____

Name ___________________________________

Directions Use this online job application form to answer the questions below.

<table>
<tr><th colspan="2">Lincoln Library Association
SUMMER INTERNSHIP EMPLOYMENT APPLICATION</th></tr>
<tr><td>1. PERSONAL INFORMATION
Name
Address
Telephone
Date You Can Start Working</td><td>2. EDUCATION
Name and Location of School

Grade You Will Complete This Year</td></tr>
<tr><td>3. JOB EXPERIENCE
Job Title
Employer</td><td>4. OTHER SKILLS</td></tr>
<tr><td colspan="2">5. REFERENCE
Name
Telephone
Relationship</td></tr>
<tr><td colspan="2">6. WHY DO YOU WANT THIS JOB?</td></tr>
</table>

6. What is the purpose of this application?

____

____

7. Why would the library ask for a reference?

____

____

8. In what section would you say when you could start your internship?

____

____

9. In which of the six sections of the application would you give information about skills you would bring to a position at the library?

____

10. What would be a good answer to the question in box number 6?

____

Home Activity Your child learned about order forms and applications. Use the Internet to look up an online application. Have your child point out the different parts of an application.

Name

Family Times

Summary

My Brother Martin: A Sister Remembers Growing Up with the Rev. Dr. Martin Luther King Jr.

Few people know about what Martin Luther King Jr. was like as a child. His older sister, Christine, tells stories of their childhood, full of love and fun. She remembers when her little brother "M.L." told their mother, "One day, I am going to turn this world upside down."

Activity

Everyday Leaders Together, discuss how you can be a leader every day. List the types of things you can do at school and at home to show that you are a good leader.

Comprehension Skill

Cause and Effect

A **cause** is why something happens. An **effect** is what happens. Sometimes one effect becomes the cause that can lead to another effect, which leads to another, and so on. This is called a chain of events.

Activity

Chain Reaction Set up a chain reaction with items such as dominoes, balls, and blocks. After placing the items in their positions, write up a short report that explains each phase of the reaction. Then, watch the reaction unfold.

Lesson Vocabulary

Words to Know

Knowing the meanings of these words is important to reading *My Brother Martin*. Practice using these words.

Vocabulary Words

ancestors people from whom you are descended, such as your great-grandparents

avoided kept away from; kept out of the way of

generations periods of about thirty years, or the time from the birth of one generation to the birth of the next generation

minister member of the clergy; spiritual guide; pastor

numerous very many

pulpit platform or raised structure in a church from which the minister preaches

shielding protecting; defending

Grammar

Conjunctions

A **conjunction** is a word that can join words, phrases, or whole sentences. *For example: and, or, but.* You can use conjunctions to make compound sentences. *For example: I made the sandwiches and Jason got the iced tea.* "I made the sandwiches" and "Jason got the iced tea" are two complete sentences, joined into a compound sentence using the *conjunction* "and."

Activity

Conjunction Squares Play this conjunction game with a family member. Write down the conjunctions *and, but,* and *or* on separate squares of paper. Mix the squares up, and turn them face-down. The first player says a simple sentence. *For example: I went to the store.* Then, the second player must turn over one of the other squares and use the conjunction to put the two sentences together. *For example: but I forgot my wallet.* Continue with the game, switching roles every other round.

Practice Tested Spelling Words

______	______	______	______
______	______	______	______
______	______	______	______
______	______	______	______
______	______	______	______

Name ______________________________

Cause and Effect

- A **cause** is why something happens. An **effect** is what happens.
- Clue words such as *because, so,* and *since* sometimes signal a cause-effect relationship.
- Sometimes one effect can become the cause of another effect, which causes another, and so on. This is called a chain of events.

Directions Read the following story. Then complete the diagram.

One day some time ago, a boy named Jack was doing homework. His mother began to examine Jack's textbook. A puzzled look clouded her face. She noticed that the book was worn and missing a dozen pages.

The next day, she told the school's principal that Jack deserved better materials. He agreed, but said that only schools in white districts got new texts. Schools in African American areas got old, damaged books.

So Jack's mother met with a lawyer. They filed a legal case, claiming unequal and unfair treatment toward Jack. A judge decided that Jack's mother was right. The board of education agreed to revise the system for providing materials to schools in the district.

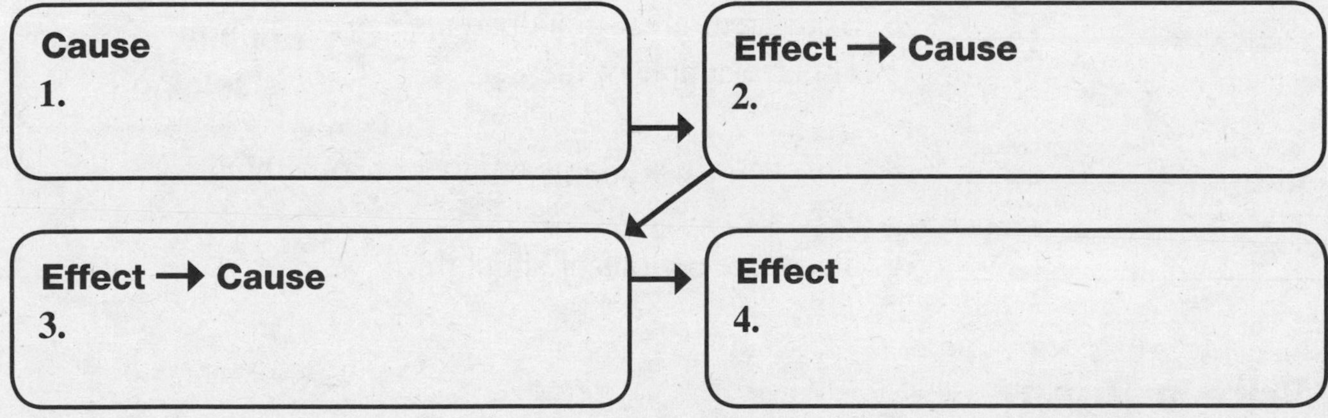

5. When do you think this fictional story takes place? Use the information from the text and your prior knowledge to answer the question.

____

____

School + Home **Home Activity** Your child used a graphic organizer to determine causes and effects. Read a story together. Use a graphic organizer like the one above to map out the causes and effects in the story.

Name ___________________________________

Vocabulary

Directions Draw a line to connect each word on the left with its definition on the right.

1. avoided	very many
2. numerous	platform in a church from which the minister preaches
3. pulpit	protecting
4. minister	member of the clergy
5. shielding	kept away from

Directions Choose the word from the box that best matches each clue. Write the word on the line.

Check the Words You Know

___ancestors
___avoided
___generations
___minister
___numerous
___pulpit
___shielding

_______________ **6.** You probably tried to do this when you were about to run into something or someone.

_______________ **7.** This person works in a church.

_______________ **8.** Your great-great-grandparents are an example of these.

_______________ **9.** This describes a large number of something.

_______________ **10.** These are periods of about thirty years.

Write a Poem

Pretend you have just heard Dr. Martin Luther King Jr. speak at a civil rights meeting. Write a poem about the event. Use as many vocabulary words as you can.

Home Activity Your child identified and used vocabulary words from *My Brother Martin.* Have your child draw pictures that represent the meanings of the words from the selection.

Name ______________________________

Vocabulary • Word Structure

- An **ending** is a letter or letters added to the end of a base word. Recognizing an ending will help you figure out the word's meaning.
- The ending *–ed* is added to a verb to make it past tense. The ending *–ing* makes a verb tell about present or ongoing actions. The ending *–s* makes a noun plural.

Directions Read the following letter. Then answer the questions below.

Dear Dr. King,

I saw you speak today in front of numerous people. I could tell that you truly care about shielding people from danger today and making sure future generations are safe, as well. I know it must be hard to talk about equal rights when some people in this country are against it. You could have avoided the jail time you spent by just living out your days as a minister. However, you believed that change would not come that way. I admire your courage.

Sincerely,
Mrs. Roberta Watson

1. How does the ending of *generations* change the base word's meaning?

____

2. What is the word ending in *avoided*? What does the word mean?

____

3. What does *shielding* mean? If you replaced the ending with *–ed,* how would the meaning change?

____

____

4. Why does the writer of the letter use *–ed* instead of *–ing* for the base word *believed*?

____

5. The word *numerous* ends with an *s.* Is this a word ending? Explain.

____

Home Activity Your child identified the meanings of words using word endings. Read a story together. Have your child show you how to define words by covering up their endings, defining the base words, and then putting the meanings together.

Fact and Opinion

Directions Read the following article. Then answer the questions below.

It is amazing how much the country changed in the twenty-five years after World War II. People came together and fought for what they believed in. They looked at the unfair laws and changed them. At one time, African Americans could not sit in the same areas, drink from the same drinking fountains, or get the same jobs as white people could. It is ridiculous how the country allowed certain people to be treated this way.

African Americans banded together and took action that showed the nation that things needed to be changed. For example, they marched through the streets singing freedom songs, and they refused to ride buses that had segregated seating. The protestors did not rest until freedom was guaranteed.

1. Underline a statement of fact found in the article.
2. How could you prove if the statement was true or false?

____

____

3. Circle a statement of opinion from the article.
4. Is the statement of opinion valid? How do you know?

____

____

____

5. On a separate sheet of paper, write a paragraph about a new rule you would like to make in your school. As you explain why this rule would be good, use at least two statements of fact and two statements of opinion.

Home Activity Your child identified statements of fact and opinion in an article. Together, write a short article that gives both facts and opinions about the community in which you live. Remind your child of the importance of using valid statements of fact and opinion.

Name ______________________________

Cause and Effect

- A **cause** is why something happens. An **effect** is what happens.
- Sometimes one effect can become the cause of another effect, which causes another, and so on. This is called a chain of events.

Directions Read the following article. Then answer the questions below.

In February of 1960, four African American college students in North Carolina took a seat at a lunch counter where only white customers could sit. No one served them, but the young men said they would not leave the seats. The four men stayed there until the store closed.

This was a sit-in, or peaceful protest in which people refuse to move. News about what the students had done spread quickly. Other college students in North Carolina began their own sit-ins. Soon cities in the South—and even in the North—were announcing that sit-ins had occurred there too. The four original students had started a powerful movement.

1. What do you think was the cause of the four students not being served?

____

2. What effect resulted from the lack of service at the counter?

____

3. What was an effect of the spreading news about the sit-in?

____

4. How did this effect become another cause in a chain of events?

____

5. Using the text and your prior knowledge, how would you describe the long-term effect of the sit-in?

____

____

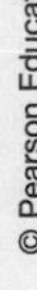

Home Activity Your child found the causes and effects in a passage. Read a story or article together and identify the major events. Then use the questions "What happened?" and "Why did it happen?" to talk about the causes and effects of these events.

Name ________________________________

Cause and Effect

- A **cause** is why something happens. An **effect** is what happens.
- Clue words such as *because, so,* and *since* sometimes signal a cause-effect relationship.
- Sometimes one effect can become the cause of another effect, which causes another, and so on. This is called a chain of events.

Directions Read the following passage. Then complete the diagram below.

The workers who picked strawberries for a fruit company were tired and fed up. They were paid very little and treated unfairly. The workers went to talk to the managers about it, but they wouldn't listen.

One day the workers had enough and went on strike. They said that they would no longer pick strawberries if things did not change. The managers lost money each day the workers refused to work. After three days, the managers finally decided to talk over the problem with the workers. In the end, the two sides made an agreement that solved the problem.

Cause
1. The workers were paid ________________________________

↓

Effect ⟶ Cause
2. They tried to ________________________________

↓

Effect ⟶ Cause
3. The workers went on ________________________________

↓

Effect ⟶ Cause
4. ________________________________

↓

Effect
5. ________________________________

Home Activity Your child used a graphic organizer to identify causes and effects in an article. Together, share memories of times when you stood up for something you believed in. Discuss the causes and effects that occurred as these events unfolded.

Name ______________________________

Take Notes/Paraphrase and Synthesize/ Record Findings

Taking notes and **recording findings** about key information in a text can help you understand and remember the text better. It can also help you organize information to study for a test or to include in a research paper. When you take notes, **paraphrase,** or put what you read into your own words. Try to **synthesize,** or combine, information as you take notes. This will allow you to include all of the author's ideas as well as important details. Use key words, phrases, or short sentences.

Directions Read the article below. Record notes on a separate sheet of paper, then use them to answer the questions that follow.

Like Dr. Martin Luther King Jr., Cesar Chavez knew that equal rights were worth fighting for. He spent most of his adult life trying to do what he believed was right.

Chavez was born in 1927 in Arizona. When he was ten years old, his family lost its farm during the Great Depression. He and his family became migrant workers, moving from place to place in search of farm work. Later, Chavez joined the U.S. Navy, married, and settled down in California.

Chavez began working to improve social conditions when he became a member of the Community Service Organization. This group worked to fight discrimination against people of Hispanic background. Chavez spoke out against this discrimination, and he urged Latino citizens to use their power as voters. He believed that Latinos' votes could make the government take notice of needs in their community.

Chavez knew that one particular group of Latinos especially needed his help—the migrant workers. He started an organization to help farm workers receive the pay, benefits, and treatment they deserved.

He realized that the first challenge was getting the attention of people across the nation. He believed strongly in the idea of peaceful protest. Chavez helped convey the issues of farm work by staging strikes. Also, he urged consumers to stop buying products from companies that mistreated migrant farm workers. Another method of protesting was fasts. During a fast, a person does not eat food. Chavez once protested by fasting for thirty-six days.

Cesar Chavez never became a wealthy man. The purpose of his work was justice, not fame. He simply cared about helping others.

1. How is this article organized?

____

2. Paraphrase the first sentence in the article.

____

____

Name ______________________________

Directions Refer to your notes to help you answer the questions below.

3. Why is it important to take note of the fact that Chavez was a migrant worker?

____

____

4. Is the detail about Chavez joining the U.S. Navy important enough to include in your notes? Why or why not?

____

5. What did Chavez do with the Community Service Organization?

____

6. What methods of peaceful protest did Chavez use?

____

7. Why is it important to write down only the most important ideas when note-taking?

____

____

8. When taking notes for a report, it is important to write down the title and author of the book or article you are reading. Why do you need to do this?

____

____

9. Descibe a graphic organizer you might use to organize your notes.

____

____

10. Copy a section of your notes from the article in the lines below.

____

____

Home Activity Your child learned how to take notes and synthesize and paraphrase information. Read an article or story aloud to him or her. After each sentence, help your child to paraphrase it. See how many sentences he or she can paraphrase.

Name

Family Times

Summary

Jim Thorpe's Bright Path

It wasn't easy for Jim Thorpe to become a famous and respected athlete. As an American Indian, he was discriminated against and separated from his family. His twin brother died when they were only nine years old. His mother and father also died when he was still in school. But he learned to move forward with his life because he was so inspired by his family and his people.

Activity

Stories of Perseverance Perseverance is the ability to stick to a purpose even though it's hard. Jim Thorpe showed perseverance by staying in school even though it was difficult for him. Discuss with your family times when you have showed perseverance.

Comprehension Skill

Fact and Opinion

A **statement of fact** can be proved true or false. **Statements of opinion** are judgments, beliefs, or ways of thinking about something.

Activity

Text Talk Together with a family member, discuss the kinds of texts in which you might read statements of fact and statements of opinions. Could you ever see both kinds of statements in the same article?

Lesson Vocabulary

Words to Know

Knowing the meanings of these words is important to reading *Jim Thorpe's Bright Path.* Practice using these words.

Vocabulary Words

boarding school school with buildings where the pupils live during the school term

dormitory a building with many rooms for sleeping in. Many colleges have dormitories for students whose homes are elsewhere.

endurance power to last and to withstand hard wear

manual done with the hands

reservation land set aside by the government for a special purpose

society the people of any particular time or place

Grammar

Capitalization

You already know that you need a **capital letter** at the beginning of a sentence or as the first letter in a name, but you also use capitalization in other places too. For instance, you must also capitalize names of organizations, publications such as newspapers and magazines, titles of works of art, and professional titles. *For example: the Plant Trees Foundation, the Chicago Crier, the Mona Lisa, Doctor Barnes.*

Activity

A Capital Letter Pretend you are writing a letter to the editor of your local newspaper. Together with a family member, address an envelope to the editor using the rules of capitalization. The return name and address should be yours. Get the editor's name and address from the newspaper.

Practice Tested Spelling Words

Name ______________________________

Fact and Opinion

- A **statement of fact** can be proved true or false. A **statement of opinion** is a judgment, belief, or way of thinking about something.
- Evaluate statements of opinion by using the text, your prior knowledge, and logic. Based on what you know or have read, ask: Is the statement of opinion valid—is it supported well? Or is it faulty, having little or no support?

Directions Read the following passage. Then complete the chart below.

In 1922, Jim Thorpe led a professional football team called the Oorang Indians. All of its members were Native Americans. The team was part of the National Football League in 1922 and 1923. The team won only a few games over two years. Frankly, they were not very good. Unfortunately, the team was owned by a selfish man named Walter Lingo. After the second season, Lingo took his money away from the team, ending it for good.

Statement	How to Check Statement of Fact / Support for Statement of Opinion	If a Statement of Opinion: Valid or Faulty?
Jim Thorpe led a professional football team called the Oorang Indians.	**1.**	
Unfortunately, the team was owned by a selfish man named Walter Lingo.	**2.**	**3.**
Frankly, they were not very good.	**4.**	**5.**

Home Activity Your child used a graphic organizer to identify statements of fact and statements of opinion. Take turns making statements of opinion about your family. Decide together whether they are faulty or valid based on information you supply.

Name ___________________________________

Vocabulary

Directions Choose the word from the box that best matches each definition. Write the word on the line.

Check the Words You Know
___boarding school
___dormitory
___endurance
___manual
___reservation
___society

__________________ **1.** the people of any particular time or place

__________________ **2.** a building with many rooms in which people sleep

__________________ **3.** power to withstand hard wear

__________________ **4.** done with the hands

__________________ **5.** land set aside by the government for a special purpose

Directions Choose the word from the box that best completes each sentence. Write the word on the line shown to the left.

__________________ **6.** Because I attended ___, I spent long stretches of time away from home.

__________________ **7.** Cars have either a ___ or an automatic transmission.

__________________ **8.** You have to have a lot of ___ to run marathons.

__________________ **9.** Years ago, the rules of ___ were very strict.

__________________ **10.** At college, Janet enjoyed living in a ____.

Write a Description

Write a description of how a boarding school might be different from your present school. Use as many vocabulary words as you can.

Home Activity Your child identified and used vocabulary words from *Jim Thorpe's Bright Path.* Together, make up your own fill-in-the-blank sentences (like those that appear in the second activity), using the vocabulary words from the selection.

Name ______________________________

Vocabulary • Dictionary/Glossary

- **Dictionaries** and **glossaries** provide alphabetical lists of words and their meanings.
- While reading, a reader may come across unfamiliar words, or familiar words used in unfamiliar ways. If this happens, use a dictionary or glossary to find the meaning.

Directions Read the following passage. Then answer the questions below, using a dictionary or glossary.

Since there was no school on Leslie's reservation, she attended a boarding school. Leslie was glad to go away to school, because otherwise she must get a job like her brothers. They earned their living doing manual labor, but Leslie was not particularly good with her hands.

At school every spring, Leslie played tennis. All year she looked forward to picking up a tennis racket. During bad weather, she even practiced hitting a ball against the walls of her small dormitory room. Leslie had big goals in life. She wanted to be a professional tennis player.

1. What is the meaning of *reservation* as it is used in the story?

____

2. What is the meaning of *manual* as it is used in the passage? What is another meaning for this word?

____

____

3. What meaning of *goals* makes sense in this story?

____

4. In this passage, what is the meaning of the word *racket*?

____

5. Choose a word with multiple meanings from the story. Write a sentence using the word in a different way from the way it is used in the passage.

____

Home Activity Your child used a dictionary or glossary to find the intended meanings of multiple-meaning words. Write down a list of multiple-meaning words. Take turns acting out and guessing the different meanings of the words.

Name ____________________

Graphic Sources

Directions Study the following graphic source. Then answer the questions below.

Football Field

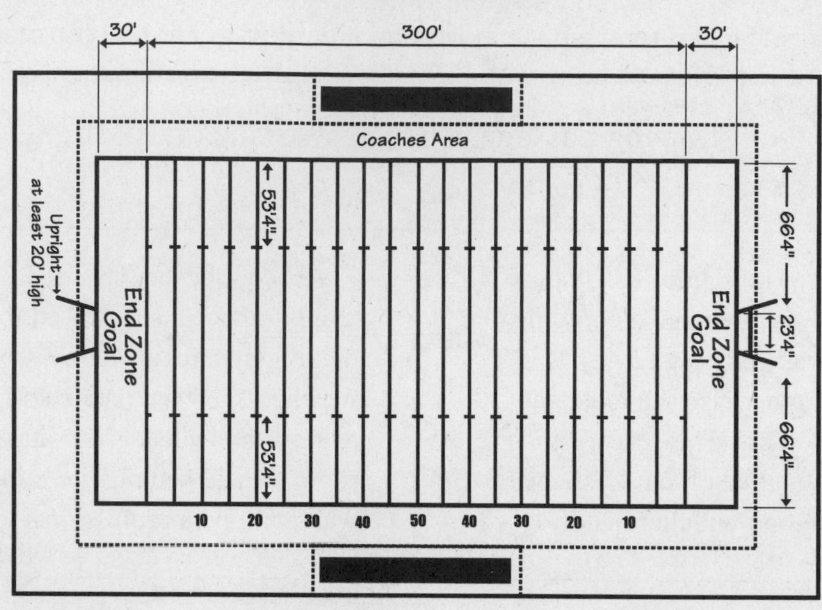

1. What is pictured in this graphic source?

2. In what way might a graphic source like this help a reader?

3. How would you describe the location of the goals on the field?

4. How long is the field, including both end zones?

5. On a separate sheet of paper, write a paragraph that could accompany this graphic source.

Home Activity Your child used a graphic source to answer questions. Together, design a graphic source that could accompany an article you have read in a newspaper or magazine.

Name ______________________________

Fact and Opinion

- A **statement of fact** can be proved true or false. A **statement of opinion** is a judgment, belief, or way of thinking about something.
- Evaluate statements of opinion by using the text, your prior knowledge, and logic. Based on what you know or have read, ask: Is the statement of opinion valid—is it supported well? Or is it faulty, having little or no support?

Directions Read the following passage. Then answer the questions below.

Louis Sockalexis was born in the town of Old Town, Maine, in 1871. As a young Penobscot boy, Louis played a lot of baseball. He went on to success on college baseball teams at the College of the Holy Cross and the University of Notre Dame. Eventually, he joined a major league baseball team called the Cleveland Spiders. This was an important moment in history. Never before had a Native American played professional baseball. At first, baseball fans of that era were probably shocked to see him play on the same field with other professional players.

Louis Sockalexis was very talented. People liked to watch him throw and bat with his powerful arms. After playing professional baseball, Sockalexis returned to Old Town and taught other Penobscot boys how to play the game.

1. Circle a statement of fact from the passage.
2. How could you check this statement?

____

____

3. Underline a statement of opinion from the passage.
4. Is this statement valid or faulty? How do you know?

____

____

5. How did the author arrange the information in this passage?

____

Home Activity Your child identified statements of fact and statements of opinion in a nonfiction passage. Choose an editorial to read. Before reading, skim the passage together, taking special note of how it is organized. After reading, underline or highlight the statements of fact and statements of opinion in the editorial.

Name ____________________

Fact and Opinion

- A **statement of fact** can be proved true or false. A **statement of opinion** is a judgment, belief, or way of thinking about something.
- Evaluate statements of opinion by using the text, your prior knowledge, and logic. Based on what you know or have read, ask: Is the statement of opinion valid—is it supported well? Or is it faulty, having little or no support?

Directions Read the following passage. Then complete the diagram.

Lieutenant Richard H. Pratt believed Native Americans needed education to help them join American society. In 1879, he opened Carlisle Indian School. Glenn S."Pop" Warner, a famous coach who worked there, trained two future Olympic athletes, Jim Thorpe and Lewis Tewanima. "Pop" Warner was good enough to make anyone an Olympian. Jim Thorpe became one of the best athletes of all time, playing in professional football and professional baseball leagues. In 1904, Pratt became Brigadier General and retired from the school.

Eventually, people came to believe that the school hurt the traditions of Native Americans, and it was closed in 1918.

Statement	How to Check Statement of Fact / Support for Statement of Opinion	If a Statement of Opinion: Valid or Faulty?
In 1879, he opened Carlisle Indian School.	**1.** Look in an encyclopedia or reference book about ____________	
"Pop" Warner was good enough to make anyone an Olympian.	**2.** ____________	**3.** ____________
Jim Thorpe became one of the best athletes of all time.	**4.** ____________	**5.** ____________

Home Activity Your child identified and analyzed statements of fact and statements of opinion in a nonfiction article. Together, look out the window and describe the weather with statements of fact and opinion. Talk about why the statements of opinion are valid or faulty.

Name ________________________________

Magazines/Periodicals

- A **periodical** is a publication printed at regular times, such as every week or every month. A **magazine** is a type of periodical. Magazines contain a variety of articles, including news stories, feature stories, editorials, and regular opinion columns, as well as advertisements.
- Most magazines organize articles by order of interest. They present important or high-interest stories first. A magazine's table of contents lists the various articles it contains.
- Most magazine articles follow the 5Ws and H format—that is, the reader learns the Who? What? When? Where? Why? and How? of a topic.

Directions Read the magazine article below. Then answer the questions on the next page.

INTERVIEWS

"The Secret of Williamson's Success"
by R. L. Dawson

Every time I sit down to write this monthly column, I find that I am pleasantly surprised by the character of the people in sports.

This month I had the chance to interview Bobby Edstrom, who plays for the Meadow College Tigers. Bobby is a football player who stands six feet five inches tall and weighs three hundred pounds. When you see him, you automatically think that if you offended him, he could stomp all over you in two seconds flat.

We sat down in his coach's office to talk. It was the beginning of training in the late days of summer. He was wearing a Tigers T-shirt and jeans. He looked very comfortable and welcoming. Suddenly I didn't feel so nervous anymore. I began by asking him about his background and how he got to be such a good football player. I was amazed at his answer.

You see, I thought Bobby was one of those "natural athletes"—the ones who are stars from their earliest days on the playground. That was not the case with Bobby. He struggled in high school. He almost did not make the team his sophomore year.

When I asked him how he got to where he is today, he said two words: "Coach Williamson." Bobby Edstrom's high school coach, Leonard Williamson, told him that practicing hard, even when you are struggling, can get you to where you want to be. This coach encouraged Bobby every step of the way. He never allowed Bobby to think that he could not achieve his goals. A tear came to Bobby's eye as he talked about his coach. I asked if Bobby had ever had a chance to thank his coach, and he said that he hadn't. Coach Williamson had moved away from town, and Bobby lost contact with him.

Well, Bobby, chances are that Coach Williamson will read this column. I think that you can consider this a sincere, if overdue, thank-you card to an important and inspiring teacher.

Name ________________________________

1. What is the title or headline of this article?

2. Who wrote this article?

3. In what part or section of the magazine does this article appear?

4. What kind of article is this selection? How do you know?

5. Who is the "who" in this article?

6. What is the "what" in this article?

7. In what kind of magazine might this article appear?

8. How is this article different from an article reporting on recent football scores?

9. Do you think this interview would appear before or after news stories? Why?

10. Why do you think the title of the article is "The Secret of Williamson's Success" even though the interview is with Bobby Edstrom?

Home Activity Your child read and analyzed a magazine article. Together, examine the cover of a magazine. Invite your child to predict the content of the magazine's articles based on the information and graphics on the cover. Make another prediction based on the table of contents. Finally, browse through the magazine together to confirm predictions.

Name ______________________

Family Times

Summary

How Tía Lola Came to ~~Visit~~ Stay

One day Miguel's Tía Lola starts to paint the family's home purple and their landlord, the Colonel, orders them to paint it white or move out. Tía Lola designs purple and white uniforms for Miguel's baseball team and names the team after the Colonel. The Colonel is so happy that he forgets about the color of the house.

Activity

Agree to Disagree Together with a family member, discuss moments when you had disagreements with others and how you worked them out.

Comprehension Skill

Theme and Character

The **theme** is the underlying meaning of a story. The author may state the theme directly, but more often, the reader has to think about the story in order to figure out the theme. **Characters** are the people or animals in a story.

Activity

My Favorite Themes Think about three or four of your favorite books or stories. What are their themes? Discuss with a family member why you like stories with these themes.

Lesson Vocabulary

Words to Know

Knowing the meanings of these words is important to reading *How Tía Lola Came to ~~Visit~~ Stay*. Practice using these words.

Vocabulary Words

affords gives as an effect or a result; provides; yields

colonel a military rank below general

glint a gleam; flash

lurking hiding or moving about in a secret and sly manner

palettes thin boards, usually oval or oblong, with a thumb hole at one end, used by painters to lay and mix colors on

quaint strange or odd in an interesting, pleasing, or amusing way

resemblance similar appearance; likeness

Grammar

Commas

Commas are a type of punctuation used inside a sentence. In a group of items, commas are used to separate the items and to make the sentence clearer. *For example: They went swimming, biking, and fishing.* Commas are also used to set off indications that someone is being directly addressed in your writing. *For example: Mom, may I go outside?* You may also see commas after introductory words like *yes*, *no*, or *well*. *For example: Yes, I do like dancing.*

Activity

Their Favorite Things Ask a family member what three of his or her favorite movies are. Write a sentence that tells the names of the movies. Be careful to put commas in the right places.

Practice Tested Spelling Words

Name ___________________________________

Character and Theme

- **Characters** are people or animals in a story.
- The **theme** is the underlying meaning of a story. The author may state the theme directly, but more often, the reader has to use facts from the story in order to figure out the theme.

Directions Read the following story. Then complete the diagram below.

When Nana came to live at her daughter's house, she knew she did things differently from her daughter's daughter. She didn't want to embarrass her. So she changed her hair style so it looked more like the ones in the magazines. She exchanged her dark dresses for more colorful sweaters and pants. Nana even tried to speak like her granddaughter. She imitated phrases she heard on television, but when she said them, they sounded funny to her ears. One night, Nana made dinner and tried to cook the foods she thought her granddaughter would like.

Her grandaughter said, "Nana, thank you for trying to change for me, but I love you just the way you are."

With that, Nana went back to her comfortable dresses, the way she always spoke, and her beloved recipes. But she liked her new hair style!

Character	Nana
Goal	**1.**
Plot Events	Nana changes her hair style. **2.** **3.**
Theme	**4.**
Support	The phrases she imitates sound funny. **5.**

Home Activity Your child read a short passage and used a graphic organizer to identify the characters and theme in a story. Tell your child a family story. Have your child identify the theme of the story.

Name ______________________________

Vocabulary

Directions Draw a line to connect each word on the left with its definition on the right.

1. resemblance	moving about in a sly manner
2. affords	a military rank below general
3. glint	similar appearance; likeness
4. lurking	a gleam; flash
5. colonel	provides; yields

Check the Words You Know

- ___affords
- ___colonel
- ___glint
- ___lurking
- ___palettes
- ___quaint
- ___resemblance

Directions Choose the word from the box that matches each clue. Write the word on the line.

__________________ **6.** An artist would use these.

__________________ **7.** You might see this if you look at a mother and a daughter.

__________________ **8.** A diamond might show this when it reflects light.

__________________ **9.** An alligator watching its prey might be doing this.

__________________ **10.** A tiny cottage built for dolls might be described this way.

Write a Conversation

Pretend a relative has just moved in with your family. Write a conversation you would have with this person. Use as many vocabulary words as you can.

Home Activity Your child identified and used vocabulary words from *How Tía Lola Came to Stay.* Make up a story with your child about two people, an artist and a colonel, from different worlds. Use the vocabulary words from the selection.

Name ____________________

Vocabulary • Context Clues

When you are reading and see an unfamiliar word, you can use **context clues,** or words around the unfamiliar word, to figure out its meaning.

Directions Read the following passage. Then answer the questions below.

All Amalia ever wanted to do was paint. One day, her aunt said she was looking for a nanny for her children. Amalia liked her little cousins so she asked her aunt if she could be the nanny. Being a nanny affords, or allows, Amalia plenty of time for painting.

Amalia and her cousins live in a quaint town with old-fashioned houses and cobblestone streets. One day, she caught the glint, or gleam, of light on a puddle. She was inspired by its resemblance, or likeness, to a mirror. When Amalia returned home, she mixed the paints on her palette to paint the light on the puddle.

1. What context clue helps you to figure out the meaning of *affords?*

____

2. What context clues help you to figure out the meaning of *quaint?*

____

____

3. One context clue for *glint* is *gleam.* If you didn't know what *gleam* meant, how could you figure out the meaning from the context?

____

____

4. What context clue gives you the meaning of *palette?*

____

5. Write your own sentence using a context clue for the word *resemblance.*

____

____

Home Activity Your child read a short passage and used context clues to identify the meanings of unfamiliar words. Read a challenging story together. When you find an unfamiliar word, have your child locate context clues. If they do not exist, help your child to paraphrase the information around the unfamiliar word.

Name ______________________________

Author's Purpose

Directions Read the following passage. Then answer the questions below.

Learn About the World Without Leaving Your Home

Learning about a different culture is not only interesting but also fun! Imagine a holiday that you really enjoy celebrating. Many cultures celebrate the coming of a new year, the gaining of independence, or the birth of an important leader. But each culture celebrates in a different way and even on different days. By learning about the similarities and differences among cultures, many people come to have a better understanding of other people.

You don't even have to leave home to start exploring. You can look in the newspaper or on the Internet to find out more. You can also watch programs on television or listen to CDs with music from the culture you are learning about. Why not get started today?

1. What kinds of ideas are expressed in this passage?

____

2. What is the purpose of the title?

____

____

3. What do you think is the author's purpose for this passage? Why do you think so?

____

____

4. What do you think the author's second purpose is for this passage? Why do you think so?

____

____

5. Do you think the author met his or her purpose? Why or why not?

____

____

Home Activity Your child read a short passage and identified the author's purpose. Together, write a short story to entertain your readers. Before writing, decide on which ideas you will use and how you will organize them.

Name ______________________

Character and Theme

- **Characters** are people or animals in a story.
- The **theme** is the underlying meaning of a story. The author may state the theme directly, but more often, the reader has to use facts from the story to figure it out.

Directions Read the following story. Then answer the questions below.

All of Luis's friends loved baseball. Unfortunately, he thought it was boring. Of course, he had never played in a real game, but he knew it had to be awful. So when the baseball season started, Luis had no friends to hang out with. His mother said if he couldn't find anything to do with his free time, then he would have to do some chores.

Luis knew he wouldn't like playing baseball, but at least he would be with his friends and not cleaning his room. Luis's first day of practice was long and difficult. But soon Luis couldn't wait to play baseball after school. He could hardly believe that the sport was now his favorite!

1. What type of person is Luis in the beginning of the story?

____

____

2. Why does Luis decide to play baseball?

____

3. How has Luis changed by the end of the story?

____

____

4. What is the theme of this story?

____

5. Summarize the story in one or two sentences.

____

____

Home Activity Your child has identified elements of character and theme in a story to write a summary of it. Read a story together. Summarize the difference between two of the characters' goals in the story.

Name ___________________________________

Character and Theme

- **Characters** are people or animals in a story.
- The **theme** is the underlying meaning of a story. The author may state the theme directly, but more often, the reader has to use facts from the story in order to figure out the theme.

Directions Read the following story. Then complete the diagram below.

Jung wasn't sure how she would ever learn the new language. It was so different from her own. The letters were unfamiliar, and the sounds were strange to her ears. But she wanted to learn it so she would feel at home in her new country. Jung spoke it whenever she could. At her job, Jung tried to use the new language with everyone. She spoke using simple and short sentences. Sometimes people were confused by what she said, but they encouraged her to keep trying. Jung went to classes twice a week. Even though she knew it could take a long time to speak the language well, Jung would not give up.

Character	**1.** ______________________________
Goal	**2.** She wanted to ______________________________
Plot Events	She spoke the new language at her job. **3.** She went ______________________________ ______________________________
Theme	**4.** Never ______________________________
Support	Jung did not give up when people did not understand her. **5.** Even though it would take a long time to learn, ______________ ______________________________

Home Activity Your child read a short passage and used a graphic organizer to identify character and theme. Write a short story together about overcoming an obstacle. Before writing, discuss the theme or message you would like to tell the readers. Then plan how you will get the point across in the story.

Name ______________________________

Dictionary/Glossary

A **dictionary** is a book of words and their meanings. A **glossary** is a short dictionary at the back of some books. It has definitions of words used in the book. Dictionaries and glossaries are organized in alphabetical order. **Entry words,** the words in dark type in both dictionaries and glossaries, might be broken into syllables. For each entry word, you might find a **pronunciation key,** the **part of speech,** the **definition,** a sentence, and how the spelling changes when endings are added.

Directions Study the dictionary and glossary entries below. Then answer the questions that follow.

Dictionary Entries	Glossary Entries
cul-ture: (kul cher), 1. *n.,* elegance; sophistication 2. *n.,* traditions and customs of a group of people; *The Italian culture is known for its food.* 3. *n.* developing land and crops; *v.* cul-tured, cul-tur-ing **Cum-ber-land:** (kum ber lend), *n.*, a river that flows in Kentucky and Tennessee; it connects to the Ohio River. **cum-ber-some:** (kum ber sum), *adj.*, difficult to control; bulky; awkward; *adv.*, cum-ber-some-ly	**cul•ture** (kul cher), noun, the customs of a group of people (p. 98) **curb** (kerb), noun, a border of hard material, like stone or concrete, on the edge of a street (p. 53) **de•cep•tive** (di sep tiv), adjective, deceiving or misleading (p.22) **deep** (dēp) adjective, difficult to understand (p. 40)

1. What is one difference between a dictionary and a glossary?

____

____

2. What is the entry word before *Cumberland*? Why does it come before?

____

____

Name ________________________________

Directions Use dictionary and glossary entries to answer the following questions.

3. What is the pronunciation of *curb?* What tells you that this is the pronunciation?

____

4. Where will you find out an entry word's part of speech? In a dictionary, how would you know if a word is a noun?

____

____

5. What part of speech is *cumbersomely?*

____

6. In a glossary, what do you think the page numbers after the definitions mean?

____

7. The dictionary shows several definitions for the word *culture*. Why do you think there is only one in the glossary?

____

____

8. What do you think the words in a glossary have in common?

____

____

9. In the dictionary, what is the purpose of the sentences that are in *italics?* Write a sentence that could be added to the definition of *cumbersome* to show how it is used.

____

____

10. Describe when you would use a glossary rather than a dictionary.

____

____

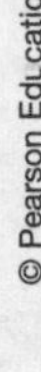

Home Activity Your child learned how to use dictionary and glossary entries. Choose a word from a dictionary page. Memorize its definition, part of speech, etc. Give your child the dictionary opened to that page. Have your child ask you "yes" and "no" questions to try to figure out the word you chose. For example, "Is the word a noun?"

Name

Family Times

Summary

To Fly: The Story of the Wright Brothers

When Orville and Wilbur Wright were young, they enjoyed playing with helicopter toys and building high-flying kites. Eventually, they started a printing business and a bicycle business to make money, but they never forgot about flying. They researched past inventions and ran experiments, which helped them to successfully fly their homemade aircraft on a memorable day in 1903.

Activity

Favorite Scene Reread *To Fly.* Choose your favorite part of the story. Write this part in the form of a scene in a play, assigning dialogue to characters instead of narration. Together, write out the script and perform it.

Comprehension Skill

Generalize

To **generalize** means to make a special kind of conclusion. A generalization is a statement that applies to many examples that all have something in common. Generalizations are called **valid** if they are well supported, and **faulty** if they are not.

Activity

Family Generalizations Think about what your family members have in common, and then write a generalization about them. Together with a family member, write a few sentences in which you support your generalization.

Lesson Vocabulary

Words to Know

Knowing the meanings of these words is important to reading *To Fly: The Story of the Wright Brothers.* Practice using these words.

Vocabulary Words

cradle a frame to support weight

drag 1. the force acting on an object in motion, in a direction opposite to the object's motion. **2.** to pull or move along heavily or slowly; to pull or draw along the ground

flex to bend

glider a winged aircraft without an engine; Rising air currents keep it up in the air.

hangars buildings for storing aircraft

rudder a flat piece of wood or metal hinged vertically to the rear end of an aircraft and used to steer it

stalled stopped or brought to a standstill, usually against your wish

Grammar

Quotations and Quotation Marks

A speaker's exact words are called a **quotation.** When you write a quotation, use **quotation marks** (" ") at the beginning and end of the speaker's exact words. Begin the quotation with a capital letter. *For example: "I'm telling Mom!" said Alice. Grandpa smiled and said, "You learn something new every day."*

Activity

You Always Say Together, discuss phrases that your family members say frequently. They may be original statements or quotations that they like to repeat. Make a book of family quotations by writing down these words of wisdom on paper that has been folded in half like a book. Don't forget to use proper quotation marks.

Practice Tested Spelling Words

______	______	______	______
______	______	______	______
______	______	______	______
______	______	______	______
______	______	______	______

Name ______________________________

Generalize

- A **generalization** is a broad statement or rule that applies to many examples.
- Valid generalizations are supported by facts. Faulty ones are not supported by facts.

Directions Read the following passage. Then complete the diagram.

Balloons aren't just colorful globes, they are actually useful tools. First, they helped advance our knowledge of flight. Experiments with hot-air balloons gave people ideas on how to build other flying machines. Second, balloons have been used in the military. Soldiers were placed in hot-air balloons to observe enemies during wars. Finally, balloons have played a part in science. They can be sent high above the ground to test weather conditions.

Valid Generalization

1.

Support

2.

3.

4.

5. What questions did you ask yourself to help you complete the graphic organizer?

____

____

Home Activity Your child used a graphic organizer to find a generalization and support. Have your child make a generalization about his or her favorite school subject. Ask your child to come up with support to back up the generalization.

Name ______________________________

Vocabulary

Directions Draw a line to connect the word on the left with its meaning on the right.

1. flex	aircraft without an engine
2. cradle	stopped
3. hangars	to bend
4. stalled	a frame to support weight
5. glider	buildings to store aircrafts

Check the Words You Know

___cradle
___drag
___flex
___glider
___hangars
___rudder
___stalled

Directions Choose the word from the box that best matches each clue. Write the word on the line shown to the left.

________________ **6.** I used the ___ to steer the aircraft.

________________ **7.** There was little___ working against the airplane.

________________ **8.** ___ the wing so that it is curved.

________________ **9.** We visited the____ to see where all the airplanes were being held.

________________ **10.** The ___ used the speed of the wind to fly.

Write a News Report

Pretend you had just witnessed the flight of the first aircraft. Write a report about the event using as many of the vocabulary words as you can.

School + Home **Home Activity** Your child identified and used vocabulary words from *To Fly: The Story of the Wright Brothers.* With your child, make up a short story about learning how to fly an airplane. Use the vocabulary words from the selection.

Name ______________________________

Vocabulary • Context Clues

- An unfamiliar word is a word you do not know. Sometimes you can use context clues—the words and sentences around the unfamiliar word—to help you figure out the meaning of the word.

Directions Read the following story. Then answer the questions below.

Carlos loved making airplanes. He made gliders, engineless aircrafts, out of paper. He even had hangars to store them in. Sure, they were cardboard boxes, but they looked just like the real buildings for aircrafts. One day he went outside with his friend Robin to fly his paper glider, *The High Flyer.* On the first try, *The High Flyer* could hardly go anywhere. "The drag is too strong," said Carlos. "What do you mean?" asked Robin. "The force pushing against the glider is too much for it. See, it has stalled, or stopped, and fallen again," said Carlos. "I have an idea," said Robin. Robin took the glider and refolded it to make the wings sleeker. The wings would not bend, or flex, so easily now. On the next try, the glider flew through the air with little trouble. "How did you know to do that?" asked Carlos. Robin smiled. "I might not know everything about science, but I do know how to make a good paper airplane."

1. What kind of aircraft is a *glider*? How do you know?

____

____

2. What are stored in real *hangars*?

____

3. How does the context tell you what *drag* means?

____

4. What does the word *stalled* mean in this story?

____

5. Write a sentence that uses context clues to reveal the meaning of *flex*.

____

Home Activity Your child used context clues to identify the meanings of unfamiliar words. Challenge your child to write a paragraph that includes context clues that reveal the meanings of difficult words.

Name ______________________

Graphic Sources

Directions Study the time line below and answer the following questions.

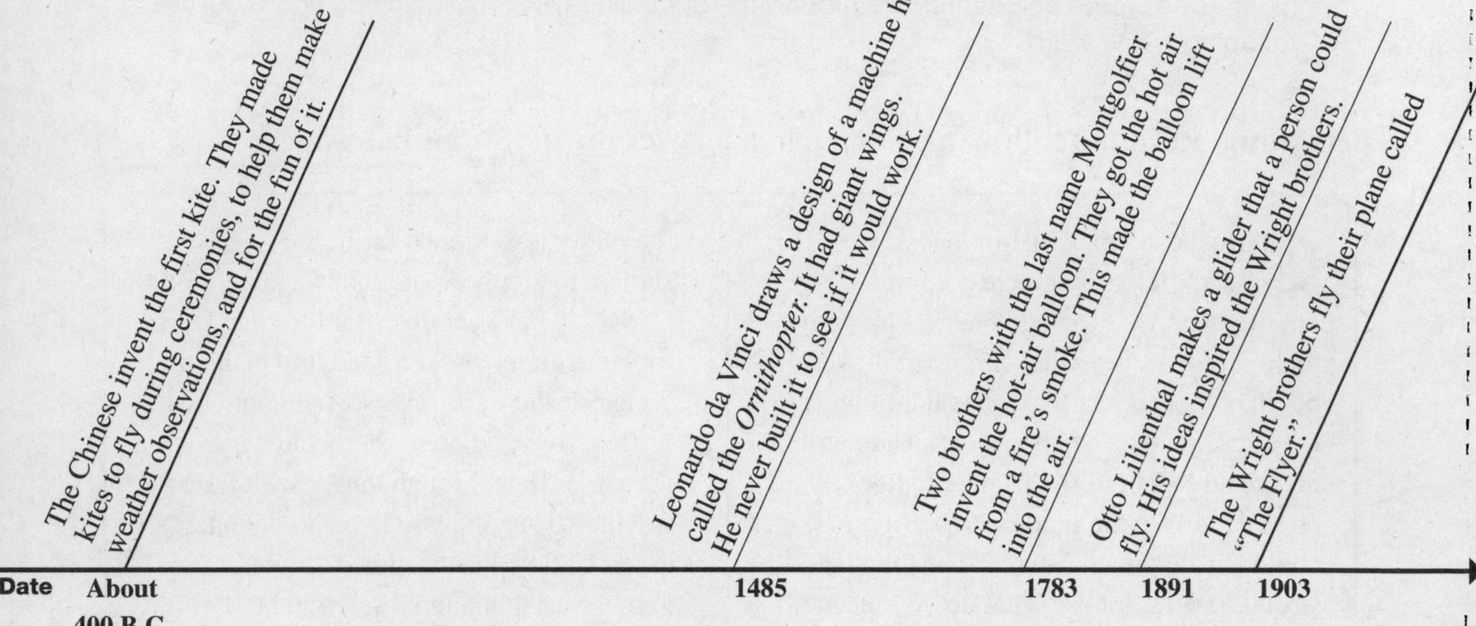

1. What does this graphic source tell you?

____

2. How does this graphic source help you to understand the information?

____

____

3. When was the first hot-air balloon invented?

____

4. How many years passed between when the *Ornithopter* was designed and the Wright brothers' flight?

____

5. On a separate sheet of paper, draw a graphic source that could accompany an article on hot-air balloons.

Home Activity Your child used a graphic source to answer questions. Find a graphic source in a book, newspaper, or magazine. Have your child study it and then explain it to you.

Name ______________________________

Generalize

- A **generalization** is a broad statement or rule that applies to many examples.
- Valid generalizations are supported by facts. Faulty ones are not supported by facts.

Directions Read the passage. Then answer the questions below.

Vanessa was a stubborn girl. When she had an opinion about something, it was hard to make her let go of it or change it, even when it was faulty. For example, she believed that airplanes were more trouble than what they were worth because they were always late. Her friend Bill couldn't believe she felt this way. "How many times have you flown on an airplane?" he asked Vanessa. "Three," she said, "and we've been late every time." "Well," he said, "think about the millions of people who fly every day. Think about the millions of times that people have had on-time or early flights. Just because you have had a few late arrivals, doesn't mean that airplane transportation isn't worth it." Vanessa wasn't sure what to say after that.

1. What generalization does Vanessa make?

____

2. What is Vanessa's support for her generalization?

____

____

3. Why is Vanessa's generalization faulty?

____

4. What is a generalization that Bill might make?

____

5. How did asking yourself questions help you to understand the passage?

____

____

Home Activity Your child asked himself or herself questions to identify generalizations. Read a story together. Pause and let your child write down questions that he or she has. Then, pretend you and your child are holding a book club meeting. Have your child play the club leader by using the questions to open up discussion about the story.

Name ______________________

Generalize

- A **generalization** is a broad statement or rule that applies to many examples.
- Valid generalizations are supported by facts. Faulty ones are not supported by facts.

Directions Read the following passage. Complete the diagram by finding a generalization and its support.

Have you ever thought about how inventors come up with their inventions? Many inventors have gotten an idea from their own lives. Eli Whitney saw a cat bring some feathers through a cage's bars. This helped him to create the cotton gin. Catherine Ryan invented locking nuts that keep bolts in place after seeing how her ring would get stuck on her finger. George de Mestral came up with his famous idea for making fasteners from the cockleburs on his dog's fur. Look around you, because a great idea may be closer than you think!

Valid Generalization

1. Many inventors ______________________

Support

2. Eli Whitney ______________________

____

3. Catherine Ryan ______________________

____

4. George de Mestral ______________________

____

5. What question did you ask yourself during reading?

____

Home Activity Your child used a graphic organizer to find generalizations. Play a game in which you both take turns making generalizations about members of your family. Guess if the generalizations are faulty or valid and explain why.

Name ____________________________________

Online Manual

- A **manual** and a handbook are the same. A grammar handbook you use is a manual for using language, for example. A manual can be a book or it can appear online. It contains instructions on how to do something. Manuals may have a table of contents, an index, sections, photos or illustrations, summaries, and explanations of vocabulary.
- Manuals should be read carefully before attempting the procedure. They often have warnings about a procedure, explaining any danger involved.

Directions Study this page from an online manual.

FLIGHT SIMULATOR 5000 OWNER'S MANUAL

- Search By Subject
- Introduction
- Installation
- Running the Program
- Diagrams
- Helpful Hints
- Glossary of Terms
- Contact Us

Pressing the **Menu** key will always take you back to the Main Menu screen. There you will find other program options. To see an illustration of the Main Menu screen and the instructions on how to use it, click on *Diagrams* in the left tool bar.

The **Arrow** keys allow you to navigate the airplane in the direction you wish.

The **Quit** key is used to end the session. If you hit **Quit** twice, you will automatically shut down the program.

Never allow liquid to come in contact with your key pad. It may cause electric shock.

Name ____________________

Directions Use the manual to answer the questions.

1. What is this manual for?

2. What does the diagram show you?

3. Where could you go if you did not understand a word used in the manual?

4. Why would you use the Search bar?

5. What happens when you press the Quit key twice?

6. In what situation would you use the Contact bar?

7. What does the **W!** mean?

8. Where can you go to learn more about the Menu screen?

9. How is an online manual different from a manual in book form?

10. Why is it important to read a manual before you use a product?

Home Activity Your child learned about online manuals. Find a print manual around your home. Have your child explain to you the different sections of the manual.

Name

Family Times

Summary

The Man Who Went to the Far Side of the Moon: The Story of Apollo 11 Astronaut Michael Collins

In 1969, Michael Collins circled the moon in a command module while two other astronauts made their historic landing. Even though Collins did not get to walk on the moon, he knew that every part of being an astronaut, from seeing the Earth from miles above to eating freeze-dried food from a pouch, was an experience to remember.

Activity

A Spacey Poem Imagine you are witnessing the wonders of space firsthand. You are one of the few people to land on the moon. Together, write a poem about your experience in space. Use vivid language to make your poem interesting.

Comprehension Skill

Graphic Sources

Graphic sources show information in a visual way. Maps, charts, tables, diagrams, and pictures are some examples of graphic sources.

Activity

A Picture Says A Thousand Words
Imagine you are writing a guidebook about your favorite hobby, sport, or activity. Think about a graphic source that you could include so that the reader would understand the information you provided in the book. Draw and label that graphic source.

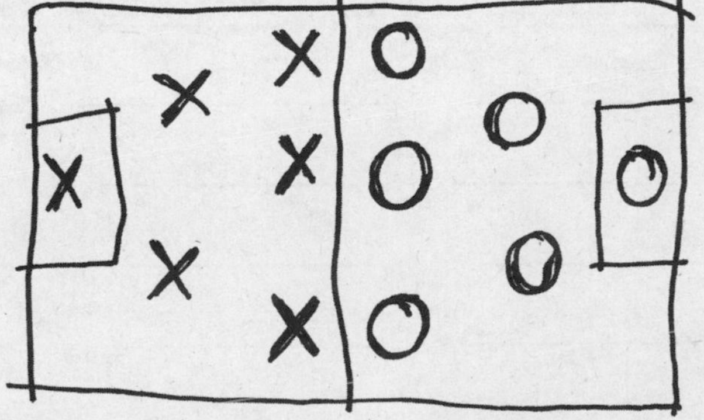

Lesson Vocabulary

Words to Know

Knowing the meanings of these words is important to reading *The Man Who Went to the Far Side of the Moon*. Practice using these words.

Vocabulary Words

astronauts pilots or members of the crew of a spacecraft

capsule the enclosed front section of a rocket made to carry instruments, astronauts, etc., into space

hatch a trapdoor covering an opening in an aircraft's or ship's deck

horizon line where the earth and sky seem to meet; skyline; You cannot see beyond the horizon.

lunar of or like the moon

module a self-contained unit or system within a larger system, often designed for a particular function

quarantine detention, isolation, and other measures taken to prevent the spread of an infectious disease

Grammar

Titles

Titles of books, articles, songs, poems, and other pieces need special attention. The main words in the title are capitalized no matter what kind of piece it is. When you write the title of a book, play, movie, or magazine, you should underline it. *For example: Puzzles Today Magazine.* The title of a short story, article, chapter, song, or poem is put in quotation marks (" "). *For example: "This Land is Your Land."* In print, you will usually see book and magazine titles in *italics*.

Activity

Personal Favorites Think about your favorite books, magazines, movies, songs, short stories, and poems. Write the titles down on a list. Use correct capitalization and punctuation. Now, ask family members what their favorites are and add them to your list.

Practice Tested Spelling Words

________	________	________	________
________	________	________	________
________	________	________	________
________	________	________	________
________	________	________	________

Name ______________________________

Graphic Sources

- A **graphic source** of information is something that shows information visually.
- Looking at graphic sources before you read will help you see what the text is about. Looking at them again during reading will help you understand the text.

Directions Study the following graphic source. Then answer the questions below.

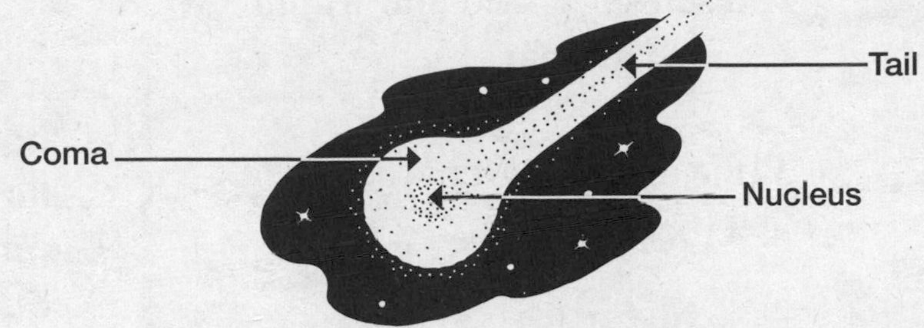

The Parts of a Comet

The comet is made up of three parts. Ice, gases, rocks, and dust form the *nucleus.* More dust and gases create the *coma,* or cloud, that surrounds the nucleus. The nucleus and the coma create the comet's head. Finally, the *tail* is the result of the dust and gases that are spread by solar winds.

1. What does this graphic source show you?

____

2. What type of article might include this graphic source?

____

____

3. Which parts make up the head of the comet?

____

4. Describe the coma of a comet.

____

5. How does the diagram help you to understand the information in the caption?

____

____

Home Activity Your child used a graphic source to answer questions about a text. Find an article that contains a graphic source in a newspaper or magazine. Have your child look at the graphic source before and during reading. Together, talk about how the graphic source makes the text more understandable.

Name ____________________________________

Vocabulary

Directions Choose the word from the box that best matches each definition. Write the word on the line.

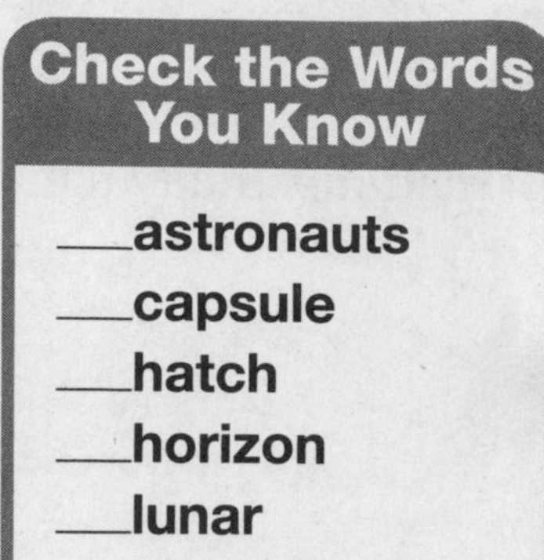

_______________ **1.** the line where the Earth and sky seem to meet

_______________ **2.** a self-contained unit within a larger system

_______________ **3.** the enclosed front section of a rocket

_______________ **4.** of, like, or about the moon

_______________ **5.** isolation to prevent the spread of an infectious disease

Directions Circle the word or words that have the same or nearly the same meaning as the first word in each group.

6. horizon	skyline	sunset	sphere
7. capsule	train	ship	pod
8. astronauts	waiters	teachers	space crew
9. quarantine	freedom	isolation	disease
10. hatch	trapdoor	closet	cabinet

Write a Story

On a separate sheet of paper, write a story about traveling in space. Describe what you see and do during the journey. Include as many vocabulary words as you can.

Home Activity Your child identified and used vocabulary words from *The Man Who Went to the Far Side of the Moon.* With your child, read an article about space or space exploration. Discuss the article, using the vocabulary words from this selection.

Name ______________________________

Vocabulary • Context Clues

- When you are reading you may run across words whose meanings you know, but whose meanings do not make sense in the sentence.
- **Homonyms** are words that are spelled the same but have different meanings.

Directions Read the following passage. Then answer the questions below.

Sandy Robinson, an astronaut, slipped through the hatch and into the capsule. She was ready for her mission—researching rocks on the moon. Two years ago, Sandy orbited the moon in a single-person module while other crew members walked on the moon's surface. Some people said it wasn't fair. This time, though, Sandy would walk on the moon herself.

Sandy made sure she was ready. Then she lowered the landing gear safely on the surface of thc moon. Sandy made sure her space suit was fitted properly. She could hardly bear the nervous feeling in her stomach. Then the door opened.

1. In this passage, what is the meaning of the homonym *hatch?* How do you know?

____

____

2. How do you know *fair* does not mean "a gathering of buyers and sellers"?

____

3. What context clues help you understand the meaning of the word *suit*?

____

____

4. Are the words *two, to,* and *too* homonyms? Why or why not?

____

5. Explain why you believe that the word *bear* is—or is not—a homonym. How could you learn if it is or not?

____

____

Home Activity Your child used context clues to identify meanings of homonyms. Together, choose a handful of homonyms. Then write a poem that uses all various meanings of the homonyms.

Fact and Opinion

Directions Read the following passage. Then answer the questions below.

My favorite part of our solar system is the sun. It is amazing! The sun is a star made of gases. It sits right in the middle of the solar system. As Earth rotates on its axis, the sun provides our planet with the light and heat we need for life to survive.

It seems to me that the sun must be the largest star in the sky. If you took the volume of Earth and multiplied it by about 1.3 million, you would get the sun's volume. Many scientists, though, think that it is only about medium size.

The center of the sun is very hot. Its temperature ranges between ten and twenty million degrees Celsius.

The sun is such an interesting star, I think everyone should learn more about it.

1. Underline a statement of fact found in the passage.

2. How do you know this is a statement of fact?

____

____

3. Circle a statement of opinion found in the passage.

4. How do you know this is a statement of opinion?

____

____

5. On a separate sheet of paper, write a paragraph about a subject you know well. Use at least two statements of fact and two statements of opinion in the paragraph.

Home Activity Your child identified statements of fact and opinion in a passage. Write statements of fact and statements of opinion on folded pieces of paper. Together, take turns distinguishing which statements are factual and which are based in opinion.

Name ______________________________

Graphic Sources

- A **graphic source** of information is something that shows information visually.
- Looking at graphic sources before you read will help you see what the text is about. Looking at them again during reading will help you understand the text.

Directions Study the following graphic source. Then answer the questions below.

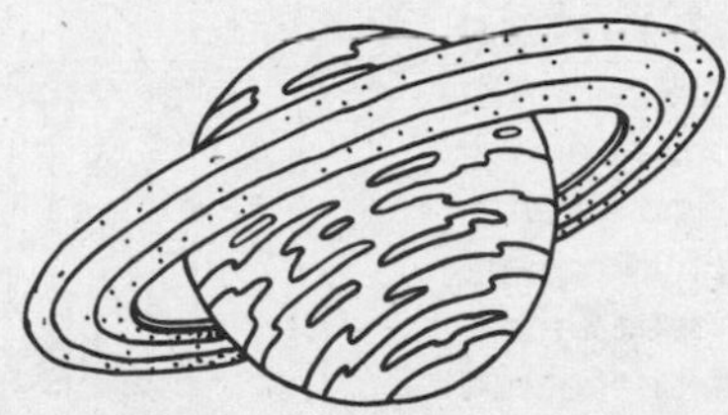

Saturn is one of the planets in our solar system. Gases make up the planet, and rock and ice create the rings around it. We can see these rings because they are very bright. NASA built a spacecraft called *Cassini* to help scientists learn about Saturn's rings and its moons by orbiting the planet and gathering data.

1. Predict the topic of the article in which this graphic source might appear.

____

2. Why can we see the rings around Saturn?

____

3. Why did NASA build *Cassini?*

____

____

4. How does the graphic source help you understand the text of the caption?

____

____

5. Why would it be helpful to preview this graphic before reading the article?

____

____

Home Activity Your child used a graphic source to answer questions about a text. Invite him or her to study a graphic source in an article very closely and then explain it to you.

Name ______________________________

Graphic Sources

- A **graphic source** is something that shows information visually.
- Looking at graphic sources before you read will help you see what the text is about. Looking at them again during reading will help you understand the text.

Directions Study the following graphic source. Then answer the questions below.

Parts of the Space Shuttle

The space shuttle has three main parts. The *solid rocket boosters* provide power and help the shuttle lift into the air. The *external tank* holds fuels, such as liquid hydrogen and liquid oxygen, that are released to the main engines. The *orbiter* is the spacecraft that holds the astronauts and the supplies for their mission.

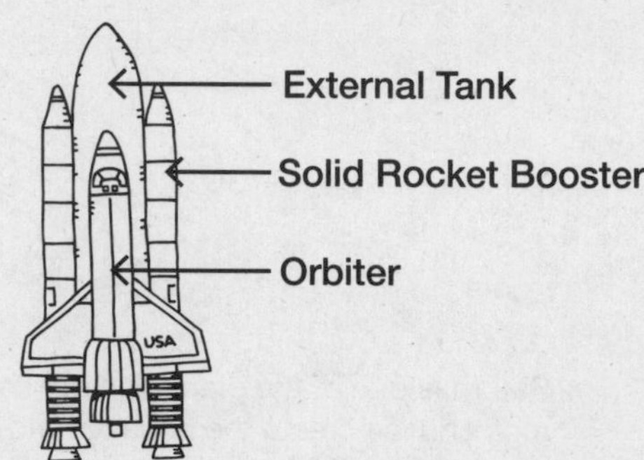

1. What is the topic of this graphic source?

____

2. Where do the astronauts live during the mission?

____

3. How many rocket boosters are there on the space shuttle?

____

4. What does the external tank hold?

____

____

5. The diagram shows the parts of the space shuttle. What information does the caption add to the diagram?

____

____

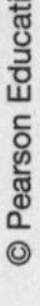

Home Activity Your child used a graphic source to answer questions. Invite your child to design a graphic source that could illustrate an article about your family.

Name ______________________________

Encyclopedia

An **encyclopedia** gives general information about many different subjects. The information in an encyclopedia is organized alphabetically by topic in a set of volumes, or books. An **entry** is the information on a particular topic. An entry begins with an **entry word** that names the topic. If you can't find an entry for a particular topic in an encyclopedia, you may need to think of another **key word** to help you locate the information.

Directions Read the encyclopedia entries below. Then answer the questions on the next page.

Entry 1

CONSTELLATION
A cluster of stars that seem to form a visual pattern in the sky. Many constellations were named long ago. Their names come from ancient myths. For example, the constellations Perseus and Orion were named for important people in myths, and other constellations were named for mythical animals like Cygnus the Swan and Leo the Lion. There are eighty-eight named constellations.

Some of the most famous star formations are part of larger star groups. For example, the Big Dipper is part of the larger constellation Ursa Major. Similarly, the Little Dipper is part of the constellation Ursa Minor.

See also entries for the following constellations: *Andromeda; Cygnus the Swan; Draco the Dragon; Hercules; Leo the Lion; Libra the Balance.*

Entry 2

MARS
A planet in our solar system. In terms of distance from the sun, Mars is the fourth planet. Mars is red, and at times appears to be very bright. The diameter of Mars is about half the size of the diameter of Earth. The atmosphere on Mars is made of carbon dioxide, argon, and nitrogen gases. The temperatures on the surface of the planet range from around 80 degrees Fahrenheit during the day to about –100 degrees Fahrenheit at night.

The surface of Mars looks like a desert, yet there are also craters, canyons, and volcanoes on it. The planet seems to experience a change of seasons. Scientists hold this view based on the fact that polar caps—made of ice or possibly dry ice—seem to shrink during certain times of the year. Scientists have not discovered any living things on Mars.

See also entries for *planet, solar system,* and *space.*

Name ______________________

1. What is the entry word for Entry 1?

____

2. If this encyclopedia contains twenty-six volumes (one volume for each letter of the alphabet), in which volume would you find Entry 1? Entry 2?

____

3. How many constellations have been named?

____

4. What color is Mars?

____

5. Where do the names of the constellations come from?

____

____

6. If you wished to look at a chart comparing Mars to other planets, where might you look in this encyclopedia?

____

7. What are some of the physical features of Mars?

____

8. In which larger star groups can you find the Big Dipper and the Little Dipper?

____

9. Why does Entry 1 end with a suggestion to look also at six other entries?

____

____

10. Do you think it is important to use an encyclopedia with a recent date of publication? Why or why not?

____

Home Activity Your child used encyclopedia entries to answer questions. Look up an unfamiliar subject in a volume of an encyclopedia. After your child finds the entry word, have him or her read and summarize the entry for you.